RENEWALS 691-4574

DATE DUE

Demco, Inc. 38-293

DILEMMAS IN THE STUDY OF INFORMATION

Recent Titles in
Contributions in Librarianship and Information Science

DILEMMAS IN THE STUDY OF INFORMATION

Exploring the Boundaries of Information Science

S. D. NEILL

CONTRIBUTIONS IN LIBRARIANSHIP AND
INFORMATION SCIENCE,
NUMBER 70
Paul Wasserman, *Series Editor*

GREENWOOD PRESS
New York • Westport, Connecticut • London

Library of Congress Cataloging-in-Publication Data

Neill, S. D. (Samuel D.).
    Dilemmas in the study of information : exploring the boundaries of
information science / S. D. Neill.
        p.   cm.—(Contributions in librarianship and information
science, ISSN 0084–9243 ; no. 70.)
    Includes bibliographical references and index.
    ISBN 0–313–27734–6 (alk. paper)
    1. Information science—Philosophy. 2. Library science—
Philosophy. I. Title. II. Series.
Z665.N415 1992
020'.1—dc20   91–24835

British Library Cataloguing in Publication Data is available.

Library of Congress Catalog Card Number: 91–24835
ISBN: 0–313–27734–6
ISSN: 0084–9243

First published in 1992

Greenwood Press, 88 Post Road West, Westport, CT 06881
An imprint of Greenwood Publishing Group, Inc.

Printed in the United States of America

The paper used in this book complies with the
Permanent Paper Standard issued by the National
Information Standards Organization (Z39.48–1984).

10 9 8 7 6 5 4 3 2 1

Copyright Acknowledgments

The author and publisher are grateful to Aslib, The Association for Information Management
for use of the following materials:

S. D. Neill, "The Dilemma of the Subjective in Information Organisation and Retrieval,"
Journal of Documentation 43, no. 3 (September 1987): 193–211.

S. D. Neill, "Body English: The Dilemma of the Physical in the Objectification of Subjective
Knowledge Structures: The Role of the Body in Thinking," *Journal of Documentation* 46,
no. 1 (March 1990): 1–15.

This book is dedicated to the
memory of my father, Robert "Bob" Neill
(Old Silvertop)

I once heard him tell a man who was
adamant he was right: "There's no one
born who hasn't made a mistake."

Contents

Acknowledgments

The first two chapters previously appeared in the *Journal of Documentation*, published by Aslib, The Association for Information Management. Permission to reprint them here, with some slight revisions, has been granted and is appreciated. I also wish to thank Katy Tonkovic for patiently working this manuscript into her daily schedule and Paul Wasserman for planting the idea that I should write a book.

Introduction

THE CONTEXT

There was a story in the *New York Times Magazine* by Bruce Selcraig in September 1990 entitled "Reverend Wildmon's War on the Arts." Reverend Wildmon had been fighting against sex and violence on TV for many years, writing members of Congress and organizing boycotts of products of companies that advertised on the offending programs. Wildmon had established a mass-mailing "information system," and as Selcraig informed his readers, Wildmon knew "his enemies' techniques and jargon well" and could "talk market shares and Nielsen ratings" with any of his opponents (p. 25). Here was a man who knew something about information and how to use it. If at times he fell victim to "selective and sloppy research," he was certainly not alone, as I show in this book, particularly in chapters 4 and 8 and, if philosophers are to be believed, in chapter 9.

Reverend Wildmon's career as a crusader against the sins of the media began when he suffered a case of information overload—the wrong kind of information. To quote from Selcraig:

During the Christmas holidays of 1976 he and his family were gathered around the television one night. When they "got into a program and there was a scene of adultery, . . . we changed the channel; and we got into another program and somebody called somebody else an S.O.B., except they didn't use the initials; changed the channel again; got into a mystery program and then a scene came on, one man had another man tied down and was working him over with a hammer. Asked the children to turn the set off and decided that I would do something about it." (p. 43)

There was too much of that kind of "information" and his way of "managing" it was to get it off the air. I address other overload problems and how people manage, in spite of the warnings of the futurologists, in chapter 6.

Wildmon is an example of an information phenomenon rarely studied in the discipline of information science, yet there is no question that information gathering and dissemination is involved. Perhaps information scientists think nothing can be done about characters like Wildmon—certainly not by information scientists. But here is a case where information is being used as decision-making data, and Manfred Kochen (1983) defined the meaning of the concept of information (in the 1980s) as "decision-relevant data" (p. 278). Kochen's opening sentence in this article in the *Annual Review of Information Science and Technology* (ARIST) is revealing: "Information and society is not a scientific topic" (p. 277). Perhaps that's why information scientists avoid it. But information divorced or abstracted from society is meaningless. Kochen's purpose was voiced in the following: "I have assumed that the readers [of ARIST] are mostly information professionals, and I have argued that acquiring and using knowledge about the effective use of knowledge is one of their major responsibilities" (p. 277). It is this argument, in the form of a question, that runs as a theme through this book. It is an argument posed as a dilemma because the *use* of information is not generally seen as part of the information scientist's responsibility in spite of the statement—in the "Criteria for Information Science" of the Institute of Information Scientists—that information science "includes the study of information from its generation to its exploitation" (Vickery and Vickery 1987, p. 361). P. S. Kawata (1989), in the third edition of his text on documentation in India, was even more specific. The "pivot" of information science, he wrote, "should be the phenomena of information transfer/communication" (p. 5), including "use, abuse and impact on individuals and groups in different contexts" (p. 4). It is also my contention that information use problems are, in certain instances, insoluble dilemmas. At least I depict them as insoluble. I do so because they are information problems grounded in human nature and can be solved only by altering that nature.

The first two chapters set the stage, describing, in the context of specific problems of information science, the cognitive aspect of human beings. Chapters 3, 4, and 5 describe information problems of use and misuse arising out of the natural flaws in human cognition and character. Human beings are imperfect by design, or if you follow the story of the Fall, the perfect design was flawed by the desire to know everything. Humans are not rational animals. They are reasoning beings. Their reasoning uses information, and some of the results are told in the chapters in this book.

In a sense, information itself is the subject of chapters 6 and 7, but all information is the product of human working—and we must understand overload and complexity if we are to understand the role of information in the reasoning process. All of this applies to chapter 8—the problem of doing research in the social sciences and in information science in particular. Any study of the human reasoning process is fraught with difficulties, especially if one intends to be scientific in the sense of science as measurement (accurate, predictive measurement). The information product of information science must be viewed in the light of the nature of information *work*—which is an art, not a science, and to study an art, one must use the methods of the humanities. Whenever one is in the position of having to interpret words (in queries) and relate them to literature (information sources), one is dealing with the art of expression. Also, since there is no scientific structure of knowledge, that is, no structure set in stone, one must interpret the expression of knowledge placement by those who index documents and those who fit them into classification schemes. There is nothing scientific about either of these very human activities. This too is a dilemma for information scientists.

OTHER APPROACHES

Brent Ruben (1985), then the director of the doctoral program at the School of Communication, Information, and Library Studies at Rutgers University, identified the concerns of "information and library studies" as "the organization, management, storage, and retrieval of data," and the emphasis of communication studies as "the process whereby data of all varieties are originated, transmitted, and transformed and used by individuals" (p. 19). He concluded his essay by suggesting that the concept of information could be a linking device for a "cross-disciplinary research agenda" (p. 22). The series of volumes in which this article appeared was edited by Ruben (1985; 1988; Ruben and Lievrouw 1990), and its purpose was to broaden the study of information from symbol, to processing, to the media of transmission, to its uses and the outcomes of its uses. Others, including information scientists themselves, have expressed a similar opinion. Brian Vickery and Alina Vickery (1987), in their very fine text on the field, said, "It has become increasingly clear that only by widening its 'knowledge base' can information science establish a solid foundation for future development" (p. v). A. J. Meadows (1990) identified an area of study close to that with which I am concerned: "Perhaps a comprehensive theory of how humans communicate will provide a theoretical foundation needed by information science" (p. 63).

The emphasis on uses and consequences in a sizable number of the papers in Ruben's volumes parallels the message I convey in this work. Brenda Dervin (1977) called on librarians to be aware of the product of their information retrieval efforts—the use made of information—in order to better understand what people did with what they took from books so that the provision of the stored record could be improved and would make more sense. George Gerbner's (1988) first sentence is a cautionary note for librarians and information scientists: "The concept of information, divorced from social and cultural contexts and functions, is misleading and potentially mischievous" (p. 3).

The mischief is that information retrieval systems constructed in a vacuum simply won't work. The efforts of information scientists to learn about the information needs and experiences of scholars (Garvey 1979; Case 1986) and managers (Wilson 1988; Iselin 1990) need to be expanded to the rest of the world of information users—that is, to everyone.

There is a keen awareness of the realities of information use in Robert Lee Chartrand and James Morentz's (1979) report of a 1977 seminar series, but the realities come out in the comments on the seminar presentations mainly because many of the participants were in government positions or had been in or connected to the Congress and so knew how decisions were made in the political arena. There is mention, in passing, of information overload, the quality of information, and the complexity of institutions. Each of these issues I develop at length in separate chapters. The need to know users and their uses (and misuses) of information is strongly supported by Al Linden in Chartrand and Morentz (1979). Linden was responsible for the library and statistical functions at the Federal Energy Administration. In the midst of making a comment, he said:

The point I am making is that perhaps we in the information business should tell our bosses "No, you don't need all that information. Why don't you go back to the good old days where you made the gut decision based on your intuition and a limited amount of input. You might be better off!" Until we in the information business develop better ways of packaging our products, instead of always selling our capability, we will not have fulfilled our role in the organization. (p. 46)

Better packaging can come only from an understanding of the way information is used.

Perhaps the work most directly relevant to the theme I present is Barbara Tuchman's *The March of Folly: From Troy to Vietnam* (1984). Each of the historical failures she describes was chosen with one criterion rigidly enforced: the losing decision makers had to have had in hand all the necessary information to avoid making the wrong choice. Here is the dilemma. How do we get people to use information well? Is it possible? Whose responsibility is it? Kochen (1983) placed that responsibility before the readers of ARIST. John Swan (1990) raised the issue of lies, distortions, and fraud in the context of the responsibility of librarians to provide access, not the responsibility of information scientists to study such phenomena. It is my opinion that information retrieval and information systems and libraries are barren inasmuch as they are not informed by a knowledge of the way information is used and abused by human beings in the process of living.

This work, then, is sandwiched between Kochen and Tuchman—a ham-and-lettuce sandwich prefaced by a cool beer and concluded down by the river.

REFERENCES

Case, Donald Owen. "Collection and Organization of Written Information by Social Scientists and Humanists: A Review and Exploratory Study." *Journal of Information Science* 12 (3): 97–104 (1986).

Chartrand, Robert Lee, and James W. Morentz, Jr. *Information Technology Serving Society.* Oxford, N.Y.: Pergamon Press, 1979.

Dervin, Brenda. "Useful Theory for Librarianship: Communication, Not Information." *Drexel Library Quarterly* 13 (3): 16–32 (July 1977).

Garvey, William D. *Communication: The Essence of Science.* Oxford, N.Y.: Pergamon Press, 1979.

Gerbner, George. "Telling Stories in the Information Age." In Brent D. Ruben, ed., *Information and Behavior*, Vol. 2, 3–12. New Brunswick, N.J.: Transaction Books, 1988.

Iselin, Errol R. "Information, Uncertainty, and Managerial Decision Quality: An Experimental Investigation." *Journal of Information Science* 16 (4): 239–48 (1990).

Kawata, P. S. *Fundamentals of Documentation.* 3d ed. New Delhi: Sterling Publishers Private, 1989.

Kochen, Manfred. "Information and Society." *Annual Review of Information Science and Technology* 18: 277–304 (1983).

Meadows, A. J. "Theory in Information Science." *Journal of Information Science* 16(1): 59–63 (1990).

Ruben, Brent D. "The Coming of the Information Age: Information, Technology, and the Study of Behavior." In Brent D. Ruben, ed., *Information and Behavior*, Vol. 1, 3–26. New Brunswick, N.J.: Transaction Books, 1985.

———, ed. *Information and Behavior.* 2 vols. New Brunswick, N.J.: Transaction Books, 1985, 1988.

Ruben, Brent D., and Leah A. Lievrouw, eds. *Mediation, Information, and Communication: Information and Behavior, Volume 3.* New Brunswick, N.J.: Transaction Publishers, 1990.

Selcraig, Bruce. "Reverend Wildmon's War on the Arts." *New York Times Magazine*, Sept. 2, 1990, 22–25, 43, 52–53.

Swan, John C. "Rehumanizing Information: An Alternative Future." *Library Journal* 115 (14): 178–82 (Sept. 1, 1990).

Tuchman, Barbara W. *The March of Folly: From Troy to Vietnam.* New York: Knopf, 1984.

Vickery, Brian C., and Alina Vickery. *Information Science in Theory and Practice.* London: Butterworth, 1987.

Wilson, Tom. "Information, Managers, and Information Technology." *Argus* 17(2): 47–50 (June 1988).

1

The Dilemma of the Subjective in Information Organization and Retrieval

Southwestern Ontario hangs down into the northern American states like a windblown icicle off an exposed eaves trough. Summers in this part of Canada can be as hot and humid as an African jungle. That is why it is always good to get home from work and sit under the large green leaves of the maple. Late in the day there can be a light breeze to stir the leaves so that one can sit amid the flickering shadows and guard against heat prostration with a cold beer. It is edifying, as well as aesthetically satisfying, to watch the shadows of the leaves on the old wooden deck. The symbolism of the play of light and dark cannot be avoided.

Although the past is gone and is irretrievable for the purpose of making changes in it, the past is not completely irretrievable for the purpose of effecting change in one's self. And just as our own lives provide information for use, so do the lives of others as recorded in print or film.

Of course, all the lives that influence us, factual and fictional, our own and those of the people we know, suffer a sea change when we think on them and absorb and adapt their impact in daily living. We process what we perceive and believe in a way that changes not only our present thinking but also the information itself, even our own memories.

In a sense, then, the true information, as it was when it happened, is as irretrievable as the pools of light and the shadows of leaves when we try to pluck them from the wooden deck. Yet the dancing sunlight and the cooling shadows are as real as the cold beer as it flows over the tongue. And if one attaches a symbolic meaning to those flickering shadows, that meaning is as real as anything else in the world.

The play of light and dark has power
to hold the mind;
for life is dancing light and shade
and like attracts its kind.

Such abstract symbolism is as useful as any information we use to solve problems.

Waiting for an operation
in the hospital
is fertile soil for fear to bloom.
But fear's somewhat assuaged
by the light and shadow
of a windblown tree
playing in a corner of the room.
The light flickers,
flashing among the shadows,
swift and clear,
like hope breaking, striking, splashing
through heavy leaves of fear.

INTRODUCTION

Brenda Dervin and Karl Popper view the nature of information from widely different vantage points. Nevertheless, it can be shown that they agree about what information is. It is my intention to clarify their positions about information and so come to an understanding of its nature and its place in information science.

I have chosen Dervin and Popper not only because they have strongly held theories about information but also because of the increasing influence each of these "outsiders" is having in our field. For instance, Popper's postulated World 3, *Objective Knowledge* (1972), has been used by a number of writers in library and information science: B. C. Brookes (1980), Alfredo Serrai (1981), Paul Leonard Gallina (1983), and S. D. Neill (1985). Don Swanson (1980) incorporated Popper's work into a discussion of the kind of access to recorded information that would best facilitate the growth of knowledge and, as we shall see in chapter 7, into his searches for unknown or undiscovered information.

Dervin's influence on librarianship began with her 1977 article "Useful Theory for Librarianship." At that time, Dervin was with the Department of Communication at the University of Washington in Seattle. Her workshops on neutral questioning and her research into information needs (1984) and the use of libraries (1985) derive from her interest in the process of communication between the mass media and people of all kinds as they manage the ordinary, and sometimes extraordinary, procedures of day-to-day living.

DERVIN'S BACKGROUND

In 1976, Dervin et al. published the results of a large-scale study of information seeking in "recent troublesome situations" of 465 citizens of Seattle—265 from the general population, 100 Asians, and 100 blacks. One of the findings was that respondents used a wide variety of gap-bridging tactics, with the expected high emphasis on informal networks and low emphasis on formal networks. This latter finding was interpreted (Dervin 1983b) not as proof that people would not use formal systems but rather "as an indication that formal systems as they are now designed do not intersect well with gap-bridging needs" (p. 18). Most questions people asked in their troublesome situations had some relation to themselves or others, rather than being questions that could be answered satisfactorily with facts from reference tools. The knowledge or information gaps were of a personal nature, what we now call coping or community information questions (Dervin 1976).

This study brought into high visibility the fact that most people do not get the help they need for everyday problems from the various communication devices designed to provide knowledge and information to communities. The people surveyed did not use newspapers, radios, schools, or libraries to get the missing information. Dervin therefore began to examine the formal communication system to find out why such important information was not being provided or was not perceived as being provided.

In an article relating her work to librarianship, Dervin (1977) stressed that the user did not get "star billing" in the measurement of library services. She said that library research in the past had viewed the "collateral" of libraries as media packages and not as information and had viewed individual users as types, stereotypes of certain groups who would ask certain kinds of questions. The user's uniqueness was not considered, and it was assumed that packaged information would answer the need. "The core assumption [of the tradition] is that information exists independent of human action and that its value lies in describing reality," and because information has its own order and organization, "diverse citizens must bend to the information in order to use it" (p. 20). Putting it bluntly, librarians operated in a Procrustean manner to fit the user into a sociodemographic as well as a knowledge classification bed.

Dervin has consistently depicted the typical information system as a failure, and this failure is attributed to blindness to differences between individuals and how people "make" information. Experts organize information in the shadow of their own perspectives: "Experts make judgments as to how their 'information' will help. They deem some observations as 'information,' others as 'entertainment,' some as 'factual,' others as 'opinion.' They isolate topical entry points or keywords which should allow user entry and then find that the ability of users to find what they want does not improve" (Dervin 1983a, p. 27).

DERVIN'S MODEL OF THE PERSON

Dervin focuses on the fact that individuals do not merely adapt to the environment but are creative in their response. There is an interpretive process going on that is constrained and directed by the current situation, as qualified by time and space factors, and by individuals' gaps in knowledge about their immediate world.

She divides information into three kinds: (1) information that describes reality; (2) the ideas individuals have in their minds, their image of reality; and (3) the behavior that selects from and uses the first kind of information and that creates from this the personal, subjective picture of reality.

Dervin (1977) established some categories of "Information 3," such as decisioning, liking-disliking, and relating to others to take advice. It is difficult to think of such activities as a kind of information, but I think the point is that different individuals will create different pictures or ideas from the same external information because of personal, affective, and social inclinations and conditions.

Dervin sees the traditional understanding of "information which describes reality" in the context of a media campaign in which a message is being shot at an audience like a bullet. If the audience does not understand the message, the fault lies in the abilities or attitudes of the audience. Dervin rejects the assumption that there is information that describes reality completely; thus we have the interpreting individual trying to make sense with incomplete information and therefore having to create some part of the answer to fill the gap in order to continue.

We seem to have a model of a Being needing to make sense out of the objects and information in the world in order to survive. The objects and information have value as tools, not in or for themselves. Each individual is found in an historical present carrying an individual biography and individual goals. The individual's history and situation act as filters in the processing of the individual's observations so that meaning is internal and unique.

DERVIN'S CONSTRUCTIVIST THEORY OF INFORMATION

Dervin comes to her conclusions about information, it must be remembered, as a student of communication. She is arguing against the theory that messages cause impacts or meanings. Under this theory, a source sends a message, which is then seen to exist much as a brick exists, and if the message hits the target, it ought to have an effect, that is, be understood. Any misunderstanding is the receiver's fault, whether caused by level of education, attitude, or some social or physical barrier.

The assumptions behind this bullet, or hypodermic, theory of communication are identified in all of Dervin's writings. One example follows:

The assumption—that messages should have a direct impact—rests on a number of other implicit assumptions. It assumes, for example, that messages can have a direct impact, that somehow they can get into receivers the same way they left the sources, and that they produce in all receivers the same impact. It assumes that a message is received the same way by source and receiver and by one receiver and the next receiver. It assumes that there is nothing unique about the receiver that will impact his or her use of the message. It assumes that there are no cognitive processes intervening between message and use.

At root, behind all these assumptions, is a core assumption dealing with the nature of information, that information can be dumped into people's heads as if people's heads were empty buckets. To make this assumption it must be assumed that information is a thing rather than a construction, that it exists independently of observers and has an inherent, correct, absolute, and isomorphic relationship to the reality it describes. Within the context of these assumptions, it is reasonable to expect that a receiver exposed to information should *ipso facto* respond. (Dervin 1981, p. 74)

One thing should be clarified before going on. Although Dervin does not make the point, it is important to see that there are two separate assumptions being set up for demolition here: (1) information exists independently of observers; and (2) information is an absolutely correct match for the reality it is intended to describe. There is no necessary or logical connection between the two. One can assume information exists externally to observers and not assume that it describes reality accurately and completely.

To continue, Dervin (1981) has described an alternative conception in which information is understood not as a thing but as a construction: "The core assumption in this alternative is that information is not a thing. Instead all information is seen as a product of human observing. All human observing is assumed to be constrained by the limits of human perceptual equipment, by the control exerted on perception by time and place" (p. 75).

From this, Dervin concluded that information provides only an incomplete picture of reality and exists to a "significant degree" internally, as part of individual frames of reference. The conclusion that information is incomplete "postulates that there are fundamental and pervasive discontinuities or gaps in life and phenomena" (Dervin, Jacobson, and Nilan 1982, p. 424), and the condition of gap applies "not only to direct experience with reality, but to indirect experience attended to via messages and signals" (p. 425). This idea of gap sets up the need and motivation for seeking information.

Dervin (1983b) made the statement that sense-making assumes that all information is subjective: "Since it is assumed that all information producing is internally guided and since it is generally accepted that all human observing is constrained, sense-making further assumes that *all information is subjective*" (p. 4, Dervin's emphasis). However, after discussing various constraints on human observing, namely time, space, and physiology, she qualified the statement that all information is subjective in such a way as to lead us to read her use of the word *subjective* as *subjectively constructed*: "Information seeking and use are posited as 'constructing' activities—as personal creating of sense. It is assumed that all information is simply the sense made by individuals at specific moments in time-space. Some 'information' becomes agreed upon and is termed 'fact' for a given time-frame at least. Others are controversial and are called 'opinion' or 'delusion' depending on the socio-political context and/or the charity of the observer" (Dervin 1983b, p. 4). Although Dervin placed factual or objective knowledge in quotation marks ("some 'information' "), she unquestionably recognized that there is a kind of information out there, external to human beings (but created by them), and that sense-making or constructing involves "information sharing interactions." For sharing to take place, there must be an external something to be shared—in this case, the "product" of human observing.

With this glimmering of light on the full nature of Dervin's concept of information, we need to note the goal of Dervin's research, which is to invent communication alternatives and assess their utility. As a result, she has produced what she calls "practice communication inventions." She started a *Good News Newspaper* because her research indicated that people emphasized the "good and hopeful" uses of answers to questions. She also designed "infosheets" for a doctor's office, a school system, and a medical clinic. The infosheets were intended to answer common questions asked by people in these situations, questions gathered from the people themselves. The answers were formed from a variety of sources, not just experts, and checked for relevance and comprehensibility. There is little doubt that the information in these sheets, written to address the needs of individuals in specific situations, was external to the users, even though *some* users were involved in constructing the contents.

In the introduction to her discussion of the infosheets, Dervin wrote that, in order for individuals to make effective sense, they "need to receive information that is transmitted subjectively." They "need to get a picture of the different senses different people have made in a variety of situations so they can locate themselves" (Dervin 1983b, p. 25). Of course, the senses made by different people in various situations generally end up in places other than infosheets, namely in articles and books. Dervin just happened to be immediately concerned about current problematic situations that people do not always understand as clearly as they would like, such as undergoing cancer treatment or the purposes and procedures of a blood donor clinic.

What is meant by information "transmitted subjectively" is explained by reference to the situations-gaps-uses model in which the individual is understood to be located in a unique time-space context. In this circumstance, the individual has questions about what is going on or, in other words, has gaps or information needs. The answers provide information that is used to produce "newly created sense" (Dervin 1983b, p. 8), unique to that individual's time-space life moment. That is, Dervin does not mean that the information is *transmitted* subjectively but that the information transmitted, for example, on any infosheet, is based, or ought to be based, on the subjective needs that are discovered by asking the individuals who are experiencing the situation themselves, rather than asking an expert to transmit what the expert assumes is needed. More generally, Dervin is saying that information comes from a subjective source and is transformed by another subjective process performed by the receiver. She has developed a research program designed to predict "not how people are moved by messages but rather how people move to make sense of messages" (Dervin 1983b, p. 6).

DESCRIPTION OF POPPER'S WORLD 3

The following description of Popper's World 3 (W3), a "world" in which information exists external to the mind, relies heavily on Neill (1982). In coming to an understanding of W3, one must recognize that a simple definition can be used only as a key. Popper did, after all, write a great deal about it, and his *Objective Knowledge* is a long discussion of the various problems raised by the concept. Nevertheless, we can begin with a single sentence from Popper (1972): "We can call the physical world 'World 1,' the world of our conscious experiences 'World 2,' and the world of the logical *contents* of books, libraries, computer memories, and such like, 'World 3' " (p. 74).

World 1 is not a problem. The clearest way to see the difference between Worlds 2 and 3 is to think of W2 as a state of mind, a disposition to act, or as acts of thought or thought *processes*, and W3 as the *products* of thought. Putting it another way, Popper (1976) wrote:

Thoughts in the sense of contents or statements in themselves and *thoughts in the sense of thought processes* belong to *two entirely different "Worlds".* . . . The decisive thing seems to me that we can put objective thoughts—that is, theories—before us in such a way that we can criticise them and argue about them. To do so we must formulate them in some more or less permanent (especially linguistic) form. (pp. 181, 182).

In a general sense, more than theories are included in W3—all the products of the human mind, such as tools, institutions, works of art, and in an even broader sense, myths and fictions—"all human products into which we have injected some of our ideas" (Popper 1976, pp. 187, 195).

At times, Popper extends W3 into the realm of as-yet-undiscovered ideas. He is concerned to take into account the potential new theories and ideas that can come from individual interaction with the record. I will not take W3 this far, leaving that to Swanson (1986), but I will restrict it to the logical contents of human artifacts—ideas that have been objectified. Indeed, *objectified* knowledge is preferable to *objective* knowledge as a term, since *objective* carries the connotation of "true" knowledge, whether arrived at empirically or by consensus. Objectified knowledge is also more appropriate for Dervin's "facts," "opinions," and "delusions."

Crucial to W3's external existence is its autonomous nature. Once thoughts are in W3, they become autonomous objects in the sense that they are not controlled or influenced by the individual who produced them; they are independent of their authors. Jason Farradane (1961) recognized the W2 and W3 aspects of knowledge when he struggled with the problem of structuring a classification of documents and pinpointed the autonomous nature of W3: "The ideal structure to be made will not have the elusive nature of thought in action; that would be impossible. We are, however, dealing with recorded thought, what has been said or written, and is thereafter to be dealt with if at all in unchanged form" (p. 128).

Anthony O'Hear (1980) mounted a rather weak argument against the autonomous nature of W3. He began with this quotation from George Lukacs: "Only when the objectified forms in society acquire functions that bring the essence of man into conflict with his existence, only when man's nature is subjugated, deformed and crippled can we speak of an objective societal condition of alienation and, as inexorable consequence, of all the subjective marks of an internal alienation." O'Hear comments: "I take this to be saying that it is when we allow our institutions to take on lives of their own, seemingly independent of and possibly contrary to our wishes, desires or control (i.e., from Popper's point of view, flourishing in World 3), that we need to be reminded that they are ultimately only ours, based in our ways of thinking and behaving, and controllable by us if we have the will to take control of them" (pp. 198–99).

To say that we can control our institutions "if we have the will" to do so is also to say that if we do not have the will to do so, the institutions will control our actions. We design institutions to exert control—rules of parliamentary procedure are ideas of behavior in debate that we create to control certain situations. Pyramidal structures, or other management systems, are designed and put into place to act as impartial (autonomous) controls of behavior in organizations. No one is saying, and certainly not Popper, that these theories of management and institutional structures cannot be changed if they don't work—if they are "falsified."

Popper (1972) usually spoke of W3 as being "largely" autonomous:

But the autonomy is only partial: the new problems lead to new creations or constructions . . . and may thus add new objects to the third world. And every such step will create new unintended facts; new unexpected problems; and often also *new refutations*. There is also a most important feed-back effect from our creations upon ourselves; from the third world upon the second world. For the new emergent problems stimulate us to new creations. (pp. 118–19)

What is to be understood by this? I have touched on it before when discussing Popper's extension of W3 into discoveries not yet made. The new facts, problems, and refutations come from W2 interacting with a new object in W3, for example, the ideas in a book or the design of a computer system. Relationships are seen that were not seen before the W3 object was encountered. Popper seems to be saying that because new ideas and theories are sparked by W3 objectified knowledge, and that because some new theories will refute old ones, somehow W3 is not completely autonomous. But this is simply confusing the process of creating or, as Dervin would have it, constructing new ideas from ideas already existing as products.

The ideas in the "text" sit waiting, whether that text is a book or an architectural structure. There is a meaning that individuals can, in general, understand as others do, but each individual can also make unique meanings from the work depending on the individual's biography.

Popper's difficulty here is directly relevant to Dervin's proposition that information is not external to people's minds. To be external means to be autonomous, no longer subject to alteration by the author or creator. Redesigning, revising, and making new editions all produce new W3 objects. The old editions, even if they have only been spoken, have still acted, still existed, and still do exist if they have not been completely destroyed. Popper seems to be suggesting that because we get ideas from reading or debating, what we have read or heard is no longer, or is not completely, autonomous. Yet others may read the same work or hear the same words and create ideas that differ from anyone else's ideas.

O'Hear (1980) raised another objection:

Certainly the thought experiments used by Popper to establish the independent existence of World 3 do not show that it is capable of autonomous development. In the first experiment, all our machines, tools and subjective knowledge of how to use them is destroyed, but not our libraries or our capacity to learn from them. In the second, our machines, tools and knowledge of how to use them is destroyed as before, and also our libraries. In the first case, civilization will re-emerge after some pain, but in the second, because the libraries are destroyed, any such re-emergence will take many millenia. The conclusion is that this shows the reality, significance and autonomy of the objective knowledge stored in the libraries. But it could equally well be argued that the experiments point to the uselessness of what is stored in libraries, independent of the ability people have to use them (which, significantly, is preserved in the first experiment). Outside the context of the specific human life and reactions in which it makes sense, all that libraries contain is a mass of undeciphered scripts. Be that as it may, the experiments singularly fail to show any degree of autonomy of human behavior in the knowledge stored, for libraries do not develop on their own at all. (p. 199)

The whole point O'Hear is making is that W3 does not develop and therefore fails to show any degree of autonomy of human behavior. But no one has said that W3 develops, or can exhibit any human behavior.

The real criticism is that contents of books are just physical objects, ink on paper. But even when we find symbols and languages such as Linear B, we know from our own language experience that there is meaning in the marks. Even scripts from the past in a language we understand have to be edited and analyzed by scholars to get at what was meant at the time of writing. Sometimes we agree on meanings, and such works become "definitive" editions. Sometimes there is debate, but the meaning is merely hidden from us. It is still there. Popper (1972) clarified his position: "Thus I do admit that in order to belong to the third world of objective knowledge, a book should—in principle, or virtually—be capable of being grasped (or deciphered, or understood, or 'known') by somebody. But I do not admit more" (p. 116). The content must be logical, must make sense.

When we say that music exists in the score, or ideas exist in the language printed, we can say, in a way, that the music and ideas exist over and above the physical marks on the page. If we say, however, that they exist just "in a way," implying that they do not really exist outside of a mind, then we are saying that the music and ideas do not exist in the score and in the printed words.

The question then arises, how can we translate the notes and the words on the page into musical sounds and into ideas if they do not exist in the signs on the paper? The fact that many diverse individuals can play the music and read the words to make similar sounds and meanings so that the music and words can be recognized as this piece or that work and can be talked about in an intelligent way, with the understanding that the reference is to a specific score or text, seems to me to be a good enough reason to support the existence of music and ideas in printed signs—an existence separate from the interpretation of individual minds. Calling renderings or readings *interpretations* implies interpretations of some text that can be given different meanings but that is still a text to work from, to share. It is similar to the contrast between the meaning we impose on light and shadow and the meaning that is intrinsic to music in its notation and words in print. We read meaning into the works of nature; we invent notes and letters and invest them with conventional meanings in a way peculiar to our species.

The world of ideas—recorded ideas of objectified thought—is a world made by humans. It is not the world of nature. Nor, in spite of Popper, is it the world of ideas that have not yet been thought, whatever that might be. Here, I speak only of the record, including all forms of record, as long as it contains thought uttered, outered, objectified in some way. Because these are human artifacts, they might be considered a lower order of existence than created (God-created) works, such as the brain or a stone. But this question does not concern us. Our purpose is to establish W3 and then work with it. Since we, as information scientists, are working with it anyway, we might as well understand it as best we can.

DERVIN AND POPPER: THE SHARED WORLD

From a phenomenological point of view, Dervin is trying to have it both ways. Her human beings are contextualized in space and time, with histories that have led to their present problem situations. Although each person has a unique history, each is also part of a particular society and a community within that society, and as we gather from her research, each can be part of a common problem situation (blood donor clinic, cancer treatment patient). In spite of the commonness, Dervin insists that information is highly subjective and therefore unique.

But we do share a public world of street signs and texts, of practices and institutions, a world whose communal nature we must accept if any communication is to take place. In a report to the Club of Rome, Hiroshi Inose and John Pierce (1984) remind us: "Communication takes place only between persons within a common context; in this context they may share a common aim, a common problem, a common curiosity, a common interest. In other words, they must share a community of interest that is important or fascinating to both (or all)" (pp. 129–30).

It is the meaning in texts and tools that individuals interpret. It is this meaning that resides in Popper's "logical content" of books and other human artifacts. Inose and Pierce came to make the summary statement above in a discussion of the difficulties of machine translation and artificial intelligence (AI). To translate well, a machine needs to "understand" what it is translating. However, this understanding comes from what we have in common in our lives, minds, and language. A book on physics or politics exists in the context of the physics or politics of its time. Programming all the background knowledge entailed in the words "its time" is the goal of those working on fifth-generation computers.

The common knowledge we store in memory is an internalization of W3—as poetry, laws, regulations, customs. The process of thinking, of trying to understand, of interpretation, is Dervin's (1977) "Information 3." She described Information 3 as how a person gets informed—the behaviors used to select, use, and create an understanding or world picture. She identified these behaviors as decisioning, liking-disliking, and taking advice. Decision making was described in some detail: "A particular individual, finding himself in a particular situation, may approach that situation by decision*ing*. He screens his 'reality' for alternative means. He looks for relevant comparison attributes. He completes his decision matrix. He makes a decision" (p. 23). It seems possible to include the other two categories of Information 3 under the "alternative means," since taking advice is a means and liking-disliking is a motivation for choosing one alternative over another. What we have, of course, is the process of thinking—Popper's W2.

We cannot ignore W2, "the elusive nature of thought in action," the problem of interpretations and points of view. The psychological issues arising from the interaction of W2 and W3 are as much a part of the world of librarians and information scientists as are the graphic records. It is this elusive nature that concerns Dervin, because it is here that we find people constructing their own meanings of words and ideas. Popper's (1972) subjectivism is similar to constructivism. He wrote: "The activities or processes covered by the umbrella term 'understanding' are subjective or personal or psychological activities. They must be distinguished from the (more or less successful) *outcome* of these activities, from their result: the 'final state' (for the time being) of understanding, the *interpretation*" (pp. 162–63). Here is a clear distinction between process and product.

Popper's general schema of problem solving includes the problem's background, and this problem situation entails the activity of understanding that, as for all intellectual activities, consists of second-world processes. This goes back to Popper's opposition to the bucket theory of minds. Indeed, much of Popper's epistemology sounds like Dervin's. Here is his (1972) discussion of sense data:

Classical epistemology which takes our sense perceptions as "given," as the "data" from which our theories have to be constructed by some process of induction, can only be described as pre-Darwinian. It fails to take account of the fact that the alleged data are in fact adaptive reactions, and therefore interpretations which incorporate theories and prejudices and which, like theories, are impregnated with conjectural expectations: that there can be no pure perception, no pure datum; exactly as there can be no pure observational language, since all languages are impregnated with theories and myths. (pp. 145–46)

Dervin tells us there is no pure message because the message as prepared by experts is clouded by the experts' prejudices or the loaded meanings of the experts' language.

Much of Popper's (1972) discussion refers to the natural world, but he includes the way we know and how knowledge grows: "The epistemological idealist is right, in my view, in insisting that all knowledge, and the growth of knowledge—the genesis of the mutation of our ideas—stem from themselves, and that without these self-begotten ideas there would be no knowledge" (p. 68, footnote). Dervin would totally agree with this. It is the burden of her message. What she has left out—for rhetorical reasons, I am sure—is the concept in the following sentence: "He [the idealist] is wrong in failing to see that without elimination of these mutations through clashing with the environment there would not only be no incitement to new ideas, but no knowledge of anything" (p. 68, footnote). The environment, including the everyday world of things and the shared environment of W3, is essential for knowledge growth both in the cultural body of knowledge and in the growth of the individual's knowledge.

Popper emphasizes the other side of the problem situation. Where Dervin said we make decisions about what information is relevant, and what parts of a message are useful, based on our unique, subjective perception of a personal problem, Popper (1972) said: "We always pick out our problem against a third-world *background*. This background consists of at least a *language*, which always incorporates many theories in the very structure of its usages. . . . A problem, together with its background . . . constitutes what I call a *problem situation*" (p. 165). Nor does Popper ignore the personal:

I am ready to admit, however, that there are certain subjective experiences or attitudes which do play a part in the process of understanding. I have in mind such things as *emphasis*: the picking out of a problem or a theory as important, even though it may not be precisely the problem or theory under investigation; or the opposite: the *dismissal* of some theory as irrelevant rather than as false; or, say, as irrelevant to the discussion at a certain stage, even though it may be important at another stage; or perhaps even the dismissal of a theory as false *and* as too irrelevant for being discussed explicitly. (pp. 166–67)

Popper was referring to scientific types of problems, but the analysis easily fits Dervin's information seekers. Perhaps the difference in emphasis lies in the nature of the problems—the one aiming for scientific, impartial objectivity, the other being personal and emotion-laden.

Popper suggested that the act of understanding was the same as problem solving and consisted of World 2 processes. He put it all together this way:

Yet the subjective work involved can be analysed, and has to be analysed, as an operation with third-world objects. It is an operation that establishes in some cases a kind of familiarity with these objects, and with the handling of these objects. To use an analogy, it can be compared with the activities of a builder of bridges or houses: in trying to solve some practical problem he operates with, or handles, simple structural units, or more complex structural units, with the help of simple or else sophisticated tools. (p. 166)

What could be more constructivist than that? But perhaps this is enough to show that the philosophical positions of Dervin and Popper are not unlike the moving patterns of light and shadow made by flickering leaves, here and there falling across each other in the play of thought.

THE DILEMMA OF THE SUBJECTIVE IN KNOWLEDGE MANAGEMENT

In the mid-sixties, after years of study and development of indexing and classification systems, the realization dawned that the inquirer's bias or point of view was preventing the attainment of the ideal. During one of the early conferences on classification research, Eric de Grolier (1965) was "struck one night" with the idea that "it was very important to study the questions posed by the users and to deduce from those questions the useful classifications" (p. 12). Later, we shall come across N. J. Belkin, T. Seeger, and G. Wersig (1983) still wrestling with this problem.

S. R. Ranganathan (1965), creating the language of classification theory as he founded libraries and library science in India, was aware of the problem of linearly organizing books on shelves while having to devise a classification scheme to satisfy the multidimensional universe of knowledge. His solution was to find "the most helpful sequence" by consulting experts for a consensus. But he knew this was insufficient and suffered "sleepless nights and nightmares" as he struggled with the "maddening" problem (pp. 33–34).

Jason Farradane, who spent forty years investigating the problems of indexing and classification, was well aware of the uniqueness of each inquirer. He saw too that the text, once published, was separate from the author, an implicit recognition of Popper's W3. Recognizing the individuality of the indexer, the author (as abstract writer), and the user, he wrote: "Some loss of information, or bias is however, inescapable: even the original author will have introduced some bias of viewpoint, not to be overcome by machine reading. Furthermore, the future applications of a given paper cannot be foreseen, and work undertaken in one field may prove to be of value in another subject which no method of indexing can anticipate" (Farradane, Poulton, and Datta 1965, pp. 287–88). Foreshadowing Dervin as well as the current problems in information retrieval, Farradane (1961) early saw, as noted above, that "the ideal index or classification structure will not have the elusive nature of thought in action" (p. 128).

While this confrontation between the individual and the text was going on in indexing and classification, Robert Taylor was engaged in the research that would result in his classic article on the reference interview. Taylor (1968), describing his work in terms Dervin would use later, said it was "an early effort to understand better the communications functions of libraries and similar types of information centres" (p. 179). His view of the inquirer as one who comes to the library "to fill out his picture of the world" (p. 181) is similar to Dervin's sense-making. He was aware that library systems were "more concerned with the descriptions of physical objects (books, papers, etc.), than assistance to the user in defining his subject." This he saw as an important and critical differentiation, "for present systems are object-oriented (static) rather than inquiry-oriented (dynamic)" (p. 192).

Taylor's five filters, through which a librarian sifts the inquirer's question, take into consideration the individual qualities of the user. This is especially true of the filters relating to objectives and motivation and the personal characteristics of the inquirer. Taylor even suggested a "neutral" question, not unlike some of those devised by Dervin, which was related to the intended *use* of the information: "from such questions as 'what do you intend to do with this information?' additional concepts, phrases, and terms" (p. 192) useful in specifying the subject could be extracted.

However, because his research took place in a library and not on the street or in a blood donor clinic, Taylor had to include the collection as an object, or agent, in his analysis. Thus he saw that the librarian is "a translator, interpreting and restructuring the inquiry so it fits the files as they are organized by his library" (p. 186). There was no avoiding the fact that the question had to be built into the system—"the system including the information specialist and all the relevant files" (p. 186). At the same time, he saw that the keys to the collection—the classification systems and indexes— were too sophisticated for users, at least as the keys then existed (p. 188).

Considering all of this, it was not unnatural, perhaps, that Allen Kent (1974) would include indexing among his unsolvable problems in information science. He recognized that definitions of concepts "are in the eyes of the beholder" and not in that which is beheld. The decision regarding the significance of an article or concept "must be made by an individual [i.e., the indexer] who is, or must pose as, a judge (for all time to come) of the value of what is presented" (p. 304). He identified the crucial problem:

The problem of designing an information system would be a trivial one if (a) each event impinging on the consciousness of man were to result in identical streams of observation; (b) each observer were to use identical words in identical configurations to describe each such event; and (c) everyone interested in learning of the event were to use identical terminology in phrasing his questions. Common sense suggests, and experiment confirms, that a person does not always make the same choice when faced with the same options, even when the circumstances of choice seem in all relevant respects to be the same. (pp. 306–7)

Unsolvable problems are not shelved. They seem to fascinate. Thus, T. D. Wilson (1981), reviewing studies of user information needs, was forced to admit that "information use (which ought to point most directly to the needs experienced by people) is one of the most neglected areas" (p. 5). How information is used was one area identified by Douglas Zweizig and Dervin (1977) as needing research. Wilson (1981) recognized that "information may also satisfy affective needs, such as the need for security, for achievement, or for dominance" (p. 9). Dervin (1983b) listed a wide variety of information uses, most of which are affective in nature. For example, she wrote that in her research, individuals said the information helped them to get ideas, get skills, get motivated, get control, avoid a bad situation, get pleasure, or get connected to others (p. 61).

Wilson (1981) stated that we must shift our research focus "from an examination of the information sources and systems used by the information seeker to an exploration of the role of information in the user's everyday life in his work organisation or social setting" (p. 11). By uncovering the facts of the everyday lives of the people being studied, we will come to understand the needs that exist, the meaning that information has in their lives, and thus we will come to design more effective systems.

BELKIN AND INFORMATION RETRIEVAL

One of the clearest examples of the concern for the difficulties of including the idiosyncrasies of the individual user into the planning of an information service is N. J. Belkin's work on anomalous states of knowledge. In a discussion of the problems of retrieval in a typical information retrieval (IR) system, Belkin, R. N. Oddy, and H. M. Brooks (1982) entered a concise description that recalls Dervin's critique. They wrote:

The user must be able to specify all of the relevant aspects of the problem, in order for the system to work optimally. If they are not stated, then documents treating these concepts (relations) cannot be retrieved (since they do not match what was specified), or will be ranked only very low in terms of probability or degree of relevance (since they match the specification only poorly). The best-match principle depends upon the assumption of equivalence between expression of need and document text in that it treats the representation of need as a representation of the document ideal for resolving that need. (p. 63)

Dervin (1977) described the assumption this way: "The user comes to the library with a request and it is assumed that there is some universal truth value about the user's situation. The user's unique situation, then, is treated as a typical or normatively defined situation and is thus made amenable to a match in an information system designed normatively" (p. 19).

Belkin, Oddy, and Brooks contended that the best-match principle was untenable. An information need relates to a problem resolution. It is not a need in itself. The background of the problem might not be clear. As they said:

There are certainly occasions when one might be able to specify precisely what information is required to bring the state of knowledge to a structure adequate for resolution of the problem, but it seems obvious that the more usual situation will be that in which what is appropriate for the purpose is not known in advance. In such a situation, the best-match strategy does not seem a reasonable first choice for IR purposes. (Belkin, Oddy, and Brooks 1982, p. 63)

The cognitive orientation taken by Belkin, Oddy, and Brooks suggested that interactions of humans with one another, with the physical world, and with themselves are mediated by their states of knowledge about themselves and about the world with which they interact. The authors also looked at the IR situation as a "recipient-controlled communication system, aimed at resolving the expressed information needs of humans, primarily via texts produced by other human beings" (p. 65). Their "mediation" is not unlike the constructivist theory of information, and recipient control is mindful of the current receiver-oriented ideas about communication. Before leaving this point, we should note that Belkin, Oddy, and Brooks recognize W3 when they specify that information needs are expressed and that answers come primarily through texts produced by other human beings.

Working on the design of the information system called Projekt INSTRAT, Belkin, T. Seeger, and G. Wersig (1983) expanded on the dynamic nature of the information processing of humans: "Since the problem treatment processes are dynamic, information precision should be a service that has the possibility of adapting itself to different or changing states of the problem" (p. 154). It is, perhaps, logical that once the information retrieval problem has been seen as an "anomalous state of knowledge" (ASK), which is identical to Dervin's "gap," there would be a progression to the unique and changing aspects of humans as knowers and information users. Thus Belkin's human being is very close to Dervin's. Dervin (1977) says: "The same person in the 'same' situation on two different days will not see the situation in the same way" (p. 27).

Taking such a position on the changing world of the user's psychological state pushes IR research toward a consideration of affective as well as cognitive information needs. Belkin, Seeger, and Wersig (1983) wrote, "There is no specific 'information need,' but there are people in problematic situations where at different states of the problem treatment process different kinds of information provision may be helpful." That is, "situations where information provision can help the individual in problem management are not restricted to simple reference, document or fact finding, but may require advice, counselling, proof, identity reassurance, and so on" (p. 154).

In the Projekt INSTRAT information provision model, W3 is a fact. The mechanism will have a model of the world, that is, a knowledge or data base. Responses will depend on "the mechanism's perception of what aspects of its world are relevant to the particular user in the particular situation" (p. 157). A 1980 conference paper of Dervin's is cited as a theory on the need to include a model of the functions of the user in any analysis of the functions of an information mechanism. This recalls De Grolier's midnight insight to construct classification systems from users' questions.

It is interesting, and indicative of the communication/information-gathering problem in general, that Belkin's work was not cited by Linda Smith and Amy Warner (1984) in their taxonomy of representations of, among other things, queries, terms, and documents. More important, Smith and Warner identified a need for the discipline to construct a representation of the user, and it is here that the work of Belkin seems most relevant. Of course, Dervin's research is fundamental to the development of a user representation, both philosophically and practically. The discussion by Smith and Warner clearly recognized Dervin's kind of argument and illustrated the concern of library and information retrieval practitioners. They wrote:

Van Rijsbergen has observed, that a major stumbling block in designing effective IR systems is the uncertainty about how to incorporate knowledge about users into our system design. . . . At present most systems are neutral: given a query, the same response will result regardless of who has submitted that query. Implicit in this design is the assumption that all users can be represented in the same way, that the interaction and the particular response can be standard for all users. Although this assumption may be reasonable where the user group is relatively homogeneous and well trained, it becomes questionable when a more heterogeneous group of users can be anticipated. Hollnagel and Woods have recently suggested that the user representation should not only be matched to the user's cognitive characteristics, but also be dynamic. This is because a user may change over time, because the nature of the user's task may change dynamically, and because there may be different populations of users. (p. 118)

It is fascinating that the work of Dervin and Belkin, both widely published, should have been completely missed.

CONCLUSION

In their practice, librarians have developed systems of organization and of access to collections of books. Most librarians still work with books, not information. Special librarians, in industrial and scientific research organizations, dealing mainly with journal and report literature, have had to be concerned about smaller packages of knowledge. Thinkers such as Ranganathan, Farradane, Taylor, and Belkin have worried more about access to smaller items of information than have so-called traditional librarians, whose collections have been accessible using large-scope subject categories such as the Library of Congress Subject Headings (LCSH) and the general classification schemes.

The early cataloguers were not unaware of the problem of individual point of view. C. A. Cutter (1876) wrote: "It is true that no system of classification can bring together all related works. The arrangement that suits one man's investigations is a hindrance to another's" (p. 530). Nor is the catalogue any better: "No catalogue can exhibit all possible connections of thought. Enough if it exhibit the most common, and give some clew for tracing the rarer ones. Those that claim perfection for any system show that they have no idea of the difficulties to be overcome" (p. 541).

Melvil Dewey (1876), addicted to the practical and the economic, was fully aware that his system was not perfect: "The impossibility of making a satisfactory classification of all knowledge as preserved in books, has been appreciated from the first, and nothing of the kind attempted. . . . Theoretically, the division of every subject into just nine heads is absurd" (p. 625).

The current rethinking of intellectual access to knowledge stores arises from several sources: research programs based on cognitive science theories such as Dervin's, machine information system designs such as Belkin's, and the merging of AI and IR as exemplified in Smith and Warner's taxonomy—all wrestling with the difficulties of serving individual needs. These are radically different vectors for librarianship and for the discipline of information science because of the move away from stores of packages of knowledge to stores of knowledge and information per se—in W3 text to be sure, but stored in invisible electronic pulses and not in physical packages to be shelved.

The history of the development of intellectual access to the store of knowledge is a history of the tension between the fluid uniqueness of the individual inquirer and the essential stability and concreteness of the store of knowledge itself. One of the most important problems facing the next generation of information scientists will be the relative fluidity of information stored electronically. The potential for losing first editions of any publication—with the ability we have in a computer to erase, correct, or change without leaving a paper trail—threatens the credibility of publishers and authors when the corrections cannot be checked against the originals. There is, of course, the promise, which Belkin and others are working to bring to fruition, that the fluidity of the computer will make it a more appropriate store of knowledge for the searching process of the unique and fluid inquirer.

However, as long as the store has to be accessed in graphic (print or picture) form, the problem of linking individual and store will remain; that is, as long as we must use our five senses to perceive the world. As Cutter noted, it is a difficulty in the nature of things. Information does exist "out there," and we must deal with it from "in here."

NOTE

The author wishes to thank Patricia Dewdney, Paul Gallina, and Michael Heine for commenting on an earlier version of this chapter.

REFERENCES

Belkin, N. J., R. N. Oddy, and H. M. Brooks. "ASK for Information Retrieval, Part 1: Background and Theory. *Journal of Documentation* 38(2):61–71 (1982).

Belkin, N. J., T. Seeger, and G. Wersig. "Distributed Expert Problem Treatment as a Model for Information System Analysis and Design." *Journal of Information Science* 5(5): 153–67 (Feb. 1983).

Brookes, B. C. "The Foundations of Information Science, Part 1: Philosophical Aspects." *Journal of Information Science* 2(5): 125–33, (Oct. 1980).

Cutter, C. A. "Library Catalogues." In *Public Libraries in the United States of America: Their History, Condition, and Management*, 526–622. Special report, Department of the Interior, Bureau of Education. Washington, D.C.: Government Printing Office, 1876.

De Grolier, Eric. "Current Trends in Theory and Practice of Classification." In Pauline Atherton, ed., *Classification Research*, 9–14, Copenhagen: Lungaard, 1965.

Dervin, Brenda. "The Everyday Information Needs of the Average Citizen: A Taxonomy for Analysis." In Manfred Kochen and Joseph C. Donohue, eds., *Information for the Community*, 19–38. Chicago: American Library Association, 1976.

———. *The Information Needs of Californians—1984, Report No. 2: Context Summary, Conclusions, Implications, Applications*. Sacramento: California State Library, 1984.

———. "Mass Communicating: Changing Conceptions of the Audience." In Ronald E. Rice and William J. Paisley, eds., *Public Communication Campaigns*, 71–87. Beverly Hills, Calif.: Sage Publications, 1981.

———. "More Will Be Less Unless: The Scientific Humanization of Information Systems." *National Forum* 63(3): 25–27 (1983a).

———. *An Overview of Sense-making Research: Concepts, Methods, and Results to Date*. Presented at the International Communications Association Annual Meeting, Dallas, May 1983. Seattle: School of Communications, University of Washington, 1983b.

———. "Useful Theory for Librarianship: Communication Not Information." *Drexel Library Quarterly* 13(3): 16–32 (July 1977).

Dervin, Brenda, and Benson Fraser. *How Libraries Help*. Sacramento: California State Library, 1985.

Dervin, Brenda, Thomas L. Jacobson, and Michael S. Nilan. "Measuring Aspects of Information-Seeking: A Test of Quantitative/Qualitative Methodology." In M. Burgoon, eds., *Communication Yearbook 6*, 419–44. Beverly Hills, Calif.: Sage Publications, 1982.

Dervin, B., D. Zweizig, M. Banister, M. Gabriel, M. Hall, E. Kwan, and C. Kwan, with J. Bowes and K. Stamm. *The Development of Strategies for Dealing with the Information Needs of Urban Residents, Phase 1: The Citizen Study*. Final report on Project No. L0035JA, Grant No. OEG–0–74–7308 for U.S. Office of Education, Office of Libraries and Learning Resources. Washington, D.C.: U.S. Office of Education, 1976.

Dewey, Melvil. "A Decimal Classification and Subject Index." In *Public Libraries in the United States of America: Their History, Condition, and Management*, 623–48. Special report, Department of the Interior, Bureau of Education. Washington, D.C.: Government Printing Office, 1876.

Farradane, Jason. "Fundamental Fallacies and New Needs in Classification." In D. J. Foskett and B. I. Palmer, eds., *The Sayers Memorial Volume*, 120–35. London: Library Association, 1961.

Farradane, J., R. K. Poulton, and S. Datta. "Problems in Analysis and Terminology for Information Retrieval." *Journal of Documentation* 21(4): 287–90 (1965).

Gallina, Paul Leonard. "Karl Popper's 3 Worlds and Some Consideration for Information Science." In *Proceedings of the 11th Annual CAIS Conference, Halifax, May 24–26, 1983*, pp. 195–203. Perth, Ontario: Canadian Association for Information Science, 1983.

Inose, Hiroshi, and John R. Pierce. *Information Technology and Civilisation*. New York: W. H. Freeman & Co., 1984. (A report to the Club of Rome Conference, Tokyo, 1982.)

Kent, Allen. "Unsolvable Problems." In Anthony Debons, ed., *Information Science: Search for Identity*," 299–311. Proceedings of the 1972 NATO Advanced Study Institute in Information Science, Seven Springs, Champion, Penn., August 12–20, 1972. New York: Dekker, 1974.

Neill, S. D. "Brookes, Popper, and Objective Knowledge." *Journal of Information Science* 4(1):33–39 (March 1982).

———. "The Reference Process and the Philosophy of Karl Popper." *RQ* 24(3): 309–19 (Spring 1985).

O'Hear, Anthony. *Karl Popper*. London: Routledge & Kegan Paul, 1980.

Popper, Karl. *Objective Knowledge: An Evolutionary Approach*. London: Oxford University Press, 1972.

———. *Unended Quest: An Intellectual Autobiography*. LaSalle, Ill.: Open Court Publishing Co., 1976.

Ranganathan, S. R. *The Colon Classification*. New Brunswick, N.J.: Rutgers University Graduate School of Library Science, 1965.

Serrai, Alfredo. *Temi di attualita bibliotecaria*. Rome: Burzone, 1981.

Smith, Linda C., Amy J. Warner. "A Taxonomy of Representations in Information Retrieval System Design." *Journal of Information Science* 8(3): 113–21. (April 1984)

Swanson, Don R. "Libraries and the Growth of Knowledge." *Library Quarterly* 50(1): 112–34 (1980).

———. "Undiscovered Public Knowledge." *Library Quarterly* 56(2): 103–18 (April 1986).

Taylor, R. S. "Question-Negotiation and Information Seeking in Libraries." *College and Research Libraries* 29(3): 178–94 (May 1968).

Wilson, T. D. "On User Studies and Information Needs." *Journal of Documentation* 37(1): 3–15 (1981).

Zweizig, Douglas, and Brenda Dervin. "Public Library Use, Users, Uses: Advances in Knowledge of the Characteristics and Needs of the Adult Clientele of American Public Libraries." In Melvin J. Voight and Michael H. Harris, eds., *Advances in Librarianship*, Vol. 7, 231–55. New York: Academic Press, 1977.

2

The Dilemma of the Physical in the Objectification of Subjective Knowledge Structures: The Role of the Body in Thinking

INTRODUCTION

If the librarian must concentrate on the store of knowledge in graphic forms, the information scientist must concentrate on the design of storage and retrieval systems that will produce information at the time of need and appropriate to the person or persons in need. Computer systems, being a kind of anti-environment for human intelligence, have highlighted the way humans process knowledge and information (for convenience, I use these words interchangeably, but I have differentiated them in Neill 1985). However, no matter how easily computers manipulate their electronic components, and therefore information, computers and humans differ in one essential way that directly affects thinking. This factor cannot be forgotten, since it is the peculiarity of human thinking processes that lies behind the episodes of information use given throughout this book to illustrate the dilemmas faced by information scientists. It is this factor that is described in this chapter.

THINKING

Some years ago I published a brief description of ways in which scholars thought that did not involve the use of words (Neill 1980). One example showed how a historian could reconstruct an event in his imagination and, like an actor in the scene, go through the thinking processes of the historical figures. Another described the work of a microbiologist as he rotated the image of a cell in his mind and, like a spectator, "saw" the missing parts. A third example, which was a little different, told how a wide receiver in football studied slow-motion movies of an opposing team to get a sense or feeling of where the defense would be at different times so that he could react without thinking. At the time, my conclusion was that the use of conceptual models of knowledge (indexing systems, trees, networks, frames, taxonomies) to represent knowledge in information retrieval systems could be restrictive and certainly incomplete because they were missing too much of the information in subjective knowledge structures, at least in *some* subjective knowledge structures.

Others have addressed some aspects of thinking that the computer can't do, concentrating on the broader context of society that impinges on meanings of words. Hiroshi Inose and John R. Pierce (1984, pp. 128–30) and Terry Winograd and Fernando Flores (1985) discuss the cultural and social layers of meaning with which each individual has enveloped the language. *Cultural* here is the broad culture of race and nation and also the local culture of region and place of work. All add conceptual layers. Winograd and Flores stated that they had not focused on aspects of intelligence directly concerned with perception and action in the physical world, not because the issues were different but because the central focus of the argument was clearer in "disembodied areas" (pp. 127–28).

Hubert L. Dreyfus (1972) and Dreyfus and Stuart E. Dreyfus (1986) discussed the role of the body in intelligent behavior, considered in terms of perception and the learning of physical skills such as riding a bicycle. My concern is the "body English" we put on thoughts—the physical or muscular substratum of the thinking process that underlies our knowledge and that is not represented in conceptual constructs such as scripts, plans, and classification schemes.

If we can only imperfectly objectify subjective knowledge structures, that is, make verbal models, because those knowledge structures have been stripped of their social and lived-in contexts, how far from that goal are we if knowledge structures have as part of their nature some physical, felt properties as well? If it can be shown that knowledge structures are, even in a small but necessary way, muscular, then not even an analogue or image component added to some future fifth-generation, knowledge-based artificial intelligence (AI) system will be able to think like a human being. In addition, the limitations of information retrieval systems using computers must be seen as clearly as possible, lest they be *expected* perfectly to match human information needs.

FEELING

There is a large literature on the use and nature of visual images in human thinking, and imaging is a clear issue in AI. In information retrieval (IR), the problem is not just representation but interactive communication. In their classic work on nonverbal communication, Jurgen Ruesch and Weldon

Kees (1956) noted, "In analogic codification, the signs are 'felt' in the body to a much greater degree than in digital codification, where feelings of localization seem to be missing" (p. 5). William G. Cole (1988) noted that an image encourages kinesthetic "memory" (p.8). Of course, in the digital codification of sounds into letters and words, the effect is to create meaning and then imaginative reaction to that meaning. Eugene Gendlin (1962) noted the difficulty of finding words to explain the localization effect:

One group of modern thinkers (Bergson, Sartre) have especially pointed out this concrete affective side of experience and its central importance in human life. They have also pointed out how difficult is the application of logic and concepts to experience as actually lived and felt. They have said that only "intuition" or actual living can grasp it adequately, while concepts and definitions can distort and deaden it. The attempt to define, they say, can turn living experience into abstractions or into dead objects of study. Thus, despite its crucial importance, felt experience has been conceptualized only vaguely, and only as it occurs at a few crucial junctures of life (for example, "encounter," "commitment"), rather than as the ever present and powerful factor it is. (p. 2)

There is a relationship here to Terry Winograd and Fernando Flores's (1985) understanding of perception, in which interaction with the environment is "always through the activity of the entire nervous system" (p. 43). Thus, "language, as a consensual domain, is a patterning of 'mutual orienting behavior,' not a collection of mechanisms in a 'language user' or a 'semantic' coupling between linguistic behavior and non-linguistic perturbations experienced by the organisms" (p. 49). Not only is language consensual, but inherent in the use of language (pp. 155, 162) is a commitment that belongs to the affective side of experience.

From an entirely different angle, H. Curtis Wright (1986), arguing against the possibility of impartiality in social science research, broadens the perspective on the place of commitment and experience in intellectual pursuits as he links thinking with action: "You cannot hover aloof and distant over the people whose subjective processes you are studying by refusing to experience the roles and functions they perform in the social order. The subjective processes which generate rational behavior in a human being must be communicated to observers through intimate familiarity with the empirical lives of the people they observe" (p. 750).

So far, the evidence presented has indicated a very general and very vague connection between the body (as flesh and emotion) and applied knowledge (as action or doing). What evidence is there to denote a closer connection between muscle (feeling) and thought?

Albert Einstein's imaginary trip on a beam of light is often used to illustrate the use of visual images in thinking. It is not as often noticed that Einstein mentioned another aspect of his thought processes. In a letter to Jacques Hadamard (1945), we find the following sentence: "The above mentioned elements are, in my case, of visual and some of muscular type" (appendix 2). Horace Freeland Judson (1980) informed us that "one great physical chemist was credited by his peers, who watched him awestruck, with the ability to think about chemical structures directly in quantum terms—so that if a proposed molecular model was too tightly packed he felt uncomfortable, as though his shoes pinched" (p. 6). Albert Rothenberg (1979) quoted Poincaré: "A host of ideas kept surging in my mind. I could almost feel them jostling one another, until two of them coalesced (*s'accrochassent*) so to speak, to form a stable combination" (p. 117). Eugene Ferguson (1977), in giving several examples of the use of visual images in thinking, oddly included this: "Michael Pupin wrote of the imaginative originality of Peter Cooper Hewitt, inventor of the mercury-vapor lamp. Those who knew him, watching him at work, felt that a part, at least, of Hewitt's thinking apparatus was in his hands" (p. 834).

Harold Rugg (1963), in a chapter on "felt thought through gestural symbol," made a somewhat unusual claim for the role of feeling in thinking:

Breaking down the total process called thinking into its steps will show how it is colored throughout by feeling. First, there is a tendency to delay response, a withholding, a gathering-together of self, which is primarily a feeling motor set; second, a grasping of relationships, fundamentally a feeling process; third, sensing and holding a continuing, directed line of thought, also a feeling process; fourth, imaginative use of symbols, probably basically a feeling process; fifth, skill in drawing diagrams and other forms of "thought models"; sixth, generalizing, using concepts. . . . Feeling is the matrix of thought. (p. 270)

D. E. Berlyne (1965) made his contribution to the phenomenon by reporting on studies of sympathetic muscular activity during thought processes. For example, "when a human being imagines himself executing a certain bodily movement, action currents occur in the muscles that the movement would use, even though the muscles are not contracting enough to produce a visible change in posture" (p. 139).

What are we dealing with here? Eugene Gendlin (1962) wrote a book about it from a psychotherapist's angle. He too quoted Hadamard:

Jacques Hadamard gives examples of mathematicians who employ dots or circles. . . . He concludes: "What may be the use of such a strange and cloudy imagery?" "I need it in order to have a simultaneous view of all elements of the argument, to hold them together, in short, to achieve that synthesis we spoke of. . . . " Here again, felt meanings function to make problem solving possible, while the symbols (dots) are mere grips, referring to felt meaning. Although Hadamard appears to make synthesis his prime principle, we shall refrain from doing so. Viewing many aspects at once and as a whole is only one vital function of felt meanings. (p. 74)

Gendlin (1962) provides another way of understanding felt meaning that is similar to the example of learning to ride a bicycle: "Suppose we are learning to dance. We may see a dance performed, we may know and be able to describe it in all sorts of symbols, but we lack the 'feel' of the action until we learn to dance" (p. 69). Transferring this physical "feel" to the level of thinking and imagination, after deep immersion, is what happens in the examples above and is identified in the words of the biologist Agnes Arber (1954): "New hypotheses come into the mind most freely when discursive reasoning (including its visual component) has been raised by intense effort to a level at which it finds itself united indissolubly with feeling and emotion. When reason and intuition attain this collaboration, the unity into which they merge appears to possess a creative power which was denied to either singly" (pp. 20–21). Susan Aylwin (1985) corroborates this: "An equally close relationship between thought and feeling is found in the experience of insight. Here the excitement accompanying the cognitive content is what tells the thinker the idea is a good one. At the moment of insight, truth is as much a matter of feeling as it is of thought" (p. 3). There is no reason to think that this experience belongs only to creative individuals who have achieved greatness. The excitement of insight applies to all thinking beings faced with the solution to a problem, when that solution is "a good one."

Winogard and Flores (1985) link management and conversation. "Every manager is primarily concerned with generating and maintaining a network of conversations for action—conversation in which requests and commitments lead to successful completion of work" (p. 144). If the phenomenon Gendlin (1978) describes in the following is imagined as taking place in an office or information center, with requests and commitments made and accepted, some idea of the play of the biological can be gained. Gendlin asks that we think of two people who are prominent in our lives (he calls them John and Helen) and let the mind go from one to the other, recalling all that is known about each:

The inner aura as you think of each person isn't made up of discrete bits of data that you consciously add together in your mind. In thinking of Helen, you don't laboriously list all her physical and personal traits one by one. You don't think, "Oh yes, Helen: she's 5'6" tall, has blond hair and brown eyes and a small mole next to her ear, talks in a high voice, gets upset easily, wants to be a playwright, likes Chinese food, needs to lose weight. . . . " Nor do you list each detail of your relationships with her.

There are undoubtedly millions of such bits of data that describe Helen as you know here, but these millions of bits aren't delivered to you one by one, as thoughts. Instead, they are given to you all at once, as felt. . . . The sense of "all about John" comes to you in the same way. (pp. 35–37)

Gendlin says all of this information is stored in the body, which is a "biological computer" (p. 37), bringing it to mind instantaneously.

D. M. Hunns (1982), discussing the way safety inspectors estimate the probability or error-producing events, concluded, "The foundation of subjective estimation is experience, direct or indirect stored in the mind of the assessor." As this population of evidence accumulates in the mind, it produces a "feel" for the frequency or probability of occurrence of a particular event. Hunns then developed the nature of this "feeling" in an interesting way. "It is as though the mind's eye views the evidence as an amorphous mass, rather like a pile of bricks, clearly feeling the bulk but not discriminating, in any numerate sense, the individual contributions from which it is formed" (p. 197). These feelings are difficult to quantify on a numerically calibrated scale, even though, Hunns says, "we can distinguish different strengths of comparative feeling" (p. 198).

It is enlightening to compare this process with the memory-based reasoning project of Craig Stanfill and David Waltz (1986), which was developed to use memory "to recall specific episodes from the past" (p. 1213). They felt that memory, rather than rules, should be the foundation of machine reasoning. "Two bodies of evidence have led us to support this hypothesis," they wrote. "The first is the study of cognition: It is difficult to conceive of thought without memory. The second is the inability of AI to achieve success in any broad domain or to effectively capture the notion of 'common sense,' much of which, we believe, is based on essentially undigested memories of past experience" (p. 1213). Memories, I might add, stored in muscles as well as brains. The machine task they tested was the recall of the pronunciation of letters and then words. Information about a set of words was programmed into the data base—a letter, the preceding four letters, the succeeding ten letters, the phoneme stress for the letter, and the preceding four phonemes and stresses. The program resulted in "a full word performance of 47 percent correct, 21 percent marginally wrong, and 32 percent wrong" (p. 1218). This level of intelligence was supported by Douglas Lenat et al. (1990). Commenting on state-of-the-art expert systems, in the context of programs with "common sense," they said, "Knowing an infinitesimal fraction as much as the human expert, the program has only the *veneer* of intelligence" (p. 32).

Relevant to one of the connotations of this book—that information science is really a humanities discipline—is this comment by Stanfill and Waltz (1986): "Knowledge acquisition, or the process of identifying and formalizing rules, remains an art" (p. 1216).

In a way not unlike that of the safety inspectors, nurses too rely on their feelings. Patricia Benner (1984) has written a work to show how excellence is based on physical experience. "The book asserts that perceptual awareness is central to good nursing judgment and that this begins with vague hunches and global assessments that initially bypass critical analysis; conceptual clarity follows more often than it precedes. Expert nurses often describe their perceptual abilities using phrases such as 'gut feeling,' a 'sense of uneasiness," or a 'feeling that things are not quite right' " (p. xviii).

Judson (1980) reports an example of a conscious need and rationale for getting the "feel" of an experience, in a conversation with Joscelyn Bell Burnell, a radio astronomer and the discoverer of pulsars.

And when it [the antenna system] was built, then it was my job to start operating it, and to analyze the data that came pouring out. They came out on a strip of paper, a long sheet of blue-squared paper that the tracing pen moved over. We got a hundred feet of chart paper every day. I operated the telescope for six months, which meant that there was three and a half miles of chart recording by the end. Anybody else would have got the computer to analyze it, but Muggins—she gestured to herself— sat down to analyze it by hand. Well, perhaps you wouldn't give it to the computer straight away, because with new equipment you want to get the feel of how it's performing and check that all's going okay. (p. 82)

Paul Dirac, the theoretical physicist who discovered antimatter, answered Judson's question "How does one recognize beauty in a theory?" with these words: "Well—you feel it, just like beauty in a picture or beauty in music. You can't describe it, it's something—and if you don't feel it, you just have to accept that you're not susceptible to it. No one can explain it to you. . . . I've found during the recent celebrations of Einstein's centenary, that Einstein had very much this same point of view" (p. 199).

LEARNING

Educational psychologists agree that learning must be based on the careful use of experience. Thus Jerome Bruner (1971) notes:

With respect to matching successive prerequisites to the "natural" limits of developing intellectual skills, most work suggests that it is often best done first through embodiment of principles in action, then by the supplement of image, and finally in symbolic form. Whether one is teaching set theory, the conservation of momentum and inertia, or the notion of representation before the law, one does well to begin with concrete actions to be performed, passing on to vivid case or paradigm instance, and coming finally to the formal description in natural language or mathematics. (p. 122)

Robert Gagné (1965), in his classic work on the kinds and conditions of learning, is even more positive:

Instruction needs to be fundamentally based on the stimulation provided by objects and events (that is, changes in objects), assuming, of course, that these objects may be people. . . . Objects and events are the stimuli from which concepts are derived. Although instruction comes to depend heavily on verbal communication, the words merely "stand for" things that may be directly observed. (p. 272)

It might be argued that Bruner and Gagné are basically concerned with learning in the elementary and secondary schools, and that is true. There is a difference between grade school and graduate school. David P. Ausubel (1968) says that after junior high school, students can acquire most new concepts and learn most new propositions by directly grasping higher-order relationships between abstractions (knowledge representations) because, at that stage, students have a body of higher-order abstractions and transactional terms. Since understanding requires reflection on what we already know, these abstractions and terms, being what we already know, can be used to postulate, for example, what is unobservable in order to explain what is observed. However, Ausubel cautions:

It would be very misleading, however, to assert that secondary school, and even older, students can *never* profit either from the use of concrete-empirical props to generate intuitive meaning, or from the use of inductive discovery and deductive problem-solving techniques to enhance such meanings. As previously suggested, generally mature students tend to function at a relatively concrete or intuitive level when confronted with a particularly *new* subject-matter area in which they are as yet totally unsophisticated. (p. 276)

The reason for the tendency to function at the concrete level is that new concepts, to be learned, must be related to the physical world, since learners do not have the ideas already established. Then, having learned the concepts, students can go on to formulate principles and propositions, blending these into whatever knowledge they already have.

Aylwin (1985), discussing representation based on actions, gives us the bottom line: "In developmental psychology enactive representations are taken to be the foundation of all subsequent intelligence, and the means whereby the most basic aspects of reality are constructed" (p. 16). She reviews the literature, showing a renewed awareness of the epistemological importance of action, and concludes that enactive imagery involves "covert action, a first-person-singular perspective, an agent and muscular tension" (p. 20).

My concern is with experience, its peculiar kind of meaning, and its use not only for verification and supplying meaning to concepts but also for innervation. *Innervation* is understood as the supplying of nerves, or what is laid down "in our bones" when, for example, we put our thoughts down on paper, or put them into words in discussion, or go through the motions to find out for ourselves what some procedure really entails. It is the process of getting the "feel of the material" in a physical sense, even when the "material" is intellectual.

REAFFERENCE

With the requisite physical experience laid in, most concepts can be easily learned through verbal symbols, reading, lectures, and discussion. Objects and physical events, however, though definable in sentences, are known in terms of their sensible manifestations. Making valid judgments about, or valid evaluations of, procedures, behaviors, processes, or spatially organized objects cannot be achieved by considering only "given" definitions, propositions, or conceptualizations. Secure judgments depend to a certain extent on the knowledge one has of one's own intellectual and behavioral idiosyncrasies. Such knowledge is gained by thinking about one's mental and physical reactions before and as they occur, for example, during the process of working through a problem with all the equipment and time constraints of some real situation. The process is not unlike a technical rehearsal for a play in which the actors and stagehands experience full costumes, lighting, and props for the first time but can stop and get things straightened out if necessary. After a good technical rehearsal, the cast and crew generally know what can go wrong and what actions to take to keep it from doing so. Knowledge comes from having been there.

The "definition" that comes from sense experience is similar to the operational definition supplied by a child who says "a hole is to dig." By experiencing procedures and actions, we get a definition, or a feeling of what to do. We get a sense of the whole, founded on a knowledge of what the furniture feels like or just how some machine sounds when it is about to break down. By going through the process of linking principles to objects, we get a sense of the structure of the physical moves that accompany the principles when we put them into words.

With the intention of acting, a person constructs an imaginary plan of intended moves—imaginary if it is the first time. This plan is subject to feedback at each step. The process of intention and feedback is *reafference*, what Jerome Bruner (1971) calls "a joint representation of action intended along with the consequence of that action" (p. 139).

Walking through any space for the purpose of, for example, siting a workstation is an intended action in itself, the consequences of which include a new consciousness of one's self in the spaces of a particular building. There is also a heightened awareness of the meaning of *workstation*, an awareness that is the focus of the physical as well as the intellectual attention. Having gone through these motions once, there is a pattern or action scheme which is laid down in brain and nerves and which provides information to feed forward—to provide an intuitive feeling for any similar decision-making situation. The information used the second and succeeding times in not imaginary, although it may be imaginative. It is information that can be felt, since it is based on experience.

THE BODY PERCEPT

In a 1963 symposium on "the body percept," held at the seventeenth International Congress of Psychology, experimental evidence was presented to show that a person's concept of his or her body is part of that person's cognitive style or way of knowing (Witkin 1965, p. 41). Part of the learning process is the relating of the body, or rather one's concept of the body, to that which is learned. This would be true especially in the case of learning the nature of objects and actions and of applying principles in operational situations.

In another study it was reported that there was evidence that each individual has a unique way of perceiving his or her body "as contrasted to nonself objects" (Fisher and Cleveland 1965, p. 48). One of the conclusions of Seymour Fisher's (1986) exhaustive analysis of the literature in this field was that "body image equivalents serve important signal functions, helping to organize information and render decisions" (vol. 1, p. 316). The point being that one of the "apparent potentials of the body image is to represent in body experience terms what is being perceived and coded at other levels of psychological feeling and attitude" (vol. 1, p. 316). Douwe Tiemersma (1989), in an historical review of the body image literature, began by highlighting the fact that "the material and mental characteristics of the body thoroughly permeate each other (p. 1). We all have to discover how we relate, physically, to new environments and situations. Such a relationship is associated with the need for feedback and with the feed-forward of intended movements in the construction of behavioral plans. Ulric Neisser (1976) explained it this way:

Information about oneself, like all other information, can only be picked up by an appropriately tuned schema. Conversely, all information that is picked up, including proprioceptive information, modifies the schema. In the case of movement through the environment, this is an orienting schema or cognitive map. This means that the cognitive map always includes the perceiver as well as the environment. Ego and world are perceptually inseparable. (pp. 116–17)

The percept one has of one's own body in a certain milieu is part of one's knowledge or understanding of that milieu. Part of the meaning of a concept is how one senses the world. There is a physical component to our knowledge that is stored in our nerves and muscles, not only in our brains. The existence of this physical quotient is one of the reasons managers *need* to communicate face to face, and why Hunns's supervisors and engineers made decisions about the probability of accidents by the feelings generated from empirical experiences, and why one's concept of query negotiation with a customer entails a consciousness of one's body, how it presents itself, and how one thinks it is seen by others, as well as a consciousness of the feelings and muscular reactions associated with the content of our knowledge structures.

PARTICIPATION

Brian Smith (1988), of Xerox Palo Alto Research Center's Intelligent Systems Laboratory, has proposed a similar idea somewhat more abstractly. He calls it "participation." His strongest description of this phenomenon is that "the physical states that realize our thoughts are caused by non-representational conditions, and engender non-representational consequences, in ways that must be coordinated with the contents of the very representational states they realize" (pp. 4–5). He expands these nonrepresentational conditions in a discussion of the fundamental constraints governing computers and representational systems in general.

Of the two basic kinds of constraints—causal relations and content relations—it is the causal relations of a system that are relevant here. Smith broke these down into three groups:

1. *Internal activity and behavior*: the relation between a system at some time and the same system shortly thereafter. This is what we've called (psychology).
2. *External connection*: actions the system takes that affect the world, and effects on the system of the world around it—the results, that is, of sensors and effectors. (Clocks have none of this, but other systems are clearly not so limited.)
3. *Background dynamics*: the progress or flow of the surrounding situation. The passage of time would be counted as one instance, as would one's conversant's behavior, or the passing visual scene. (p. 27)

This "participation" in events—internal psychological experience, actual sensory contact with things, and awareness of surrounding events and objects— is a causal connection to what we *think*. It is a part of the thoughts we have. Mental images and words are connected irrevocably to their referents in reality. George Lakoff (1987) coined the term *experientialism* to mean what Smith means by *participation*. Lakoff describes several facets of thought: it has an ecological structure and gestalt properties, is imaginative, and is embodied. The last is relevant to this chapter. "Thought is *embodied*, that is, the structures used to put together our conceptual systems grow out of bodily experience and make sense in terms of it; the core of our conceptual systems is directly grounded in perception, body movement, and experience of a physical and social character" (p. xiv).

T. S. Eliot (1948) noted the tendency of language to become more abstract and ambiguous the further the speaker got from daily experience. "A local speech on a local issue is likely to be more intelligible than one addressed to a whole nation, and we observe that the greatest muster of ambiguities is to be found in speeches which are addressed to the whole world" (pp. 87–88). Shoshana Zuboff (1988) quotes a manager who spent his early career in the navy:

I spent years and years on the bridge of a ship looking for the horizon, and gave orders based on the information my eyes gave me. With computer technology, the commander of a ship is no longer on the bridge. He is in a room filled with computers. Now he looks at the screen with a lot of information and makes decisions. He must have new ways of making sense. He must *feel* the numbers, trends and plots, and relate it to the outside, to what really happens. (p. 168, emphasis added)

THE OBJECTIFICATION OF SUBJECTIVE KNOWLEDGE STRUCTURES

Knowledge that can be turned into words or pictures can be "objectified" in various ways for communication purposes. Some part of knowledge, however, must be left behind in the body that gathered it, felt it, stored it, and massaged it. Only abstractions (print, ideographs) and models can be objectified and made into machine-readable representations. Indeed, *representations* is just the word to use. Knowledge representations are not knowledge but rather representations of knowledge.

Still, that is plenty. It is not as bad as the wheelwright makes out in the following story, told by Victor Gollancz (1950):

Duke Huan of Ch'i was reading a book at the upper end of the hall; the wheelwright was making a wheel at the lower end. Putting aside his mallet and chisel, he called to the Duke and asked him what book he was reading. "One that records the words of the Sages," answered the Duke. "Are those Sages alive?" asked the wheelwright. "Oh, no," said the Duke, "they are dead." "In that case," said the wheelwright, "what you are reading can be nothing but the lees and scum of bygone men." "How dare you, a wheelwright, find fault with the book I am reading? If you can explain your statement, I will let it pass. If not, you shall die." "Speaking as a wheelwright," he replied, "I look at the matter in this way: when I am making a wheel, if my stroke is too slow, then it bites deep but is not steady; if my stroke is too fast, then it is steady, but does not go deep. The right pace, neither slow nor fast, cannot get into the hand unless it comes from the heart. It is a thing that cannot be put into words; there is an art in it that I cannot explain to my son. That is why it is impossible for me to let him take over my work, and here I am at the age of seventy, still making wheels. In my opinion it must have been the same with the men of old. All that was worth handing on, died with them; the rest, they put into their books. That is why I said that what you were reading was the lees and scum of bygone men." (p. 292)

LIVE MODELS REPRESENTING KNOWLEDGE

I can think of but one objectification of a knowledge structure in which the model itself was alive (had nerves and muscles) and held meaning. The ancient Chinese used the body of a tortoise to represent their knowledge, placing the nine categories of actions and processes and behaviors on the head, tail, shoulders, thighs, and sides. The tortoise belonged in the north with the feminine principle, holding the meanings of multitude, mother earth, and things shaped like containers, including the belly and the tortoise (Medhurst 1846). All the other representations—trees, circles, triangles (Neill 1979)—merely indicate relationships or subjects denoted by words.

CONCLUSION

Artificial intelligence works with a variety of knowledge representations, all of which are semantic in nature—patterns of concepts, propositions, and procedures. The computer's behavioral modeling entails actions such as insert, delete, update, find, create (using a defined procedure), and request. This behavior is of the machine's workings, the electrical relays. Linda C. Smith and Amy J. Warner (1984) note that "available representations are rather limited in that they emphasize words and disregard the importance of graphics and pictures as aspects of document content" (p. 117), but see Cole (1988). Others have concluded that there are few solutions to the problem of knowledge representation (Abbott 1987) and that we are unsure about the nature of the mind—it could be a "kludge," says Christopher Cherniak (1988), that is, full of inelegant rules (p. 409). Vasant Dhar and Harold E. Pople (1987) found that their prototype systems were "inadequate in matching the behavior of experts who often resorted to reasoning based on deeper domain knowledge in explaining or rationalizing a case. . . . What generally became apparent was that the hidden assumptions, which typically went unarticulated during knowledge acquisition, often played a central role in case analyses" (pp. 553–54). Perhaps the assumptions went unarticulated because they were based on the muscular or body substratum of knowledge.

Librarians, having done a form of information retrieval for centuries, have had to develop dozens of classification schemes to model knowledge structures (Richardson 1930; Brown 1978). Some schemes are philosophical or logical, and others are based on the subjects of the literature at hand—rather than a deliberate modeling of subjective knowledge. Librarians have also devised quick and dirty indexes and thesauri.

Information scientists have given us sophisticated indexing systems such as PRECIS, SMART, and NEPHIS, all based on language structures to varying degrees.

Jason Farradane's relational operators were consciously based on subjective thought processes, and the relational operations have been shown to be not conceptually, but perceptually, grounded (Neill 1975). We do not know the final results of N.J. Belkin's work as he attempts to model inquirer and system in an exhaustive analysis of verbal protocols, although we must note that some physical aspects are recorded as well-drawn-out sounds and intonational stress. One of Belkin's problems has been the defining of experience, a subject directly relevant to the present work. His tentative conclusion makes sense and shows the extent of interaction necessary between user and system: "Interaction is necessary to successful model-building, although it is often based on *a priori* models held by the intermediary. These existing models, or stereotypes, can often hinder successful information interaction" (Belkin 1984, p. 128). Successful model-building requires cooperative experiences among the participants as they get a "feel" for one another's "models."

What does this mean for an AI or IR system? How does one get a "feel" for the internal "models" and "thoughts" of a machine? The answer is that we learn the idiosyncrasies of a machine by working with it over a long period of time. But how does a machine get a "feel" for a human being?

Part of our understanding of a machine is the feel we get of its workings. It is part of our knowledge. But the feeling is, as we have seen, inexpressible in any objective way, although we can act on the knowledge of those feelings. Without such feelings, even an intelligent machine will not be knowledgeable, nor will it have the character, values, or personality of the human information processors described in the next chapter and throughout this book.

REFERENCES

Abbott, Russell J. "Knowledge Abstraction." *Communications of the ACM* 30(8): 664–71 (1987).

Arber, Agnes. *The Mind and the Eye.* Cambridge: Cambridge University Press, 1954.

Ausubel, David P. *Educational Psychology: A Cognitive View.* New York: Holt, Rinehart & Winston, 1968.

Aylwin, Susan. *Structure in Thought and Feeling.* London: Methuen, 1985.

Belkin, N. J. "Cognitive Models and Information Transfer." *Social Science Information Studies* 4(2/3): 111–129 (1984).

Benner, Patricia. *From Novice to Expert: Excellence and Power in Clinical Nursing Practice.* Menlo Park, Calif.: Addison-Wesley, 1984.

Berlyne, D. E. *Structure and Direction in Thinking.* New York: Wiley, 1965.

Brown, K. R., comp. General Classification Schemes in a Changing World. *Proceedings of the FID Classification Symposium . . . Brussels, November 1976.* The Hague: FID, 1978.

Bruner, Jerome S. *The Relevance of Education.* New York: Norton, 1971.

Cherniak, Christopher. "Undebuggability and Cognitive Science." *Communications of the ACM* 3:4: 402–12 (1988).

Cole, William G. "Metaphor Graphics and Visual Analogy for Medical Data." Address to the University of Utah's Infofair, March 1988.

Dhar, Vasant, and Pople, Harry E. "Rule-based Versus Structure-based Models for Explaining and Generating Expert Behavior." *Communications of the ACM* 30:6: 542–55 (1987).

Dreyfus, H. L. *What computers can't do.* New York: Harper & Row, 1972.

Dreyfus, Hubert L., and Stuart E. Dreyfus. *Mind and Machine.* New York: Free Press, 1986.

Eliot, T. S. *Notes towards the Definition of Culture.* London: Faber & Faber, 1948.

Ferguson, Eugene J. "The Mind's Eye: Nonverbal Thought in Technology." *Science* 197 (4306): 827–36 (1977).

Fisher, Seymour. *Development and Structure of the Body Image*. 2 vols. Hillsdale, N.J.: Lawrence Erlbaum, Associates, Publishers, 1986.

Fisher, Seymour and Sidney E. Cleveland. "Personality, Body Perception, and Body Image Boundary." In Seymour Wapner and Heinz Werner, eds., *The Body Percept*, 48–67. New York: Random House, 1965.

Gagné, Robert M. *The Conditions of Learning*. New York: Holt, Rinehart & Winston, 1965.

Gendlin, Eugene T. *Experiencing and the Creation of Meaning*. New York: Free Press of Glencoe, 1962. (For another, relevant use of Gendlin, see Zuboff 1988, p. 31.)

———. *Focusing*. New York: Everest House, 1978.

Gollancz, Victor. *A Year of Grace*. London: Gollancz, 1950.

Hadamard, Jacques. *The Psychology of Invention in the Mathematical Field*. New York: Dover Publications, 1954.

Hunns, D. M. "Discussions around a Human Factors Data-Base, An Interim Solution: The Method of Paired Comparisons." In Arthur E. Green, ed., *High-Risk Safety Technology*, 181–215. New York: Wiley, 1982.

Inose, Hiroshi and John R. Pierce. *Information Technology and Civilization*. New York: Freeman, 1984. (A report to the Club of Rome Conference, Tokyo, 1982.)

Judson, Horace Freeland. *The Search for Solutions*. New York: Holt, Rinehart & Winston, 1980.

Lakoff, George. *Women, Fire and Dangerous Things: What Cateogires Reveal about the Mind*. Chicago: University of Chicago Press, 1987.

Lenat, Douglas B., Ramanathan V. Guha, Karen Pittman, Dexter Pratt, and Mary Shepherd. "Cyc: Toward Programs with Common Sense. *Communications of the ACM* 33(8): 32–49 (Aug. 1990).

Medhurst, W. H., Sr., trans. *Ancient China . . . the Shoo-king*. Shanghai: Mission Press, 1846.

Neill, S. D. "Books and Reading and a Singleness of Purpose." *Canadian Library Journal* 42(2): 57–62 (April 1985).

———. "Farradane's Relations as Perceptual Discriminations." *Journal of Documentation* 31(3): 144–57 (1975).

———. "McLuhan and Classification." In A. Neelameghan, ed., *Ordering Systems for Global Information Networks: Proceedings of the Third International Conference on Classification Research, Bombay, 1975*, 177–87. Bangalore: FID/CR and Sorada Ranganathan Endowment for Library Science, 1979.

———. "Mysteries of the Deep: Models of the Universe of Knowledge." *Journal of the American Society for Information Science* 31(5): 375–77 (1980).

Neisser, Ulric. *Cognitive reality*. San Francisco: Freeman, 1976.

Richardson, Ernest Cushing. *Classification*. 3d ed. Hamden, Conn.: Shoestring Press, 1930.

Rothenberg, Albert. *The Emerging Goddess: The Creative Process in Art, Science, and Other Fields*. Chicago: University of Chicago Press, 1979.

Ruesch, Jurgen, and Weldon Kees. *Nonverbal Communication*. Berkeley: University of California Press, 1956.

Rugg, Harold. *Imagination*. New York: Harper & Row, 1963.

Smith, Brian Cantwell. "The Semantics of Clocks." In J. H. Fetzer, ed., *Aspects of Artificial Intelligence*, 3–31. Dordrecht: Kluwer, 1988.

Smith, Linda C., and Amy J. Warner. "A Taxonomy of Representations in Information Retrieval System Design." *Journal of Information Science* 8(3):113–21 (1984).

Stanfill, Craig and David Waltz. "Toward Memory-based Reasoning." *Communications of the ACM* 29(12): 1213–28. (1986).

Tiemersma, Douwe. *Body Schema and Body Image*. Amsterdam: Swets & Zeitlinger, 1989.

Winograd, Terry and Fernando Flores. *Understanding Computers and Cognition: A New Foundation for Design*. Norwood, N.J.: Ablex, 1985.

Witkin, Herman A. "Development of the Body Percept and Psychological Differentiation." In Seymour Wapner and Heinz Werner, eds., *The Body Percept*, 26–47. New York: Random House, 1965.

Wright, H. Curtis. The Symbol and Its Referent: An Issue for Library Education." *Library Trends* 34(4): 729–76 (1986).

Zuboff, Shoshana. *In the Age of the Smart Machine*. New York: Basic Books, 1988.

3

The Dilemma of Human Imperfection: Character, Values, and Personality

INTRODUCTION: INFORMATION IS NOT POWER

Information is power if and only if you have the knowledge to know what it means, the will to use it, the ability to apply it, and access to a channel of communication. Channels of communication range from the broadcast media to a soapbox to whispering in someone's ear. Information can be used for evil as well as good. Sometimes knowing what information *means* causes the possessor to hide it.

All the "ifs" are functions of character, values, and personality. There are those who value money or power, who have strong personalities to push them toward those goals, who exhibit loyalty to friends and family (if no one else), whose word is good (even if only to certain people), and who can be courteous and kind under certain circumstances and ruthless under other circumstances. I suppose this defines a "good" character—when these characteristics are applied consistently and indiscriminately and on every occasion (and when other characteristics obtain as well, such as dependability, truthfulness, fairness, resoluteness, selflessness, honesty, magnanimity, self-control, and integrity). These characteristics have been valued for as long as there have been records of human thought. They are embodied in the three theological virtues of faith, hope, and charity and in Plato's cardinal virtues of prudence, justice, fortitude, and temperance (or moderation). We have not valued, on the other hand, those characteristics called, in former times, the seven deadly sins: pride, anger, lust, envy, greed, sloth, and gluttony. Some of these traits are the ingredients in the examples of human imperfection and the effects on the use of information given in this chapter.

PERSONALITY

The effect of personality and values on the use of information cannot be better illustrated than by the classic cases of T. D. Lysenko, the Russian agricultural geneticist, and Gregor Mendel, the Austrian priest who first discovered the basic principles of heredity. Lysenko dominated Soviet genetics from 1937 to 1964, in spite of the obvious uselessness of his methods of winter seed preparation (vernalization) and the fact that his methodological mistakes were clearly evident to other Soviet scientists. But Lysenko promoted himself, using, as Zhores Medvedev (1969) wrote, "a noisy campaign" (p. 14) and "political demagoguery" (p. 16). It was the appropriate time for such a character, for Stalin was in power and approved scientific speeches cast in the vocabulary of the revolution and the communism of the day. For instance, Lysenko's address to the Second All-Union Congress of Shock Collective Farmers in 1935, delivered in the presence of Stalin, contained the following sentence, which gives the tone and direction of the whole: "In fact, comrades, while vernalization created by Soviet reality could in a relatively short period of some four to five years become a whole branch of science, could fight off all the attacks of the class enemy (and there were more than a few), there still is much to do" (Medvedev 1969, p. 16). Aggressive and ruthless, Lysenko also was responsible for removing those who criticized him, simply because they did so. As Medvedev concluded, "To create a false doctrine, all that may be required is a fanatical person who has faith in the products of his own fantasy and who assumes the function of an infallible, scientific prophet" (p. 246). In the end, Lysenko and his "science" were completely discredited. The "information" that had been promoted to Russian farmers during those years helped to reduce production of grain rather than increase it and set the economy back severely.

One might think that certain social and political circumstances have to be present to support such an individual, and to repress his critics, and that is true up to a point. Lysenko's was an extreme case. But it is not only under dictatorships that domineering personalities can deceive their fellow scientists. The most famous case in the West is probably that of Sir Cyril Burt, the renowned British psychologist. There is no question that he was guilty of serious deception in his later work, where he falsified results and invented coauthors. However, in the most charitable of conclusions, Leslie Spencer Hearnshaw (1979) seemed to say that Burt was suffering from mental illness, showing "all the essential marks of a marginally paranoid personality" (p. 290). Perhaps such personality traits as those of Lysenko and Burt characterize all scientists who publish fraudulent results. Of course, the work of strong personalities is not always fraudulent. F. A. Hayek (1967) wrote of John Maynard Keynes, "Indeed the magnitude of his influence as an economist is probably at least as much due to the impressiveness of the man, the universality of his interests, and the power and persuasive charm of his personality, as to the originality and theoretical soundness of his contribution to economics" (p. 345).

Gregor Mendel was the opposite of Lysenko. "Reserved and cautious" by nature (Iltis 1932, p. 282), he shunned public discussion, and his classic paper "Experiments in Plant-Hybridization" sank into thirty years of oblivion after being published in the 1866 *Proceedings of the Brunn Society for the Study of Natural Science*. His carefulness is described in a letter he wrote to a friend about the lecture and its subsequent publication. "When last year I was asked to publish the lecture in the 'Proceedings' of the society, I agreed to do so, after I had once more looked through my notes relating to the various years of the experiment without being able to discover any sort of mistake" (Iltis 1932, p. 180). So unassuming was he that, Hugo Iltis tells us, when he was teaching, "He would sometimes give formal demonstrations of the way in which such crossings [in plants] were effected, showing how the flowers were protected from disturbing influences by paper caps. Yet he did not as a rule explain that he himself was engaged upon such experiments, so that few of his pupils knew that he was an original investigator" (p. 73).

It seems that the information available to us is as much a function of personality as it is of the activities and devices of information scientists. In the next section, subtler psychological and personality factors work against the dissemination of information, with tragic results.

CHANGING HATS: A COGNITIVE TRICK

The communication problems behind the *Challenger* space shuttle disaster of January 28, 1986, are detailed by Dorothy Winsor (1988). For several years, engineers had been concerned about the failure of the O-rings to completely seal the joints of the solid rocket boosters. It was this failure that allowed hot gases to escape from the side of the booster and burn a hole in the nearby liquid fuel tank, which then exploded. As the *Challenger* launch date neared, engineers told management that there was a very real possibility that at 50°F or below, the sealing system could fail. Winsor describes, from the report of the president's commission on the accident, how managers interpreted the information more optimistically than did the engineers, and how the "bad news" was kept within the two major contracting companies. I am drastically simplifying the story, and the whole of Winsor's article is relevant to the kinds of information problems I describe in this book.

The crucial decision started to unfold in January 1986 as the final preparations for *Challenger's* flight began. Winsor (1988) sets the scene:

A launch scheduled for January 27 was cancelled and rescheduled for the next day. The temperature at launch time was 36°F, 17° colder than it had been for any previous launch. When MTI engineers, including Ebeling, Russell, and Boisjoly, heard of the predicted low temperatures, they became alarmed enough to convince Lund, their Vice President of Engineering, to recommend that the launch be delayed until the temperature of the joints reached 53°F, the previous lowest launch temperature. In their argument, they cited the information from Russell's memo and the severe erosion from the 53°F launch the previous January. (p. 106)

Lund, Morton Thiokol International's vice president of engineering, did recommend delaying the launch in a teleconference with other managers and engineers from MTI and the Marshall Space Center, where NASA's shuttle program was headquartered. The facts presented by the engineers were not questioned, only the conclusions drawn from them. Then MTI held a private caucus off the phone. During the caucus it became obvious, Winsor tells us, that MTI was split along role lines. The engineers continued to argue against the launch.

At this point, Jerald Mason, MTI's Senior Vice President, said it was obvious that all present would not reach agreement and that a management decision would have to be made. He polled the other three vice presidents in the room, first asking Lund, who had presented the recommendation not to launch, to take off his "engineering hat" and put on his "management hat." . . . When Lund changed his role, he changed his position, and the four managers voted unanimously to launch. (p. 106)

Although no information scientist or officer was involved in this drama, the essence of the tragedy was information—its interpretation and its application. In this instance, information was not power. The peculiarities of human beings in organizations were added to the inborn dilemma of the subjective to short-circuit the potency of the facts.

Another example where the mere act of role change resulted in a different interpretation of information is found in a discussion of the British judiciary. Commenting on the release of wrongly convicted persons who had been accused of Irish-related terrorist activities, Hugo Young (1990) described the judges' "brassbound certainty" that the law had taken its proper course. He noted that lawyers, in becoming judges, "acquire this habit of certainty which admits no doubt," and yet, he pointed out, "the possibility that the system has erred is the livelihood of any barrister who finds himself in front of the Court of Appeal." But when that barrister becomes a judge, "the same proposition inexplicably seems to tend towards one in which he feels obliged to repudiate unto his final breath" (p. 6).

These role changes, which result in changes in the perception of the relevance of information and its interpretation, are not unusual. Philip Tetlock (1989) cites organizational behavior and bureaucratic policies research that "abounds" with examples of policymakers "shifting supposedly firm convictions on assuming new posts or after shifts in the prevailing political atmosphere" (p. 346). Tetlock describes how individuals, as decision makers, lose their own values to become representatives of bureaucratic constituencies: "It is typically assumed that attributes of individual decision makers cease—at this level of analysis—to be terribly important; what matters are the complex bureaucratic and political perspectives and interests that these decision makers are expected to represent. Decision makers become role incumbents; as the saying goes, 'where they stand depends on where they sit' " (pp. 345–46). Of course, we all have a tendency to shift our views and conduct depending on the social demands of the moment. We are forced to realize that the subjective element "underscores," as Tetlock puts it, "the plasticity of beliefs, attitudes, values, and feelings" (p. 346) that is the human condition. That "plasticity," however, seems to harden depending on the role, if Young's description of British judges is as accurate as it seems to be.

Manfred Kochen (1983) did not take into consideration this cognitive alteration by role change when he raised the question of the responsibility of information scientists to do something about the major problems of society. One of his examples concerned the nuclear weapons issue. "Ordinary citizens," he wrote, "appear to be more enlightened about nuclear weapons issues than military and political experts, although the latter have vastly more data, even information (decision-relevant data). However, they sorely lack knowledge and to an even greater extent, understanding and wisdom based on ethical as well as cognitive and emotional understanding" (p. 298). They probably just switched hats—from ordinary citizen to military expert.

Kochen asked "Why is this the way it is and what can we, as information scientists, do about it?" He was raising the question of boundaries—of domain. Where do information scientists draw the line? Should they study such communication problems as are exemplified in this chapter, and in other chapters in this book, or do those problems belong to the fields of communication research, sociology, psychology, and theology? If the answer is that these are *not* information science problems, then information scientists must be limited to the investigation and development of systems for information retrieval from the graphic record. Perhaps the study of information production, as bibliometrics (or informetrics), would be a feeder into the study of information systems. My intent is to help in the process of definition by pushing the boundaries under the streetlight.

ERRORS OF JUDGMENT

Judgments made about current problems are frequently, if not always, influenced by information we have about similar problems previously experienced. For instance, the O-ring erosion and weakening that caused the *Challenger* accident was not new. The fifteenth shuttle flight of January 24, 1985, was launched at a temperature of 53°F, the lowest to that time. The joint showed greater erosion than on any previous flight. Winsor (1988) suggested that, although each of the next four flights experienced joint seal problems, neither Morton Thiokol nor the Marshall Space Center seemed unduly concerned. "Perhaps the very frequency of the problem added to its acceptability because the damage kept occurring with no serious consequences" (p. 104).

The same kind of factor motivated the 1976 decision by President Gerald Ford to have the entire American population vaccinated—to prevent a recurrence of the swine flu epidemic of 1918, which had caused 450,000 deaths in the United States and twenty or thirty million worldwide (Osborn 1977, p. 90). This decision was based on an outbreak of a flu, similar to that of 1918, among soldiers at Fort Dix, even though no subsequent cases of the flu appeared anywhere else in the world (Osborn 1977, p. 92; Silverstein 1981, pp. 47, 125). The 1976 decision-making process was influenced, quite naturally, by what was known about the 1918 pandemic, which created the atmosphere for political and personal considerations in the genuine concern for public health (Silverstein 1981, pp. 32–33).

The first step in implementing the decision to immunize the nation was a discussion with the senior members of what was then the Health, Education, and Welfare Department and those of the Center for Disease Control. The magnitude of the problem of manufacturing and distributing the vaccine before the fall flu season was immense and costly and, it must be remembered, based on a *possibility* only. Arthur Silverstein (1981) reported of the meeting: "Everyone around the table realized immediately what all of this implied, and while 'We all understood the pandemic might not come,' serious discussion was preempted by anecdotes of what had happened in 1918" (p. 40).

When the secretary of HEW, David Mathews, wrote to the officer of management and budget to apprise the department that a request for funds was on its way, his note read, in part: "There is evidence there will be a major flu epidemic this fall. The indication is that we will see a return of the 1918 flu virus that is the most virulent form of flu. In 1918, a half-million people died. The projections are that this virus will kill one million Americans in 1976" (Silverstein 1981, p. 42). None of the scientific qualifications were present in this message—that the present virus was not exactly the same as that of 1918 and that there was no way of assessing the virulence or severity of the new virus.

A little over three months later, in the July 3 issue of the British journal *Lancet*, "it was reported that five of six volunteers infected with the swine flu virus had only experienced relatively mild forms of the disease, while the sixth was unaffected, suggesting that this new strain might not be as virulent as had been feared" (Silverstein 1981, p. 80). Any politician who read this article, however, would not have been convinced. The authors, A. S. Beare and J. W. Craig (1976), were tentative in their "deductions" and prefaced their discussion with the following caution: "Experiments on the virulence of microorganisms in man can never be scientifically complete and the evidence that we present on that of A/NJ/8/76 (the 'New Jersey'

virus) is not conclusive" (p. 5). As we shall see in the next chapter, inconclusive evidence, though acceptable for quotation in "the literature," has
little or no effect on those who must make political decisions and is even
less influential in changing attitudes and behaviors. Charles Erasmus (1961),
discussing change in non-industrial societies, showed how it was necessary
to provide the experience of seeing an obvious, even a spectacular, change
(as in the use of a hybrid corn seed, of a cure for yaws, or of a small motor
to help irrigation). "Cognition," he wrote, "as a causal factor in cultural
behavior takes the form of probability predictions—frequency interpretations derived from inductive experience" (p. 22). As the examples in this
section show, it is not just nontechnical or casual observers who make choices
based on frequency interpretation. Thus, in spite of the research information
in the *Lancet*, and in spite of the fact that no other cases of the flu had
appeared, there seemed to be no political or humanitarian alternative but
to go ahead with the immunization program in light of the possibility—that
is, assuming, as someone said, "a probability greater than zero" (Silverstein
1981, p. 42) that there would be a repeat of 1918. It was *that* information,
and not the facts that qualified or negated it, that influenced the decision
makers.

That circumstances beyond the control of the people involved affect their
judgments is witnessed as well by the Beirut massacre of October 23, 1983,
in which hundreds of U.S. Marines were killed when a truck loaded with
five thousand pounds of explosives crashed into the building in which the
marines were housed. As in the previous examples, the evidence that something will or will not happen was sufficiently convincing that most of the
participants can be seen to be doing their best *under the circumstances*.
Although the commission set up to analyze the disaster faulted the chain of
command and the officers on the spot for not providing adequate security
measures, the position of the commanders was a particularly complex one.
Indeed, as Benis Frank (1987) wrote in his history of the marines in Lebanon
in 1982–84, "The Commission softened these findings by recognizing a series
of circumstances beyond the control of both Colonel Geraghty and Lieutenant Colonel Gerlach which influenced their judgment and actions"
(p. 108).

The circumstances included (1) a large volume of specific threats ("at least
100 potential car bombs had been identified since the arrival of the Marine
unit," Frank 1987, p. 103), most of which never materialized; (2) the "perceived and real pressure to accomplish a unique and difficult mission"
(p. 174)—indeed, the mission "was not interpreted the same by all levels of
the chain of command" (p. 23); and (3) the fact that although the U.S. Mul-
tinational Force commander received "a large volume of intelligence warnings concerning potential terrorist threats prior to 23 October, 1983, he was
not provided with the timely intelligence, tailored to his specific operational
needs" (p. 173). These and other aspects of the situation—particularly the

different and differing religious factions with long histories of enmity—made the gathering and interpretation of information extremely difficult.

Could an information professional have done any better in these cases? We must consider that the medical people in the swine flu instance were adept at dealing with and gathering information about disease—they were specialists in that work. And we can say the same thing about those experts who dealt with the data on the *Challenger*'s rocket boosters. Would it have been possible for an *information* specialist (not an engineer) to have influenced the decision with an outsider's interpretation? We can, in the Beirut instance, look at military intelligence personnel as just that—individuals specializing in gathering and interpreting information for others to use in making decisions. Has anyone claimed that sort of IR for information science?

GREED AND THE ABUSE OF INFORMATION

If the purpose of Kochen's (1983) article was to move information science toward the study of information in the social and political realm, to move information scientists from technical services to the study of the provision and use of information in the public domain (and I think that was his goal), then information scientists must study not only information overload and mismatch (Kochen 1938, pp. 295–97) but also misleading information and the concealment of information, especially when these affect the public in general.

Perhaps the two most notable culprits in the field of misinformation or misleading information (telling half-truths or only part of the story) are text-book publishers and advertisers. The publishers of textbooks have always reflected the political and social values of the dominant groups in their respective countries, leaving out variant, deviant, unacceptable, and critical views of the culture's norms (Black 1967; Dick 1982; Nischol 1978; O'Neil 1981; Vitz 1986). Society, meaning those of us who make up society, is probably more to blame than the corporations. It is not possible to say the same in the case of the advertising business. Just as money is at the root of publishers' acquiscence to school board demands, so is it at the root of the manipulation of the truth in marketing products of all kinds. The examples I have chosen are notable instances of abuse of information because they resulted in death, illness, and broken lives.

The first example is the selling of artificial milk to mothers in third world countries by transnational corporations such as Bristol-Myers and, largest of all, Nestlé, the Swiss-based infant-formula manufacturer. In a well-documented study, Andrew Chetley (1986), active for many years in the fight to get a code to control the practices of these large corporations, details the deadly effects of bottle-feeding in countries with insufficient clean water or general hygienic conditions and with largely illiterate populations incapable of reading and following the instructions for the most effective use of artificial baby milk.

Taken to court in 1976 by the Sisters of the Precious Blood, Bristol-Myers faced sworn affidavits from people in eighteen developing countries. These statements clearly showed that "Bristol-myers was simply not telling the truth when it claimed in its 1976 Proxy Statement that its infant formula products are neither intended nor promoted for (A) private purchase where (B) chronic poverty could lead to (C) product misuse (D) harmful effects, and that the products were marketed (E) through professional personnel and (F) not directly to the consumer" (Chetley 1986, p. 51). After continued efforts to forestall action, the company agreed "to halt all direct consumer advertising and to withdraw the use of the mothercraft nurses" (p. 52).

However, the best-known case was the boycott, beginning in 1977, of Nestlé products around the world in an effort to get the company to stop "all promotion of infant formulas, including direct advertising to consumers, the distribution of free samples to health care facilities and parents, the use of company 'milk nurses,' and promotion to health workers" (p. 53). As early as 1936, Nestlé had promoted sweetened condensed milk, "a product which is totally unsuitable for infants" (p. 39), in Southeast Asia, claiming that "sweetened condensed milk is the food *par excellence* for delicate infants" (p. 40). Quoting Dr. Cecily Williams, Chetley explained the purpose of the "milk nurses": "Dr. Williams was much more scathing about company pro-motion—in particular the activity of 'milk nurses,' the sales representatives the company uses to promote their products to mothers. Then I went to Singapore and found Nestlé nurses, these girls dressed as nurses, dragging a good lactating breast out of the baby's mouth and pouring in baby milks' " (p. 40).

Radio ads in Nigeria, between 1963 and 1967, proclaimed: "Mother, be-lieve in Lactogen. . . . All things in mother's milk are also present in Lac-togen. Mother, watch the health of your baby, and give him the best, give Lactogen" (p. 40). But, where "poor socio-economic and cultural conditions prevail both early weaning and artificial feeding of infants are dangerous practices," and Chetley cited studies from different countries showing how bottle-fed infants "were three times more likely to die than breast-fed in-fants," were more likely to be "severely malnourished," and were ten times more likely to be hospitalized with gastroenteritis and pneumonia (p. 8). In 1975, the vice president of Nestlé, in a BBC TV program, responded to these criticisms: "If she continues to feed the baby with a dirty bottle and dirty water, it can lead to the death of the child. We accept no responsibility for hygienic conditions in the country and for the lack of knowledge of reading and writing" (p. 39).

In that sentence is the crucial information issue—the deliberate ignoring, if not suppression, of the necessary information about the *conditions* that would make bottle feeding less likely to lead to health problems. Nor was there any effort to inform people about the *only* conditions under which bottle feeding was necessary, that is, when breast-feeding was not possible.

A much more blatant suppression of information is the case of the promotion of the intrauterine device known as the Dalkon Shield. As told by Morton Mintz (1985), there was consistent use of false and inadequate research and suppression of unfavorable research results from the beginning to the end of the A. H. Robins pharmaceutical company's selling of the Shield between 1970 and 1974, when it was forced to withdraw the device from the market. The device caused injury to thousands of women, particularly from pelvic inflammatory disease. Even after the defective product was taken off the market, Susan Perry and Jim Dawson (1985) criticized the Federal Drug Administration for doing nothing "to see that the shield was removed from the women already wearing it" (p. 6).

Two examples will show the use of information—information known to be false and carefully selected to manipulate the truth—by human beings motivated by the greed for money. First, late in 1973, Allen J. Polon, the A. H. Robins project coordinator for the Shield, sent the following memo to Robert A. Hogsett, the manager of promotional services:

SUBJECT: Destruction of Dalkon Shield Literature

This memo is written referencing two pieces of Dalkon Shield literature which you questioned me about. The first is the eight-page advertisement titled "A. H. Robins—A Progress Report—The IUD that's changing current thinking about contraceptives. . . . " In this advertisement there is a table entitled "Clinical Results to Date" which is outdated *and parts of which are no longer valid*. Also, the labeling on the back cover is not considered complete and could cause trouble for AHR if we continued to use this advertisement.

The other advertisement in question is the earlier two-page ad with a large picture of a uterus with the Dalkon Shield inserted. This, too, is out of date for two reasons. *A pregnancy rate of 1.1 percent is stated which is not valid* and the labeling at the bottom of the second page is incomplete and no longer used.

Therefore, please *do not continue to use the two advertisements in question since both are outdated and both contain statements which are either incomplete or invalid.* (Mintz 1985, p. 83, with Mintz's emphasis)

Mintz then continued: "The A.H. Robins Company never told the medical profession or the FDA, and certainly not the public, that its Dalkon Shield project coordinator had repudiated the claims with which it had induced physicians to implant the devices in millions of women. Nor did Robins reveal that no senior executive, so far as is known, took serious issue with Polon" (p. 83).

Second, by 1973 enough experience in using the Shield had accumulated to raise research questions, and several groups applied to the Robins company for funding. Ellen J. Preston, the company's liaison with physicians, received these requests, some with preliminary data already in place. Most of them were unfavorable, and Preston "had become," as Mintz wrote, "almost zealous in her opposition to paying for research that might reflect adversely on the Shield" (p. 119). The following excerpt from a September 1973 "Clinical Project Plan Proposal" reveals a "deliberate failure to acknowledge the consequences of anything but Sales."

In my opinion our number one priority, even obligation, is to make further use of the vast amount of data in our own [ten-investigator] prospective studies. . . . Although a number of very favorable reports on the Shield have been published, some highly unfavorable data has also been published. It is my understanding that within our own data there are single studies of very favorable data which could be used to counteract some of this already published material. . . . Certainly any initial report on AHR data must include all ten studies, but we could "break out" the individual studies to show this favorable data. (p. 119)

Mintz carefully described the deficiencies of these studies, all done at speed and one of which had been denounced by Lester Preston (Ellen's husband and the director of scientific information at A.H. Robins) as a "clear-cut case of GIGO (garbage in, garbage out)" (p. 120).

POLITICS AND INFORMATION BIAS

Governments, like corporations, must keep some information secret—at least we have accepted that principle without having tested its opposite. In our business-oriented culture, we seem to have agreed that politicians can hide, manipulate, and cut information to maintain national security, in particular, and to get elected. During elections, we smile at exaggerations, biased claims, and promised benefits. Unlike the Dalkon Shield example, most of the misinformation in politics is relatively harmless, and in any case, we understand what's happening. Thus Alex Brummer (1990) can say that the British government's coordinator of information is better known as the "Minister of Banana Skins" (p. 4). But there are occasions when political motives sneak up on otherwise honorable people and affect their attitude toward information.

The British, for instance, have had centuries of trouble with the Irish, and the Irish Republican Army has resorted to terrorist tactics in the last quarter of a century in particular, killing prominent individuals—and others, who were innocent, by mistake (Spinks and Cook 1990)—by bullets and bombs. In one case of wrongful conviction, the "Maguire Seven" were jailed for possessing explosives and killing twenty-eight people in 1974. In an examination of the sentences sixteen years later, the trial judge was criticized "for failing to sum up on the forensic evidence adequately, and the Court of Appeal for refusing to accept that he had erred" (Pallister, 1990 p. 6).

The Royal Armaments Research and Development Establishment was also criticized "for failing to reveal evidence which could have influenced the jury towards an acquittal" (ibid.). Hugo Young (1990), writing on the Maguire trial in more general terms, noted: "The police, determined to secure convictions, wanted to verify too many hasty conclusions. The scientific evidence produced by the prosecution was faulty and incomplete. Like other Irish trials of the 1970s, the atmosphere was contaminated and the procedures fatally flawed, by what amounted to a political requirement" (p. 6).

In another case—the Guildford Four—detectives discovered documents, after the accused had served fifteen years in prison, suggesting that some of the confessions, on which the case stood or fell because there was no other evidence, "had been fabricated by investigating officers." The court of appeals said the investigating officers had not just "seriously misled the court . . . they must have lied" (Bennett 1990, p. 4). Ronan Bennett commented: "By any standards that is no technicality. It was the deliberate falsification of confessions against suspects on whom there was not a shred of evidence, other than their Irishness" (ibid).

Another case, which mixed politics and greed, is the story of the consignment of eight steel tubes, bound for Iraq, which were seized by British customs and which, it was later admitted, were parts of a gun barrel. James Lewis (1990) reported several instances of misinformation in the process of manufacturing and delivering the various parts of the giant gun, which had been sold to Iraq by the Canadian scientist Dr. Gerald Bull (killed by a professional gunman in March 1990). Bull's company, Space Research Corporation, had ordered the steel tubes from another company, Sheffield Forgemasters, "who were given to understand that they were intended for a petrotechnical application." A truck driver, arrested by Greek police while driving through that country with nearly thirty tons of British-made tubing, believed he was carrying "industrial machinery." It took the government eight days to admit that the eight steel tubes were parts of a gun barrel. During that time, Lewis (1990) reported, "the Department of Trade and Industry rubbished the idea privately, while refusing to say anything openly" (p. 3).

There are many cases of information cover-up by governments. The German police had information about the people who had blown up Pan Am Flight 103 over Lockerbie, Scotland. As the investigation progressed, the Germans realized that, for a brief time, they had held in custody the bomb maker, the bomber, and even the bomb itself and had released them. As Steven Emerson and Brian Duffy (1990) told the story, "Having now recognized the magnitude of their error, the German intelligence services embarked on a cover-up to hide their mistakes" (p. 74). This involved withholding from the British and American investigators the names of five of the seventeen who had been arrested, supplying sloppy translations, and not revealing that the bomb maker was, in fact, a spy working for King

Hussein of Jordan, who was concerned about the terrorists attacking Jordanians (p. 84).

Then there was the Hanford atomic plant revelations of thousands of secret files on the results of "deliberate safety lapses" (Schneider 1990), in which plant managers made no effort to protect citizens. Since 1944, when the plant began to make materials for atomic weapons, weapons-industry leaders had taken "unusual measures to assure the public that the industry, which . . . operated in more than 30 states, was entirely safe." Keith Schneider has reported that documents made public since 1988, and the Energy Department's own admissions, have made clear that the government was not always telling the truth. "The worst accidents, mishaps and releases of radiation were kept secret. In instances in which the Government experts knew the public would be exposed to large amounts of radiation, such as fallout from the atmospheric testing of atomic bombs in Nevada during the 1950's, the industry's scientists prepared flawed studies that they asserted 'proved' that the public had not been harmed" (p. 20E).

CONCLUSION

There is no reason to believe that deliberate falsification of records, destruction of files, or errors of interpretation will cease with the continuing development of the information age. Indeed, tampering with computerized information by "viruses" or "break-ins" merely promises differences in methods of coverup and manipulation. Human imperfection will remain. The question is, is it information scientists' business to study information from this point of view? Peter Drucker (1989), as a business and management person, saw the social impact of information in terms of managing—the changes for entrepreneurs, the difficulty for totalitarian regimes to control information, the transformation of the city as the ability to move people to work becomes more difficult and the ability to move ideas and information becomes easier. "The city might become an information center," he wrote, "rather than a center for work" (p. 259).

But Drucker was aware that anyone who works with knowledge must have values. Under the phrase "knowledge is power," he saw "knowledge workers in their entirety" as "rulers," as "leaders." That, he cautioned, "requires ethos, values, and morality." He went on to discuss the necessity for moral education because "knowledge people have to learn to take responsibility" (p. 238). As seen from the examples presented in this chapter, that responsibility covers a wide territory, from moral values to cognitive skills to an almost superhuman objectivity. Drucker, as a management "scientist," was prepared to address these issues. The dilemma for information scientists is whether they too have any responsibility in this area—as "knowledge people."

REFERENCES

Beare, A. S., and J. W. Craig. "Virulence for Man of a Human Influenza-A Virus Antigenically Similar to 'Classical' Swine Viruses." *Lancet*, no. 7975 (July 3, 1976), 4–5.

Bennett, Ronan. "A Cosy Whispering Campaign Blown Open." *Manchester Guardian Weekly* 143(8): p. 4 (Aug. 26, 1990).

Black, Hillel. *The American Schoolbook*. New York: William Morrow, 1967.

Brummer, Alex. "Minister Slips on His Own Banana Skin." *Manchester Guardian Weekly* 143(9): 4 (Sept. 2, 1990).

Chetley, Andrew. *The Politics of Baby Foods: Successful Challenges to an International Marketing Strategy*. New York: St. Martin's Press, 1986.

Dick, Judith. *Not in Our Schools?!!! School Book Censorship in Canada*. Ottawa: Canadian Library Association, 1982.

Drucker, Peter. *The New Realities*. New York: Harper & Row, 1989.

Emerson, Steven, and Brian Duffy. "Pan Am 103: The German Connection." *New York Times Magazine*, March 18, 1990, 28–32, 72–74, 84–87.

Erasmus, Charles. *Man Takes Control: Cultural Development and American Aid*. Minneapolis: University of Minnesota Press, 1961.

Frank, Benis M. *U.S. Marines in Lebanon, 1982–1984*. Washington, D.C.: History and Museums Division, Headquarters, U.S. Marine Corps, 1987.

Hayek, F. A. "Harrod's Life of Keynes." In his *Studies in Philosophy, Politics, and Economics*, 344–48. Chicago: University of Chicago Press, 1967.

Hearnshaw, Leslie Spencer. *Cyril Burt, Psychologist*. London: Hodder & Stoughton, 1979.

Iltis, Hugo. *The Life of Mendel*. Trans. Eden Paul and Cedar Paul. London: George Allen & Unwin, 1932.

Kochen, Manfred. "Information and Society." *Annual Review of Information Science and Technology* 18: 277–304 (1983)

Lewis, James. "Government Admits 'Pipes' Were for Gun." *Manchester Guardian Weekly* 142 (17): 3 (April 29, 1990).

Medvedev, Zhores A. *The Rise and Fall of T. D. Lysenko*. Trans. I. Michael Lerner. New York: Columbia University Press, 1969.

Mintz, Morton. *At Any Cost: Corporate Greed, Women, and the Dalkon Shield*. New York: Pantheon Books, 1985.

Nischol, K. *The Invisible Woman: Women and Girls as Portrayed in the English Language Textbooks Published by the Central Institution of English, Hyderabad*. New Delhi: Amaltas, 1978.

O'Neil, Robert M. *Classrooms in the Crossfire*. Bloomington: Indiana University Press, 1981.

Osborn, June E., ed. *History, Science, and Politics: Influenza in America, 1917–1976*. New York: Prodist, 1977.

Pallister, David. "Judges Faulted over Maguire Case." *Manchester Guardian Weekly* 143(3): 6 (July 22, 1990).

Perry, Susan, and Jim Dawson. *Nightmare: Women and the Dalkon Shield*. New York: Macmillan, 1985.

Schneider, Keith. "Now the U.S. Asks What Its Radiation Did in the Cold War." *New York Times*, July 29, 1990, 20E.

Silverstein, Arthur M. *Pure Politics and Impure Science: The Swine Flu Affair*. Baltimore: Johns Hopkins University Press, 1981.

Spinks, Peter, and Stephen Cook. "Australians Murdered by IRA in Another 'Mistake.' " *Manchester Guardian Weekly* 142 (22): 3 (June 3, 1990).

Tetlock, Philip E. "Methodological Themes and Variations." In Philip E. Tetlock et al., eds., *Behavior, Society, and Nuclear War*, 1:334–86. New York: Oxford University Press, 1989.

Vitz, Paul C. *Censorship: Evidence of Bias in Our Children's Textbooks*. Ann Arbor, Mich.: Servant Books, 1986.

Winsor, D. A. "Communication Failures Contributing to the Challenger Accident: An Example for Technical Communicators." *IEEE Transactions on Professional Communication* 31(3): 101–7 (Sept. 1988).

Young, Hugo. "False Courage of Their Convictions." *Manchester Guardian Weekly* 143(3): 6 (July 22, 1990).

4

The Dilemma of Information Ignored: Argumentation with Selected Evidence

INTRODUCTION

When Manfred Kochen (1983) identified one of the major responsibilities of information professionals to be "acquiring and using knowledge about the effective use of knowledge" (p. 277), he was not thinking about human imperfections but about opportunities. Doing something about the moral and psychological dilemmas of people is outside the discipline domain of information scientists, even though the problem affects the use of information, which *is* their domain. It would seem that the problem of the effective use of knowledge might be amenable to investigation and "solved" or treated by education—teaching people how to use information effectively. I am going to take only the extreme case of ineffective use—that is, having useful information in hand and ignoring it—which is really *no* use. This would seem to be a simpler problem to address than using information ineffectively, for there the infinite varieties of human abilities and personalities are in play *as well as* the varieties of ways of using the information. The examples I describe in this chapter will illustrate the complex nature of the problem and show how much the ignoring of information is a matter of human nature and, as a topic for information scientists to study, a dilemma.

One of Kochen's challenge areas was security and the threat of nuclear war. He thought information professionals "ought to be able to devise ways of enlightening the heated debates that surround the security dilemma." He then made a statement that seemed to say that military and political experts were ignoring the knowledge that ordinary citizens held: "Ordinary citizens appear to be more enlightened about nuclear weapons issues than military

and political experts, although the latter have vastly more data, even information (decision-relevant data). However, they sorely lack knowledge and
to an even greater extent, understanding and wisdom based on ethical as
well as cognitive and emotional understanding" (p. 298).

Those sentences were written by Manfred Kochen the concerned citizen.
If Kochen the scholar, concerned with the effective use of information, had
looked carefully at those words, he might have realized he was ignoring his
own advice. First of all, there is no evidence that ordinary citizens are more
or less enlightened than are the experts. As he said, they only "appear" to
be more enlightened because, of course, he himself agreed with their point
of view. There is no evidence that the experts are ethically rotten. The
"security dilemma" was surrounded by "heated debates." Kochen provided
an argument for the side he opposed when he referred to several "outstanding
scholars" who supported the nuclear deterrent concept. He ignored this
when, in his conclusion, he wanted to make his point in terms as strong as
possible. Human beings are like that.

One need think only about the massive amount of information used to
warn against cigarette smoking and drug abuse to realize how perverse we
are when it comes to the effective use of information. We also have great
quantities of information about the ingredients in the food we buy. Some
people teach themselves how to use this information effectively in the selection of nutritional products. Others ignore it completely. What is the
information scientist to do about these cases? Librarians can and do set up
displays of materials presenting the literature on current issues of this kind.
Presumably, in a display of the literature on nuclear arms, they would include
materials from both sides of the debate. But Kochen's concern was for information professionals to acquire and use knowledge about the effective
use of knowledge. The librarian's display of materials does not address the
use question. Indeed, the librarian's position would be that the use of the
information, effective or otherwise, is not the responsibility of the information professional. Is Kochen altering that responsibility, or, when he asks
that information professionals acquire and use knowledge *about* the effective
use of knowledge, is he asking only that studies of the 'effective use' problem
be done and the results applied in some way that would not abrogate the
rights of individuals to use knowledge any way they saw fit? That is, in the
librarian's display of materials, there would be included a handout explaining
how information can be used effectively—how, for instance, not to ignore
qualifications, how to weigh evidence, how to be honest with oneself in
seeing both sides of an argument fairly. There might also be included a list
of criteria for establishing validity, for example, based on John Williamson
(1977, pp. 5–8) or David Sackett (1981) or the Opposing Viewpoints Series
by Greenhaven Press—see Lynn Hall and Thomas Modl (1988). But that
would be *evaluating* the information, not *using* it. Having assured oneself
of the quality of the information, one still must use it, and it is there that

individual skills and subjective characteristics come into play. Can the information professional do anything about use? The question raises another dilemma, one F. W. Lancaster wouldn't touch with a ten-foot pole, at least not in 1977 when he wrote: "A library can only be evaluated in terms of whether or not it is able to provide materials sought by users at the time they are needed. What the user subsequently does with these materials is completely outside the librarian's control (and, some users might say, none of the librarian's business)" (p. 4). Can we assume he would apply this principle to all information work? What would Kochen have argued in defense of *his* position?

IGNORING GENERALITIES

However, the dilemma of people ignoring information is not going to be solved easily. After the California earthquake of October 17, 1989, the *New York Times* carried an article by Timothy Egan (1989). The following words were boxed: "Scientists and engineers had advice about quakes, but it didn't get across." The article also referred to Dr. Dwight Crandell, who had predicted the eruption of Mount St. Helen's two years before it exploded, and to geologists who had said the volcano "would erupt within a few years." The 1988 forest fire in Yellowstone National Park was also predicted. Egan wrote, "Several experts had warned that because of drought and a buildup of dry, aging trees, a major fire was overdue; they urged greater preparation." Yet after the fire, "several political leaders expressed surprise."

Californians "know" there will be earthquakes. They have been told by experts that "bigger and worse earthquakes are sure to come." Egan reported, "Some engineers apparently knew that many bridges would not withstand a big earthquake." A memo to the governor (dated October 22, 1987), warning that failure to strengthen some freeways could cost lives, never reached him. Had someone decided to ignore that memo on behalf of the governor? After the quake, the governor commissioned a study of the worth of rebuilding (retrofitting) the double-deck freeways. At the same time, the mayor of San Francisco was planning soil studies for a new double-deck freeway, the Embarcadero. Fenton Johnson (1990) commented, "Meanwhile, Caltrans [the California Department of Transportation] is well under way retrofitting the city's other double-deck freeways—all damaged in the quake, all currently shored up with wooden braces—even as a governor's panel found that these efforts may be inadequate or pointless" (p. 34).

These kinds of warnings get ignored because people can't just stand around doing nothing. Johnson described it this way: "This schizophrenic conflict between knowledge and denial—the certainty of the inevitable, and the need, after all, to go on—is characteristic of contemporary life, and not just here" (p. 33). Egan (1989) gave another reason: "Unless danger is immediate and obvious, scientists are seldom listened to." Note the kinds of warnings the experts gave—something will occur "within a few years," bigger and worse earthquakes are "sure to come" (but exactly when is not known), "a major fire was overdue," "some engineers apparently knew" (but not all engineers). These are not specific warnings. People do respond to (they do not ignore) specifics. A case in point is the Brady-Spence prediction of a giant earthquake off the coast of Central Peru (Olson 1989). The following illustrates the kind of specifics people pay attention to:

The status of the prediction is as follows. A foreshock series will commence in mid-September 1980. The time duration of this series will be approximately 328 days. There will be a total of twelve-to-thirteen foreshocks which will be temporally distributed in two active phases, each of whose time durations will be approximately 109 days. The foreshock series will terminate on July 30, 1981, with the occurrence of the mainshock ($M \geq 9.8$). . . . This event will eliminate the largest generally recognized seismic gaps in the world, e.g., the inferred rupture zones of the 1868 and 1877 great earthquakes. The event will be followed by a vigorous after shock series. My current interpretation of the spacetime seismicity patterns in central Peru also leads me to hypothesize that a second event ($M \sim 8.8$) will nucleate 276 days later (ca May 2, 1982). . . . I cannot make more precise predictions of the occurrence times of the mainshocks ($M \geq 9.8$, $M \sim 8.8$) until the initiation times of their respective foreshock series are known. I cannot overemphasize that the occurrence of the foreshock phases are necessary and sufficient for the occurrence of the predicted mainshocks. *If the foreshocks do not occur, the prediction is invalid.* (p. 47)

Brady changed the dates slightly as he collected more data from Peru, but the only qualification, the one on the foreshocks, remained the same. In Peru, in June and July of 1981, the Peruvian Civil Defense held a communications exercise and a simulation exercise of the Lima metropolitan earthquake-response plan.

Meanwhile, from the time of the first prediction in 1976, the theory was under attack, particularly by scientists with the U.S. Geological Survey (USGS), which "conducts or supports most of the basic geoscience research on earthquakes and earthquake prediction" (Olson 1989, p. 9). Brady, who developed the theory, was with the U.S. Bureau of Mines (USBM). Spence, who provided Brady with some seismicity data from Peru, was with the USGS. These two agencies, according to Olson, are "traditionally competitive." Although Brady's theory proved wrong and neither the foreshocks nor the major earthquake occurred, the information was not ignored.

IGNORING CONTRARY DATA

Olson (1989) provided an example of a very different way of ignoring information. He called it "perceptual divergence."

A classic example of perceptual divergence also came out of the March 18 meeting. At the meeting, John Filson (USGS-Reston) attempted to cast doubt on the theory underlying the Brady-Spence prediction, but the USBM representatives (Robert Marovelli and Chi-shing Wang) interpreted his comments differently. Wang prepared the memoir: "Filson, USGS: the USGS cannot endorse Brady's prediction because his prediction theory is too difficult to be understood by USGS scientists." That is, apparently not only does where you stand depend upon where you sit, but also what you hear. It is almost as if Filson, Marovelli, and Wang were at different March 18 meetings. (p. 48).

It seems to be normal for people to hear words through individual screens, basically ignoring the true meaning of the words and hearing only what conforms to one's own beliefs. In this case, the people at USGS couldn't understand a theory based on an analysis of rock structures developed from data "natural" to the USBM. We tend, in general, to read and listen to those who reinforce our own intellectual and moral positions.

An intellectual position that is assumed to be true, and believed to be true, by many university professors is that doing research is necessary to being a good teacher. Yet all the research on the relationship between the two concludes that there is little or no positive correlation. Kenneth Feldman (1987) reviewed the research and concluded, "An obvious interpretation of these results is either that, in general, the likelihood that research productivity actually benefits teaching is extremely small or that the two, for all practical purposes, are essentially unrelated" (p. 275).

David Webster (1985), in an editorial, reviewed ten studies of the relationship between research and teaching, summarizing the results that indicated there was really no relationship. Letters to the editor followed— four against and one in support of Webster's findings. What were the arguments against? One was that in more advanced courses (not introductory or low-level courses), "the students would have the benefit of the researcher's wider knowledge of the subject and personal research experience. The researcher has a clear advantage over the non-researcher in this sphere" (Cohn 1986, p. 5). Elchanan Cohn also opined that graduate students

would clearly benefit more from faculty research, for it is inconceivable how one could successfully direct graduate student research without having had substantial research experience. The complementarity between teaching and research would be particularly strong in graduate education, where the relation between teaching effectiveness and faculty research has not been studied systematically. Although my data are largely impressionistic, I would predict that a very strong correlation between teaching effectiveness and research output would be found for graduate instruction (which includes, of course, thesis preparation). (p. 5)

Webster (1986) was prepared to grant Cohn something in the thesis preparation area. But Cohn's evidence is "impressionistic." He did not search for studies of research and teaching in graduate schools, although a study by J. P. Rushton, H. G. Murray, and S. V. Paunonen (1983) had included a survey of four hundred graduate school professors and had noted that the survey found "no relationship between research productivity and student ratings of teaching" (p. 103). However, I should not ignore an aside included by the authors, from an unpublished study by one of them, which added that "graduate students tend to rate the 'researcher personality' as more effective a teacher" (p. 111). I am not arguing on one side or the other. If that were the case, I would ignore this little comment, and did so in Neill (1989).

As a matter of interest, the personality of the creative researcher was described as ambitious, enduring, seeking definiteness, dominant, showing leadership, aggressive, independent, nonmeek, and nonsupportive. These characteristics are, of course, a composite. Not every researcher would exhibit all of them. The effective teacher was described as liberal, sociable, showing leadership, extroverted, nonanxious, objective, supporting, nonauthoritarian, nondefensive, intelligent, and aesthetically sensitive. All the research agreed that a good researcher could also be a good teacher and vice versa. Nor does anyone argue that a nonresearcher *cannot* have a "researcher personality," at least in part.

Other arguments on the side of the myth that research is necessary to good teaching are (1) research motivates faculty to keep up-to-date; (2) research maintains enthusiasm, interest, and intellectual vitality; (3) research is an antidote to parochialism by bringing faculty into contact with editors and readers outside the home university; (4) an active writing program keeps faculty in touch with what students have to go through in writing essays; and (5) getting published boosts faculty morale and confidence.

Frederick Weaver (1989) listed most of these and said all were "crucial to high quality teaching" (p. 57). He gave no evidence. He did not refer to Webster, although the two wrote in the same journal. He did cite Martin Finkelstein (1984), saying that Finkelstein had shown "that the correlation between time spent at research and teaching quality is positive though small" (p. 58 n.3). Finkelstein's conclusion however, was a little more complicated:

To the extent that judgments of teaching effectiveness are based largely on its intellectual competence dimension (and this appears to be the preferred criterion of faculty), then research productivity and the expertise that it engenders and the general ability that it signals does bear a fairly small, but consistently positive, relationship to good teaching. To the extent that judgments of teaching are based on socioemotional aspects of the learning situation (and students appear more disposed to this criterion), then the expertise developed via research activity appears a largely irrelevant factor. That good research is both a necessary and sufficient condition for good teaching, then, is not resoundingly supported by the evidence. (p. 126)

Finkelstein had earlier commented on the faculty criterion preference. He proposed two "possible" explanations: (1) in judging their colleagues' classroom performance, they simply took research-related criteria into consideration, and (2) some kind of "halo-effect" was operating wherein judgments of research productivity *and* of teaching effectiveness reflected a single general ability factor (p. 123). In any case, Weaver's pronouncement that scholarly writing and publishing, which boosted morale, commitment, and confidence, was "crucial to high quality teaching" was totally inappropriate to the evidence he cited. Weaver (and Webster's letter writers) ignored the findings of research that did not square with their beliefs—beliefs that, in this case, are held by the generality of university faculty.

IGNORING INFORMATION BECAUSE OF FEAR

The history of the reaction to the AIDS disease provides excellent examples of people ignoring information because of fear. The wealth of literature on the disease grows by leaps and bounds. One brief, general work is by a writer and a psychiatrist (Hyde and Forsyth 1987). The authors open their book with a firm denial that AIDS is spread by casual contact: "Doubts, fears, apprehensions, and ignorance about AIDS continue to abound. Myths and superstitions die hard, especially when many questions remain unanswered. But even though many people cannot bring themselves to believe it, there is no evidence that AIDS is spread by casual contact" (p. 2). After detailing a number of stories in a chapter entitled "Epidemic of Fear," the authors comment: "Only through education and further research can one strike a balance between fear of the disease, sensible precautions, and concern for people who suffer from AIDS. Fear makes people 'block out' information. We need more campaigns which emphasize the lack of danger from casual contact since polls show that people are simply not listening" (p. 63).

Another work, by Dennis Altman (1986), discussed the political and ethical problems of closing bathhouses frequented by gay men. Altman's comments illustrate another reason for ignoring information:

My own observations during the course of writing this book suggested that while quite major shifts in behavior have taken place, surprising numbers of people continue to use the baths in the same way as before the epidemic. Certainly visits to the largest baths in New York (in June 1984) and Paris (November) suggested that most of the patrons were either unaware of the problem or, if aware, were deliberately ignoring the warnings. It is, of course, possible that some men may even have increased high-risk sex as a means of denying the reality of the epidemic. (p. 155)

In spite of assurance in the literature, there is still much about AIDS that is unknown, and this leaves the door open for people to ignore any or all information that is designed to quell their fears. The Opposing Viewpoints Series, mentioned before in the context of critical thinking and the effective use of information, includes a title on AIDS (Hall and Modl 1988). In that book are collected articles arguing, with and without evidence, both sides of several AIDS issues. Readers, ignoring the purpose of the series, could selectively read only those items that supported their own views.

DOUBT, HESITATION, AND CONFUSION OF GOALS

Leslie H. Gelb, the director of the Study Task Force that examined the Pentagon Papers (published under the editorship of Senator Mike Gravel in 1971), later wrote an account of the Vietnam experience while he was a senior fellow in the Brookings Foreign Policy Studies program (Gelb and Betts 1979). One chapter was devoted to an analysis of the confusion of points of view, of the variant interpretations of what was actually happening in Vietnam, and the seemingly always qualified recommendations for action (or inaction) throughout the long U.S. involvement in Indochina beginning after the Second World War. There are, in such circumstances, many examples of individuals deliberately ignoring information for any number of reasons. In my view, all of these reasons began with the doubt about purpose and specifics in a war in a distant and foreign country and the confusion and hesitation such doubt breeds.

The administration nearly always wanted good news, usually for political reasons. This naturally led to ignoring bad news. Pessimistic reports had to be qualified. Gelb and Richard Betts give a number of examples: (1) "A State Department intelligence brief of October 22, 1963, sketched such a bleak picture that McNamara and the Joint Chiefs lodged a protest with Rusk, and Rusk ended up apologizing for his errant estimators, who turned out to be exactly right" (p. 302). (2) As the United States was beginning its heavier involvement in the early 1960s, "the commander in Saigon, General Paul Harkins, decided he did not want any defeatist reporting from American officers in the provinces" (p. 304). Failure was not expected of American forces. (3) According to Gelb and Betts, Dean Acheson, who had said privately on June 17, 1952, that it was "futile and a mistake to defend Indochina in Indochina," made the public announcement the following day that Communist "aggression had been checked" and that the "tide is now moving in our favor" (p. 311). Acheson ignored his own knowledge and intuition. Not only do people hear what they want to hear, as we saw earlier, but they also say what they think (or know) others want to hear.

There was no doubt or hesitation on the part of Averell Harriman. Former Vietnam Ambassador Frederick Nolting (1988) tells the story of the efforts to get a treaty with Laos. At one point during a conversation with Harriman, Nolting asked if he had ever read Nolting's instructions ordering the U.S. mission to work with the South Vietnamese government and to consider their views. Harriman replied "that he had not, but that he knew what he was doing" (p. 83). That is, he had been directed by President Kennedy to get a "diplomatic settlement" on Laos, and he was determined to do so. Not interested in hearing any arguments against a settlement—even when the South Vietnamese were concerned about safeguarding against Viet Cong infiltration through Laos—Harriman, at a meeting with South Vietnamese President Diem, "turned off his hearing aid and closed his eyes" (p. 83). Harriman showed no doubt or hesitation, but he was far from understanding or caring about the realities of the people on the spot. He was addressing the president's political agenda, and ignoring the problems of Vietnam. The result was ignorance all around. When President Lyndon Johnson appointed Clark Clifford as secretary of defense "in part," Ole Holsti (1972) reports, "because Clifford was seen as a staunch supporter of administration policies in Vietnam," he could not have foreseen that Clifford would begin to doubt the wisdom of those policies when, according to Holsti (1972), "the Joint Chiefs of Staff were unable to provide satisfactory answers to the most basic questions about the conduct of military operations and their consequences" (pp. 209–10). Johnson then went to Dean Acheson, the former secretary of state, for advice. Acheson told the president "he was 'being led down the garden path' by the Joint Chiefs of Staff 'who don't know what they're talking about' " (pp. 210–11).

The press stories from Vietnam were watched carefully by politicians, not only to get information but also to gauge the effect on the voters. Some stories were inaccurate; others, say Gelb and Betts (1979), "painted a more accurate picture of the war than the consensus of official reporting" (p. 304). But the press ignored the less dramatic events, focusing on the fighting. When there was an opening of a hospital or a school, the press seldom bothered to go. Nolting (1988) wrote: "The mission notified the press in advance about such events, inviting journalists to accompany us, but they rarely did. Two or three reporters levelled with me, saying they could go, but their papers would not print the story; or if they did it would be on the back page" (p. 91). Nolting called this "selective reporting." Phillip Davidson (1988) talked to Robert Elegant, an experienced reporter: "Most correspondents, he asserts, were woefully ignorant of the setting of the conflict and of war in general, particularly guerilla war. Added to this ignorance was an unwarranted and inordinate sense of their own omniscience. What the correspondents did not see or believe to them did not exist—regardless of obvious evidence to the contrary" (pp. 487–88).

Selective reporting is not just the other side of the coin to selective reading. It is a more insidious information problem, for it takes away the *possibility* of choice altogether. Is it censorship? Is it lying? It is motivated by ambition, political beliefs, prejudice, frustration, or any of a number of human tendencies. It is, in any case, a dilemma for those who study information and feel a responsibility for its accuracy, comprehensiveness, and effective use.

SOME THEORY

Gelb and Betts (1979) give the following description of how the U.S. Air Force falsified and exaggerated reports:

The military, for example, was often deliberately optimistic, even to the point of falsification. It has been reported that the Air Force consistently exaggerated the effects of the bombing, in many cases not so much as a deliberate lie but because of the way the military and the military intelligence systems were organized. Although the Air Force had remarkably accurate methods of measuring bomb destruction in its photo intelligence techniques, this information was consistently played down in favor of the pilots' reports, which owing to human error as well as never-corrected duplication gave a grossly inaccurate overall picture of the military effects of the bombing. Why did the Air Force do nothing to change this system (and thus implicitly encourage it)? First, because of the intense competition among the services, and second, because of the pressures regarding promotion. (pp. 309–10)

Success was essential in the competition for funds and, at the individual level, for promotion in the ranks.

Dorothy Smith (1974) adds another factor to the reporting dilemma. Her insight is that our knowledge of society is "to a large extent mediated to us by documents of various kinds" (p. 257). We write reports, fill in forms, produce "executive summaries," all in some standardized pattern for ease of reading. Smith calls this a "documentary" reality, which is "fundamental to the practices of governing, managing and administration. . . . The primary mode of action and decision in the superstructures of business, government, the professions, and other like agencies, is in symbols, whether words, mathematical symbols or some other. It is a mode of action which depends upon a reality constituted in documentary form" (p. 257). She takes an example from Jonathan Schell's (1968) description of bombing raids in the Vietnam War: "Most of the terms used in the Bomb Damage Assessment Reports seemed to have been devised for something like a bombing raid on a large, clearly visible, stationary military base, and not for the bombing of guerilla in the setting of fields and jungle" (Smith 1974, p. 266). Schell's (1968) description of how the Forward Air Control (FAC) pilots related what they saw to what they reported is worth quoting in full:

When a FAC pilot guided an air strike onto a target that was defined by his coordinates only as a patch of jungle a hundred metres square, and was termed a "Suspected Enemy Troop Concentration," or guided an air strike onto a village that was described as an "Enemy Sniper Position," there was no meaning in a figure for the "Percentage of Target Destroyed," and little meaning in a figure for the "Percentage of Bombs on Target." Since the pilots could never know how much of the real target—the enemy troops—had been destroyed, they fell back on simply reporting how many houses had been destroyed, or how much of the hundred-metre-square patch of jungle had been torn up, as though this had been the objective of the bombing. Also, since the enemy was fighting primarily a guerrilla war, and built virtually no "military structures," the FAC pilots came to apply this term to any building that the planes happened to bomb. (p. 180)

Smith (1974) noted that when the pilots filled in the forms, "they reproduced the world as those at the top said it had to be" (p. 266). The actuality and the uniqueness of Vietnam were ignored by the form of the accounting practices.

The use of forms to collect and control information has a long and fascinating history, which is told exhaustively and well by James Beniger (1986). One of the main ideas in the "Control Revolution" is "rationalization," that is, "control can be increased not only by increasing the capability to process information but also by decreasing the amount of information to be processed" (p. 15). By means of rationalization, or preprocessing, then, control of information is made simpler, but at the cost of leaving out of the accounting process much of what can only be described as the qualitative aspects of the "things" described. Beniger (1986) provides a relevant illustration:

One example from within bureaucracy is the development of standardized paper forms. This might at first seem a contradiction, in that the proliferation of paperwork is usually associated with a growth in information to be processed, not with its reduction. Imagine how much more processing would be required, however, if each new case were recorded in an unstructured way, including every nuance and in full detail, rather than by checking boxes, filling blanks, or in some other way reducing the burdens of the bureaucratic system to only the limited range of formal, objective, and impersonal information required by standardized forms. (pp. 15–16)

So the FAC pilots in Vietnam, guiding air strikes with the aid of instructions that had little relevance to the actual task, had to improvise ways of telling where the enemy was operating. Schell (1968) described this process:

This was how Captain Reese came to think that he could spot, on the trails, grass that had been freshly bent by the passage of enemy troops, and that he could distinguish enemy houses from civilian houses by whether they were in the tree lines or not; how Lieutenant Moore came to think that he could tell a farmer from a soldier by the way he walked; and how major Billings came to believe that he could tell enemy soldiers from civilians by making a low pass over the fields and seeing who ran for cover, and that he could judge whether a wisp of smoke hanging over the woods was rising from the fire of a Montagnard or from the fire of a Vietcong soldier. (p. 181)

For a long time, the uniqueness of the war was lost for those relying on the "reality" of documents.

The information explosion demands that we reduce the quantity of information. Administrators and executives of large and small organizations want—indeed, need—to work from summaries of longer reports. David Suzuki (1987) told of one executive who preferred "graphs with colours." Suzuki commented, "It didn't surprise me, but it gets rather scary to think that decisions involving thousands of employees or millions of dollars may be made on the basis of a two-page summary of a 100 page report." In essence, the person responsible for decision making has to rely on someone else to compress reports—to choose what to leave in and what to ignore.

Any information-gathering and -recording form designed for statistical purposes has to be as simple as possible for ease of analysis. Hence as Suzuki wrote, "Questions with yes-no answers are preferred." But he went on, "The fewer the choices, the less meaningful are the answers." Complex issues are never a matter of yes or no, as we have seen in the examples in this chapter. As soon as people and their concerns are reduced to ciphers, "there is little real informational content. Most of these numbers tell us nothing about the complexities that make issues important; they hide human values, fears or hopes, social injustice or impediments to progress" (Suzuki 1987).

On the other hand, executives of companies and governments have a great deal of knowledge that they use to fill in or make sense of the bare bones of the information they receive. This is their "working knowledge" of the business they supervise. Everyone, in time, develops a working knowledge of the job performed on a daily basis. The Vietnam pilots had to work hard at it because they came unprepared; but they did develop that kind of knowledge.

Working knowledge—the knowledge we carry around in our heads for instant use (as opposed to knowledge we get from reports and books and studies)—can be used to ignore information. If new knowledge does not jibe with working knowledge, or doesn't "fit" with working knowledge because it contradicts long-held and hard-won concepts, that new knowledge can be ignored.

Mary Kennedy (1983) described several parts of working knowledge: formal evidence, empirical experiences, individual interests or goals, beliefs, and values. All are "blended together to form an integrated and organized body of knowledge" (p. 199). Kennedy found that working knowledge influenced, in two ways, what information was retained. One was that individuals used their working knowledge as "a means of identifying facts that are relevant." The second way refers to the reduction of information. When the evidence (of a research study, for example) is very complex, "working knowledge reduces the evidence to a simpler form, usually to a one-line proposition" (p. 203)—in essence, to a simpler and more retainable, and more usable, form. The process of incorporating new knowledge into working knowledge involves reduction, interpretation, and sometimes transformation and can lead to "conclusions that differ substantially from those embedded in the original findings" of research or evaluation programs (p. 193). Working knowledge, therefore, exerts a strong influence on our "reading" of evidence, causing, at times, a selective information processing that results in our ignoring elements of data contrary to our interests and, as I will illustrate in the next section, to theories that we have worked long and hard to develop—theories that have, in fact, become part of our working knowledge.

MARSHALL MCLUHAN'S USE OF BRAIN HEMISPHERE LITERATURE

McLuhan's theory that the electronic media had created a form of communication similar to oral or preliterate communication was formulated before he discovered references to the different modes of thinking attributed to the left and the right hemispheres of the brain. All of the basics of his ideas were worked out in the 1950s while he and some colleagues at the University of Toronto were working on the short-lived journal *Explorations* (Neill 1973). The ideas appeared full-blown in the popular *Understanding Media* (McLuhan 1964). On the other hand, late-twentieth-century interest in the characteristics of the two halves of the brain began "in the early 1960s" with the work of Joseph E. Bogen and Phillip J. Vogel—the radical sectioning of the corpus callosum in patients with intractable epilepsy—and with the follow-up studies by Roger Sperry (Harrington 1987, p. 280).

We must keep in mind that before McLuhan found the literature listing the functions of the left and the right halves of the brain, he had been applying his insights to events in the world by means of aphorisms—"the medium is the message," "the rear view mirror," "hot and cool media," "the global village" (a phrase encompassing the effects of the oral nature of electronic communication media). He had been using this working knowledge for two decades. My intention is to examine the selection of the hemisphericity literature that McLuhan cited and show how qualifying statements of the authors of that literature, which would have weakened or stalled McLuhan's use of their findings, were ignored.

The second chapter of Marshall and Eric McLuhan's (1988) *Laws of Media: The New Science*[1] is called "Culture and Communication: The Two Hemispheres." This chapter was a revision of McLuhan (1978). Hemisphericity is used as if it were caused by culture. The two halves of the brain are treated as if they were separate entities. The following quotations are given as examples: (1) "Visual space is the result of left-hemisphere dominance in a culture, and its use is restricted to those cultures that have immersed themselves in the phonetic alphabet and thereby suppressed the activity of the right hemisphere" (p. 69); (2) "The individual features of the face, as isolated figures, are easily noted by the left hemisphere, which cannot handle them together as a pattern. It is the 'acoustic' power of simultaneous comprehension that gives the right hemisphere the ability to recognize faces" (p. 70).

In the article that was the basis for the second chapter in *Laws*, McLuhan

Figure 4.1
Brain Hemisphere Functions

LEFT HEMISPHERE	RIGHT HEMISPHERE
Speech, Verbal	Spatial
Logical	Artistic
Mathematical	Intuitive
Linear	Holistic
Sequential	Simultaneous
Intellectual	Emotional
Worldly	Spiritual
Active	Receptive
Analytic	Synthetic
Reading, Writing	Music

(1978) wrote, "The dominance of either left or right hemisphere is largely dependent upon environmental factors" (p. 55). In *Laws*, he wrote, "Cultural dominance by either the left or the right hemisphere is largely dependent upon environmental factors" (p. 72). Based on the evidence, that statement is simply not valid. It might be that different cultures can be related to different ways of thinking about the world and that these ways of thinking can be categorized by the dichotomies listed in Figure 4.1, but these ways of thinking are variations on a common genetic foundation of brain structure and function, a foundation that cannot be altered in any fundamental way by environmental influences. Norman Geschwind (1972), footnoted in *Laws* (p. 119) as a citation from George Steiner (1975), stated, "It seems likely that the asymmetries of the brain are genetically determined" (p. 83). Either this was ignored or the reference itself was ignored, with the *Laws* footnote merely directing us to Steiner's sources.

Another source was an article by Robert J. Trotter (1976). McLuhan (1978) referred to this, and it was used again in *Laws*. Trotter summarized brain research from Broca to Sperry in a few paragraphs, then described an anthropological study of the Inuit by Solomon H. Katz (1975). The conclusion was that the Inuit were basically "right-brained" in their cognitive abilities, their art, and the structure of their language. This conclusion fit well with McLuhan's thesis that literate cultures with a phonetic alphabet are left-brained.

Figure 4.1 is based on the chart that Trotter constructed and that was used by McLuhan. In *Laws of Media*, we find the following comment on this chart: "Because the dominant feature of the left hemisphere is linearity and sequentiality, there are good reasons for calling it the 'visual' (quanti-

Figure 4.2
Meanings of Left and Right

LEFT

Controlled by right hemisphere of the
brain (primarily responsible for orientation in space; has a holistic, integrative
cognitive style for the purpose of pattern recognition and orientation; output
by expressive movement and gestures,
manipulation of objects and drawing;
spatial relationships; musical perception
and expression).

Feelings, emotions, intuition.

Receptive, passive.

RIGHT

Controlled by left hemisphere of the
brain (predominantly involved with logical, analytic thinking; verbal and mathematical thought; output by speech and
writing; comprehension of language; association of names with objects).

Reason, logic, thinking.

Expressive, aggressive.

tative) side of the brain; and because the dominant features of the right
hemisphere are the simultaneous, holistic, and synthetic, there are good
reasons for indicating it as the 'acoustic' (qualitative) side of the brain" (p. 69).

Trotter took his hemisphere functions from Katz (1975), who culled them
from the early split-brain studies of Sperry, Gazzaniga, and Bogen and from
a survey, found in the literature of anthropology, of cultural beliefs about
the left and the right sides of the body. Katz was a professor of physical
anthropology at the University of Pennsylvania and a medical scientist at
Eastern Pennsylvania Psychiatric Clinic. The literature of psychiatry and
psychotherapy has recorded lists of body characteristics for many years, both
left and right sides, top and bottom halves, front and back, without reference
to brain hemispheres. I include a list (Figure 4.2) based on Edward Smith
(1985) as illustration.

Trotter (1976) tells us that handedness has been found to be a fairly reliable
sign of "hemisphere activation" (p. 219). Because most people are right-
handed, that is, are left-brained, and "because the speech centers are almost
always located in the left hemisphere, that hemisphere has usually been
considered 'dominant' (p. 219). After noting that the Inuit language reflects
a high degree of spatial right-hemisphere orientation and that all Inuit carvers
were right-handed (p. 220), he ignored the significance of the latter "fact"
(if right-handed, then the left brain is dominant) and reported Katz's description of the work of the left hand cradling the piece being carved as
proof that the Inuit were right-brain dominant.

Criticisms of Trotter's article appeared in the "Letters" column of *Science
News* on May 8, 1976, one calling our attention to "self-fulfilling hemisphere

myths." Indeed, Katz had constructed his brain function lists *before* studying the Inuit, and Trotter pointed out what Katz had admitted, that the lists were "only intuitive at present" (p. 220). Nevertheless, Trotter and the McLuhans accepted the dichotomy of functions as scientific facts, ignoring (or misreading) the qualifications.

Another footnote in *Laws* refers to Michael Gazzaniga's (1977) review of split-brain research. Tests of patients after commissurotomy (the surgical procedure to split the two halves of the brain) indicated a dichotomy of abilities of the two hemispheres: "the complementarity of the two hemispheres became increasingly evident" (*Laws*, p. 69, footnote). The Gazzaniga article, however, was not as convincing about the strict dichotomy of functions. Gazzaniga warned that there was some evidence that hinted at a redundancy—"a redundancy which suggests that all language and all spatial functions are not strictly and exclusively lateralized to the respective left and right hemispheres" (p. 94). This was ignored.

More support for the dichotomous functioning of the brain came from the work of Joseph Bogen (1977). This was a speculative paper with the title "Some Educational Implications of Hemispheric Specialization." Bogen hedged his call for educational curricula to address right-brain learning by saying that he really wasn't sure about the nature of hemisphericity but that "for now" he "would offer the short answer: assuming two types of intelligence, rather than some larger number, [hemisphericity] not only appeals for reasons of simplicity, but it has the very important advantage of conforming with the physiology of the brain" (p. 137). By his own evidence, of course, hemisphericity conforms with the physiology of only the *split* brain.

Using Steiner's (1975) *After Babel* (a book about translation) as a source, McLuhan came to conclusions about the origins of speech and connections to hemisphericity. The relevant quotation from Steiner stated:

In an estimated 97 per cent of human adults language is controlled by the left hemisphere of the brain. The difference shows up in the anatomy of the upper surface of the temporal lobe (in 65 per cent of cases studied, the *planum temporale* on the left side of the brain was one-third longer than on the right). This asymmetry, which seems to be genetically determined, is dramatized by the fact that the great majority of human beings are right-handed. Evidence for this goes back to the earliest stone tools. No such cerebral unbalance has been found in primates or any other animal species. (pp. 280–81, quoted in *Laws* at p. 119)

Not quoted in *Laws of Media* are Steiner's sentences that followed directly afterward and that warned we were not being given scientific facts but speculation:

Unlike animal species we are out of balance with and in the world. Speech is the consequence and maintainer of this disequilibrium. Interpretation (translation) keeps the pressures of inventive excess from overwhelming and randomizing the medium.

It limits the play of private intention, of plurality in meaning, at least at a rough and ready level of functional consensus. In an ambiguity which is at one level ontological and at another ironic, idiomatic level, political or social, we speak left and act right. Translation mediates: it constrains the constant drive to dispersion. But this, too, of course, is conjecture. (pp. 281–82)

The "conjecture" qualification was ignored. In Figure 4.1, reading and writing are shown as functions of the left hemisphere. However, some confusion exists regarding the sequential or strictly linear nature of reading and writing, and in that confusion lies a hint that the right hemisphere could be involved in those activities. The "evidence" comes from an article by the Russian neurophysiologist A. K. Luria (1970). McLuhan cited this article to support the contention that the "anterior regions of the left hemisphere" are responsible for sequential analysis and therefore for the "mental process of writing a word" which entails "putting the letters in the proper sequence" (*Laws*, p. 73). At the end of his paper, however, Luria (1970) asked a question that suggested that reading and writing could also involve some spatial (right hemisphere) abilities: "What can there be in common between the capacities for orientation in space, for doing computation and for dealing with grammar and logic? Yet all three of these abilities are affected by the same lesion in the lower part of the left parietal lobe" (p. 78). Luria's answer was that computation and grammar involve a spatial factor, that is, placing numbers on one or another side of each other and, similarly, seeing words as spatially related, for example, "father's brother" and "brother's father." Here was a spatial function on the left side of the brain. This "conclusion" was either ignored or read in such a way as to allow McLuhan to "hear what he wanted to hear."

CONCLUSION

None of the examples used as evidence in this chapter are intended as negative criticism of anyone. They are illustrations of a human condition and of an information problem. Humans need to reduce information to a manageable size, and that holds regardless of the amount of information we face. That is, it is not a problem of information overload. One report of one hundred pages will be reduced, in our working knowledge, to a usable summary statement or, even, a direction, just as would the contents of a hundred such reports. The human mind classifies and categorizes and constructs models of the world as schemas or frames or exemplary episodes (stories).

It is also a natural *tendency* to see and hear what we want to see and hear, when "want" fits our interests and goals and the body of knowledge we have already structured or, more accurately, collected. Although I don't think it is possible to overcome the categorizing of information, I do think it is possible to fight the tendency to ignore information that undermines our theories.

In any case, ignoring information for whatever reason means that the quality of working knowledge is poorer. It is basically inaccurate and can lead only to false conclusions, errors, and mistakes. In some cases, this consequence might not matter. McLuhan's work can be completely ignored without harm, so "errors" by McLuhan are not as important, in one sense, as those found in the examples of AIDS or the war in Vietnam.

Nor is it unknown for people *not* to ignore information. Betty Edwards, even before the second edition of her popular book *Drawing on the Right Side of the Brain*, acknowledged in an earlier work that "recent research indicates a less-clear division of functions between the hemispheres than was thought to be the case in earlier investigations. I have coined the terms L-mode and R-mode to designate *style of thinking* rather than a more rigid conception of *location* of functions in one hemisphere or the other (Edwards 1986, p. 12). Neither Marshall nor Eric McLuhan—nor, for that matter, Bruce Powers (McLuhan and Powers 1989)—bothered to look at "recent research."

In the article by Johnson (1990) on the 1989 California earthquake, Mayor Art Agnos of San Francisco was quoted as saying on ABC's "Nightline": "If you're going to tell me I'm going to have something in the next 25 years, save the information. I don't need it" (p. 33). The "something," of course, was an earthquake. Was the mayor saying "I'm going to ignore that information?" or was he saying "Don't tell me, I already know it"? Agnos (1990) felt compelled, because of these possible interpretations, to write a letter describing all that was being done in preparation for the next quake. His opening sentence indicated his desire to be seen as ignoring nothing: "Fenton Johnson's article 'Aftershock in San Francisco' (June 17) left the mistaken impression that San Francisco's disaster planning is rooted in denial. Nothing could be further from the truth" (p. 6).

What can the information profession do to make sure information is not ignored? Conduct courses in critical thinking and careful reading? Encourage others to conduct such courses? Study communication events to understand the problem more scientifically? English teachers, psychologists, and communication theorists are already in the field. Have they made a difference? Can they? It is my contention that the dilemma of people ignoring information is a natural human tendency and will not be "solved" even for those with the best intentions; for although much ignoring is deliberate, much is accidental, unpremeditated, even involuntary. It is, after all, a dilemma.

NOTE

1. *Laws of Media* (sometimes cited as *Laws* for convenience) was prepared for publication by McLuhan's son Eric after his father's death in 1980. All of it was

written by Marshall McLuhan except the introduction and the last chapter, which Eric "worked up" from his father's notes (*Laws*, p. xi). I shall therefore use McLuhan's name in the singular when referring to this work.

REFERENCES

Agnos, Art. "Aftershock in San Francisco" (Letter to the Editor). *New York Times Magazine*, July 15, 1990, 6.

Altman, Dennis. *AIDS in the Mind of America*. Garden City, N.Y.: Anchor Press/ Doubleday, 1986.

Beniger, James R. *The Control Revolution: Technological and Economic Origins of the Information Society*. Cambridge: Harvard University Press, 1986.

Bogen, Joseph E. "Some Educational Implications of Hemispheric Specialization." In M. C. Wittrock, ed., *The Human Brain*, 133–52. Englewood Cliffs, N.J.: Prentice-Hall, 1977.

Cohn, Elchanan. "The Research-Teaching Debate" (Letter to the Editor). *Educational Record* 67(1): 4–5 (Winter 1986).

Davidson, Phillip B. *Vietnam at War: The History, 1946–1975*. Novato, Calif.: Presidio Press, 1988.

Edwards, Betty. *Drawing on the Artist Within*. New York: Simon & Schuster, 1986.

Egan, Timothy. "When Disaster Is Predictable: A Failure to Communicate." *New York Times*, Oct. 29, 1989, E4.

Feldman, Kenneth A. "Research Productivity and Scholarly Accomplishment of College Teachers As Related to Their Instructional Effectiveness: A Review and Exploration." *Research in Higher Education* 25(3): 277–98 (1987).

Finkelstein, Martin J. *The American Academic Profession: A Synthesis of Social Scientific Inquiry since World War II*. Columbus: Ohio State University, 1984.

Gazzaniga, Michael S. "Review of the Split-Brain." In M. C. Wittrock, ed., *The Human Brain*, 89–96. Englewood Cliffs, N.J.: Prentice-Hall, 1977.

Gelb, Leslie H., and Richard K. Betts *The Irony of Vietnam: The System Worked*. Washington, D.C.. Brookings Institution, 1979.

Geschwind, Norman. "Language and the Brain." *Scientific American* 226(4): 76–83 (April 1972).

Gravel, Mike. *The Pentagon Papers: The Defense Department History of United States Decisionmaking on Vietnam*. 4 vols. Boston: Beacon Press, 1971.

Hall, Lynn, and Thomas Modl, eds. *AIDS*. St. Paul, Minn.: Greenhaven Press, 1988. (The Opposing Viewpoints Series includes "critical thinking activities" and a short introduction on why it is important to consider opposing viewpoints.

Harrington, Anne. *Medicine, Mind, and the Double Brain: A Study in Nineteenth-Century Thought*. Princeton, N.J.: Princeton University Press, 1987.

Holsti, Ole R. *Crisis, Escalation, War*. Montreal: McGill-Queen's University Press, 1972.

Hyde, Margaret O., and Elizabeth H. Forsyth. *AIDS: What Does It Mean to You?* New York: Walker Co., 1987.

Johnson, Fenton. "Aftershock in San Francisco." *New York Times Magazine*, June 17, 1990, 30–34, 38.

Katz, Solomon H. "Toward a New Science of Humanity." *Zygon* 10(1): 12–31 (March 1975).

Kennedy, Mary M. "Working Knowledge." *Knowledge: Creation, Diffusion, Utilization* 5(2): 193–211 (Dec. 1983).

Kochen, Manfred. "Information and Society." *Annual Review of Information Science and Technology* 18: 277–304 (1983).

Lancaster, F. W. *The Measurement and Evaluation of Library Services.* Washington, D.C.: Information Resources Press, 1977.

Luria, A. K. "The Functional Organization of the Brain." *Scientific American* 222(3): 66–78 (March 1970).

McLuhan, Marshall. "The Brain and the Media: The 'Western' hemisphere." *Journal of Communication* 28(4): 54–60 (Autumn 1978).

————. *Understanding Media: The Extensions of Man.* New York: McGraw-Hill, 1964.

McLuhan, Marshall, and Eric McLuhan. *Laws of Media: The New Science.* Toronto: University of Toronto Press, 1988.

McLuhan, Marshall, and Bruce R. Powers. *The Global Village: Transformations in World Life and Media in the 21st Century.* New York: Oxford University Press, 1989.

Neill, S. D. "McLuhan's Media Charts Related to the Process of Communication." *AV Communication Review* 21(3): 277–97 (Fall 1973).

————. "No Significant Relationship between Research and Teaching, Research Reveals." *University Affairs* 30(4): 8 (April 1989).

Nolting, Frederick. *From Trust to Tragedy: The Political Memoirs of Frederick Nolting, Kennedy's Ambassador to Diem's Vietnam.* New York: Praeger, 1988.

Olson, Richard Stuart, with Bruno Podesta and Joanne N. Nigg. *The Politics of Earthquake Prediction.* Princeton: Princeton University Press, 1989.

Rushton, J. P., H. G. Murray, and S. V. Paunonen. "Personality, Research Creativity, and Teaching Effectiveness in University Professors." *Scientometrics* 5(2): 93–116 (March 1983).

Sackett, David L. "Evaluation: Requirements for Clinical Application." In Kenneth S. Warren, ed., *Coping with the Biomedical Literature: A Primer for the Scientist and Clinician,* 123–57. New York: Praeger, 1981.

Schell, Jonathan. *The Military Half: An Account of Destruction in Quang Ngai and Quang Tin.* New York: Knopf, 1968.

Smith, Dorothy E. "The Social Construction of Documentary Reality." *Sociological Inquiry* 44(4): 257–68 (1974).

Smith, Edward L. *The Body in Psychotherapy.* Jefferson, N.C.: McFarland & Co., 1985.

Steiner, George. *After Babel: Aspects of Language and Translation.* New York: Oxford University Press, 1975.

Suzuki, David. "The Trouble with Information." *Globe & Mail,* March 28, 1987, D4.

Trotter, Robert J. "The Other Hemisphere." *Science News* 109(14): 218–20, 223 (April 3, 1976).

Weaver, Frederick S. "Scholarship and Teaching." *Educational Record* 70(1): 55–58 (Winter 1989).

Webster, David S. "Does Research Productivity Enhance Teaching?" *Educational Record* 66(4): 60–62 (Fall 1985).

————. "The Research-Teaching Debate: The Author Responds" (Letters to the Editor). *Educational Record* 67(1): 7 (Winter 1986).

Williamson, John W. *Improving Medical Practice and Health Care: A Bibliographic Guide to Information Management in Quality Assurance and Continuing Education.* Cambridge, Mass.: Ballinger, 1977.

5

The Dilemma of the
Quality of Information:
An Incremental Death

INTRODUCTION

As a technological and consumer society, we are constantly bombarded with
information. Some of the information is good, accurate, useful, and needed;
some is junk. But someone's junk information is another's useful information.
Some information is wrong—it is misinformation, and some of *that* information is dangerous. What I am concerned with in this chapter is wrong
information, not so much the blatantly wrong information but the subtly,
deceptively, seemingly right, wrong information. I will begin by defining
quality by describing some examples from my own experience. Although
this is a very limited experience, it is the literature I know, and I will present
evidence that the literature of other disciplines is similarly threaded with
"low-grade" information.

EXAMPLES

My consciousness of the quality of information was first raised when I
reviewed a collection of essays on the theory and practice of classification
(Neill 1975). Most of my complaints were about logical contradictions and
clumsy styles of writing, which a good editor would have corrected. Perhaps
I should qualify that and say a good editor who had the time, for some
publications are hurried into print and thereafter lie in wait for the unwary
reader—waiting, one hopes, forever.

One error, found in a footnote, claimed that James Duff Brown's classification scheme began in the last decade of the eighteenth century. Brown

was born in 1862. This is an error of fact that anyone can make. It is easy to see how the author, with the number 18 in mind (from 1862 or 1890), could write eighteenth instead of nineteenth century.

Errors are of two kinds—of fact and of thinking. Errors of thinking are nearly always variations of the truth—interpretations seen by others as errors. I touch on this in chapter 9. Errors of fact ought not to happen, and although placing James Duff Brown in the eighteenth rather than the nineteenth century will make no difference to anyone, except to the student who quotes this "fact" in an essay I have to read, there isn't any question that the quality of a work is lessened when facts are wrong.

A different kind of factual error occurs when works, published hurriedly, include out-of-date information. I reviewed a collection of papers on Canadian libraries, which had been written for a conference in late February 1977. In one of the papers, we find that "the Institute of Professional Librarians of Ontario is still looking toward self-government." By the time of the conference, it was known that the IPLO had folded in the summer of 1976. This "fact" could not have been known when the paper was written, but an errata sheet would have been appropriate in this case.

There was, as well, a more serious breach of one of the criteria of quality in this collection. I refer to the necessity of including supporting evidence for statements and conclusions. One of the papers was about career choices made by librarians and how the selection or advertising for positions was done. It was a footnote that first bothered me. The authors of the paper wrote: "Librarianship, like other professions, requires a certain number of individuals to carry out the mundane, routine work of the profession. Often the non-professionals performing these tasks are members of minority groups (Neill 1978, p. 359).

At the time I wrote that review I had been in the profession for twenty-five years and had not realized that minority groups were so used. Somehow this fact had slipped past me. Perhaps, I thought, I was unaware because I had never worked in a big, multicultural city library. The reference was to Erwin O. Smigel's *The Wall Street Lawyers: Professional or Organizational Men?* (Glencoe, Ill.: Free Press, 1964), pp. 40–42. I was surprised by this source of evidence about nonprofessionals in libraries in Canada. Did Smigel talk about librarians in a book about Wall Street lawyers? On page forty-one of Smigel's work, there is a discussion of the kind of men hired to do routine work, such as keeping up with the securities laws for each of the fifty states, indexing and cataloging, and conducting factual studies. The older men, the relatives, and the less than brilliant members of the law firms who were assigned to these routine tasks were all professional lawyers. Surely they could not be the reference point for the nonprofessionals working in libraries.

And what about the use of minority groups? On page forty-two, we learn that Wall Street law firms, in order to get people who knew the local courts and their routines, hired lawyers from local law schools: "Many of them come from Jewish and Irish families." These references are completely ir-relevant to the texts they are intended to support.

This is not just a citation error. It is, on the one hand, an example of questionable evidence, to put it charitably; on the other hand, it is an example of a sham citation. In an analysis of citations in surgical journals, James Evans, Howard Nadjari, and Sherry Burchell (1990) found thirteen major and forty-one minor errors in three journals. They concluded that their evidence indicated that the authors had not checked their references, and "in many cases," the reference had not even been read (p. 1354). Blaise Cronin's (1984) analysis of the role and significance of citations mentions the 'noise' factor, which is a "direct by-product of authors' tendencies to trivial, perfunctory, redundant, or wayward citations" (p. 51). He also refers to malpractices—"of window dressing, padding and the practice of sprinkling a few citations as an afterthought as a means of enhancing the respectability of a paper" (p. 50). If an author, in the process of padding the reference list with "wayward" titles, uses those references as evidence to support conclu-sions, we can seriously question the facticity of those conclusions and the quality of the work as a whole.

Another kind of questionable evidence that breaches the evidentiary cri-terion of quality is the use of insufficient numbers and varieties of witnesses to support positions taken, advice given, or drugs recommended. In a review of a major study of Canadian public libraries (Tague and Neill 1982), examples of abuse of this criterion were included. *Project Progress*, the study re-viewed, was published by the Canadian Library Association after years of planning and fund-raising. The research, which cost $110,000, was done by the Urban Dimensions Group of Toronto. More money had been hoped for, and this sum probably had an effect on the data gathering. It was undoubtedly the largest Canadian study of its kind and was promoted enthusiastically across the country.

It is likely the small sample for the telephone interview survey (two hundred people) was a result of the amount of money collected. Two hundred people would yield a reliability factor of plus or minus 7 percent. This, perhaps, could not be helped, although it would have required the re-searchers to qualify their findings somewhat. But the most unusual aspect of the study was the reliance on in-depth interviews with eighteen uniden-tified "influential persons and decision-makers." The purpose of these in-depth interviews was to provide qualitative information to help interpret the quantitative information. That's fair enough, but some of the claims made were not supported by any evidence other than *one* of those eighteen in-dividuals. For instance, the claim in the foreword that there was a "lack of or vague definition of library purpose" seems to have been made because of the comments of one "influential person." No question about public library purpose was asked of the two hundred in the random sample or of the ninety library workers who were chosen to be interviewed.

Another sentence in the foreword stated, "Private sector information services are competing directly with public libraries, but many of our decision-makers are skeptical about our ability to compete effectively in the future." No description of these private sector information services was given. No comparison was made between the kinds of information they sold and the kinds of services provided by libraries. No question was asked of anyone about how often they used a private sector information service. In other words, no *evidence* of competition, direct or indirect, was given.

The authors of the report concluded that there would be increased government pressure on libraries for cost-effectiveness and equity in providing services. The only evidence for this statement was in the following sentences: "An informant noted that small and medium-sized libraries will come under increasing pressure to provide broader and better service in the future" and "In speaking with us about this matter, a senior politician contended that the public library service would come under increasing pressure to demonstrate greater cost effectiveness and, at the same time, achieve greater equality of, and accessibility to, services" (*Project Progress* 1981, p. 96). A study built on such flimsy evidence cannot win credibility.

Bibliometricians, in developing mathematical models, need to test them for "goodness of fit" against observed data. For example, H. S. Sichel (1985), gathered twelve data sets to test his Generalized Inverse Gaussian-Poisson distribution model against others. The data sets were counts of articles in journals, citations by authors, periodicals requested or used in libraries, and scientists nominated as renowned. It is not the quality of the mathematics that is in question. Nor, as Wassily Leontief (1977) said of econometric models, is the problem that "in all too many instances sophisticated statistical analysis is performed on a set of data whose exact meaning and validity are unknown to the author" (p. 27), although that certainly can be true. The point is that the data are sometimes hard to evaluate for validity and reliability because they come from a distance beyond even the author cited. Leontief noted, "The same well-known sets of figures are used again and again in all possible combinations to pit different theoretical models against each other in formal statistical combat" (p. 30). This is exactly what Sichel did. The purpose of the original collection of the data is irrelevant and certainly ignored.

But the quality question is the validity of the data and the author's responsibility to provide evidence of validity. John Williamson's (1977) outline of tests for validity included the question: "What is the source of the data or information upon which the article is based?" (p. 5). Sichel's (1985) collection of data sets included two references to Paul Allison's work in sociology. One of the sets, Allison (1980a), contained an anomaly—thirty-seven authors who had zero publications. Sichel commented: "The final distribution in Table 2 is radically different from the previously cited examples. It refers to the publication counts of 237 chemists during the first six years after receiving their doctorates, according to Allison. In the nature of this collection, we encounter a zero frequency of 37. These are men who have not published at all" (p. 316). Sichel was careful to say "according to Allison," as if disclaiming responsibility for the quality of the data. Sichel also cited Allison (1980b), which included not only data about the above chemists in their first two years, but also data about the number of articles published by 286 biochemists in their first three years.

Neither of Allison's articles commented on how the data had been gathered or on whether there were any qualifications attached to the numbers or other clues regarding their reliability and validity. It turns out that Allison was using figures gathered by two other people.

A footnote to Allison (1980a) informed the reader that the author was "indebted to Barbara Reskin for the use of the data reported in Table 1" (p. 434). Among others thanked for helpful suggestions was Scott Long. There were no references to works by Reskin. Scott Long's (1978) study had provided the table of biochemists' publications for Allison (1980b), and in that article Allison cited Reskin (1977), for it was in Allison's second paper that he had linked the data of Long and Reskin regarding 239 chemists (not Sichel's 237) and 286 biochemists.

Reskin (1977) thanked Allison, among others, for comments on an earlier version of her article. Her study discussed a survey of 238 (not 239 as quoted by Allison) doctoral chemists from U.S. universities between 1955 and 1961.

Long (1978), in a footnote, thanked, among others, Allison and Reskin for comments on an earlier version of his article. Long's population was male biochemists who had obtained their doctorates in the fiscal years 1957, 1958, 1962, and 1963. They were divided into two groups: (1) 134 biochemists who held teaching positions in graduate departments and were nonmovers, and (2) 47 who moved to other teaching positions. These two groups did not add up to Allison's 286 biochemists, nor was there any data that would build into Allison's table showing 59 biochemists with zero publications. Long (1978) gave but two indications that some of the biochemists in the population had not published: (1) "the strong positive effect of early publications on later publications indicates a tendency of *those who publish* to continue publishing" (p. 898, my emphasis), and (2) "thus, if a scientist has only a dissertation and a few publications, or perhaps none at all, at the time he applies for a job, it may be that less formal indicators are evaluated" (p. 900). Both these statements hinted that some had not published, but there were no numbers, and the "perhaps none at all" sounded as though Long did not have numbers he could rely on.

The abstract in Reskin's (1980) dissertation tells us the study "traces the careers of about 450 female and male doctoral chemists." The first page states there were "about 500." Table 7.3, which charts the number of publications of these 450–500 chemists from 1955 to 1970, has a total of 453—232 male and 221 female. The figures for nonpublishers are given as percentages of the two populations—7.1 percent of the 453. I worked that out as 32 who published nothing.

Where did Allison get his figures? It is possible that Allison had other papers from both Reskin and Long. He and Reskin had coauthored a paper on estimation problems, and Long, in a footnote, said he and Allison were planning more detailed study of a much larger sample of job changes. At least that was all I could think, short of writing to the author, which I did. In reply, Allison (1988) said he had worked from "original data, not with tabulations in published papers." Why, then, the discrepancy in the numbers? Allison (1980b) was careful, in his references to Long and Reskin, to use the words "For a description of the sample see . . . "; thus, readers were warned that *his* numbers were not to be found in those articles, just a description of how and why the numbers had been collected. The reader seems to have been brought to the edge of the swamp of unpublished papers and dissertations and given a vision of the invisible college awash in invisible data.

Sichel (1985) found the 37 nonpublishing chemists interesting because he could use a zero quantity to further test his mathematical model. I'm sure he went out of his way to find as many "real" data sets as he could. But it didn't really matter to him that the evidence for these 37 was, shall we say, impure.

By accident, I came across another example of the use of distant data that lead, this time, to invalid results. Following a citation trail from one article to another, I came upon T. Braun, W. S. Lyon, and E. Bujdoso's (1977) graphing of the growth of the literature of activation analysis. In this work, the growth of publications was traced to 1970. The authors noted that a study of the more recent years "awaits completion" (p. 684A). I thought this would be an interesting citation search exercise for the students in my course on advanced reference service, but first I wanted to run through it myself to see if it would work. That is, I needed to know if there was anything to find at the end of the trail. I have found it is uninspiring to give students exercises that result in zero hits.

I was led to the *Journal of Radioanalytical Chemistry*, where, in an incredibly heavy, navel-gazing article, Bujdoso, Lyon, and I. Noszlopi (1982) gave a neat and relevant summation of William Garvey (1979): "According to Garvey, about 20% of the reports and theses, and 65% of the papers in conference proceedings, will eventually appear in the form of journal papers" (p. 198). From this, it was clear that 80 percent of the reports and theses and 35 percent of the papers in conference proceedings would not appear as journal articles. I could not remember these figures from my reading of Garvey, nor could I find them in an exhaustive search.

Garvey and Belver Griffith (1972) reported that two-thirds of the technical reports produced by psychology researchers in 1962 had not been published by 1965 and that, "apparently, the contents of the vast majority of these reports were never submitted for journal publication" (p. 130). Even assuming that 100 percent of the two-thirds were *never* published, the remainder was not Bujdoso et al.'s 20%.

In a series of studies of presentations at national meetings, covering nine different fields of study, Garvey, Nan Lin, and Carnot Nelson (1970) concluded that nearly all the papers presented (all but one plus) and deemed worthy of publication by the authors would achieve some form of postmeeting publication—less than half in journals, the rest in books or technical reports (p. 36; p. 198 in Garvey 1979).

Bujdoso et al. (1982) were looking at journal publications only, but these earlier findings of Garvey and his research team were not as clear-cut as Bujdoso et al. claimed. Recognizing that the first part of Garvey (1979) was a summary of all the earlier studies, I wondered if somewhere in there were the overall conclusions that gave Bujdoso et al. their figures.

The following is the first relevant statement that we come across: "Likewise, if you select almost any major medium in the informal domain ('technical reports,' papers presented at scientific meetings, theses or dissertations, etc.) you will find that the main content of the majority of these reports eventually gets reported in journals" (Garvey 1979, p. 40). Of course, we need to know what is meant by "main content" and by "the majority." Might there be a meaning that would support Bujdoso et al.'s figure of 65 percent, even though that percentage refers only to papers in conference proceedings? If the statement meant that a majority of technical reports and theses, as well as conference proceeding papers, end up as journal articles, the 20 percent figure is not supported.

A later sentence does, roughly, lead to the 65 percent figure: "Even though our studies suggest that a majority of the material which is presented at national meetings does eventually achieve journal publication, about a third of it is never submitted to journals" (p. 50). The words "about a third" could certainly be translated into 35 percent. Garvey did not leave things there, however. After discussing what happens to the "third" that does not get into the journal literature, he made the following concluding statements: "Each year hundreds of thousands of papers are presented in the course of a few days at a few hundred national meetings, and then during the following 2 or 3 years, about half of this material is diffused into thousands of different journals. Most of the other half of this presentation material (the unpublished) is either never disseminated further or embedded in the fugitive literature" (p. 51). If Bujdoso et al. had taken this "finding" as their source, would they have said 50 percent instead of 65 percent?

Although Garvey's findings on the number of technical reports that were later published as journal articles were also confusing, they were not at all supportive of Bujdoso et al.'s 20 percent figure. In the main text, Garvey (1979) stated: "Still, 'technical reports' are considered by scientists as only interim reports. For example, the main content of almost half of the 'technical reports' produced by *scientists* end up being published as journal articles" (p. 59). In appendix A we find the figure quoted earlier (from Garvey and Griffith [1972]): "Two-thirds of the technical reports produced in 1962 had not achieved journal publication by 1965" (p. 136). What are we to make of this? That one-third is "almost half"? That the emphasis on the word *scientists* is meant to mean "not psychologists" (the subjects of the 1972 study)?

There are only two places where Garvey used a (roughly) 20 percent figure in connection with theses and reports. First: "In every discipline we have studied (physical, biological, and social sciences) we have found that a relatively large and consistent portion (between 16—20%) of the articles published by the core journals of the disciplines are based on a thesis or dissertation" (p. 61). Since this did not refer to the percentage of theses that were published in (all) journals, it cannot be the source of Bujdoso et al.'s figure. Nor can the information in the table in appendix E be the source, in spite of the caption: "Prepublication reports of main content of journal articles" (p. 208). The two columns are labeled: "Type of Prepublication Report" and "Authors/N = 3676/%." In the table, under the heading "Written," we find:

Type of Prepublication Report

Written	Authors
Technical report (distributed outside author's institution)	21.0
Thesis or dissertation	19.4

The table presents not the percentage of prepublication reports ending up as journal articles but the percentage of authors who first presented their material in these formats—some of the authors using more than one format (oral and written).

Bujdoso et al. (1982) used Garvey's "data" to establish the data base for their study of the journal literature of prompt nuclear analysis. They began with the following:

Journal papers	1030
Papers published in conference proceedings or multiauthored books	452
Reports	149

| Theses | 38 |
| Other items (mainly patents) | 16 |

By taking 20 percent of the reports and theses and 65 percent of the papers in conference proceedings ("according to Garvey"), they established their data base as 1,250 research papers (after deducting 110 review papers). They thus added 220 to their working total, and a very smoky 220 it was.

How important is it, for the results of research based on distant data, that the data reflect reality? If the answer is "not very important," since the models built from those numbers are not very finely tuned anyway and need not be more than "pretty" accurate, then we have to ask just how seriously we can take those results. That is, what credibility does such research have, based as it is on the shaky ground of distant data? Surely we must be able to assume that researchers have checked their data to make sure it is valid if they expect to be believed. More important is the fact that unless they do so, they will not be fulfilling their ultimate responsibility, which is to the Fat Lady in J. D. Salinger's (1961) *Franny and Zooey*. In the book, Franny is on the phone talking about the time she was on the radio show "Wise Child." Her brother Seymour had told her to shine her shoes, but she couldn't see why.

The studio audience were all morons, the announcer was a moron, the sponsors were morons, and I just damn well wasn't going to shine my shoes for them, I told Seymour. I said they couldn't see them *any*way, where we sat. He said to shine them anyway. He said to shine them for the Fat Lady. I didn't know what the hell he was talking about, but he had a very Seymour look on his face, and so I did it. . . . I don't think I missed more than just a couple of times. This terribly clear, clear picture of the Fat Lady formed in my mind. I had her sitting on this porch all day, swatting flies, with her radio going full-blast from morning till night. I figured the heat was terrible, and she probably had cancer, and—I don't know. Anyway, it seemed goddam clear why Seymour wanted me to shine my shoes when I went on the air. It made *sense*." (pp. 198–99).

The examples I have described were found by chance. They are not unusual. Leroy Wolins (1962) described how one of his graduate students wrote to thirty-seven authors for the data they had used in articles. Thirty-two replied. Twenty-one reported the data misplaced, lost, or inadvertently destroyed. Raw data was sent by nine authors. The data of three of the nine, Wolin reported, involved gross errors.

But it isn't only the gross errors that slip through the quality review system. It's the research that works mightily to say nothing. Michael Cooper (1972) constructed an elaborate model for evaluating information retrieval systems based on costs. His conclusion wiped out the validity of the model and, at the same time, claimed the model to be useful and meaningful:

There are a number of deficiencies in the model. The performance measure that is used in determining the optimum allocation of effort between the user and the system is simplified. In all probability, a performance measure is much more complex than this cost model assumes. Another deficiency is that the model has not yet been verified with operating data. Aside from these problems it is believed that the framework that the model presents is a useful way of evaluating retrieval systems as well as a meaningful method for arriving at an optimal allocation between user and system resources. (pp. 311–12)

Cooper's belief just isn't sufficient.

Carl Drott, Jacqueline Mancall, and Belver Griffith (1979) reworked some data from another study to show that Bradford's Law had "present applications" and "potential promise." After presenting their figures, the authors concluded that a searcher could check how well a search through the journal literature was done by comparing the actual results with those predicted by Bradford's Law. The outcome of the search, in terms of number of relevant articles and number of journals, could also be predicted *before* the search was done (p. 301). The next section of their article, "Some Recent Findings," concluded: "These findings cast doubt on the hypothesized applications of Bradford's Law which were discussed above" (p. 302). They then decided "The exact importance of Bradford's Law remains to be determined. It does, however, seem that there is great potential for future impact on a wide variety of information related situations" (p. 304). I would have to say, based on their own conclusions, that it does not "seem" that way at all.

Another example exhibiting insignificant results also illustrates how the desire to quantify can raise doubts about the quality of the research because the initial assumptions simply undermine the whole project (except for the pleasure the researchers experience in applying elegant mathematical procedures). Abraham Bookstein and Eve Podet (1986) compared various models for the prediction of library school student performance. They began by giving their rationale for the chosen measure of performance: "Performance will be defined here as graduate grade point average (GGPA). While it is true that there are other measures of success, such as likelihood of graduation and income after graduation, GGPA lends itself to study with quantitative methods" (p. 371). The authors assured us that they were really only testing the model and were not interested in giving information to educators who might want to learn something on the topic. Yet they concluded, somewhat inconclusively, "In spite of the somewhat inconclusive results, this study affirms that the probabilistic model has some value in predicting success in graduate school" (p. 387). This "affirmation" is made "regardless of the validity of the GGPA as a measure of quality" (p. 371).

No wonder Gerard Salton (1985) could say of information science, "Most of the published research in our field is probably not worth doing and ought to be forgotten" (p. 268). However, this was only an opinion, and he had "no firm data" and went on to cite forty-five worthwhile papers. These were "the few," I imagine.

MEASURING QUALITY

I have spent a great deal of time, so far, detailing what could be seen as merely sloppy work, rather than concentrating on the serious frauds of science that are dangerous to life and limb. Those have been well-covered by others (Broad and Wade 1982; Kohn 1986), and the results of such perfidiousness are *clearly* significant. But it is the *subtle* wearing down of rigor and hence quality that leads to the indirect destruction of the scientific enterprise. It is the lazy little products that kill the mind, by sowing the seeds of rot in the structure of knowledge. These seemingly unimportant slips from the very highest standards of quality work indirectly, creating a cynicism first among scholars themselves, and from them into the classroom simply by an alteration of attitude—the loss of respect for science—and then into the thinking of the general public. In the loss of quality is the loss of credibility. I imagine this is the reason the focus of the authors in *Quality in Science* (La Follette 1982), a collection of essays, was on the establishment of criteria of quality in terms of social value. As Harvey Brooks (1982) wrote in the opening chapter:

> Where output measures have been introduced, they tend to measure the internal mechanics of the research enterprise itself—scientific papers, number of citations to scientific papers, patents, Nobel and other prizes, invited papers at international meetings, and sometimes migrations of scientists. Measures of the quality or significance of these outputs are crude at best. Moreover, neither the input nor the output measures give much weight to the social function of the scientific enterprise, or provide any criteria for the assessment of its output against the social functions expected of it. (p. 1)

Manfred Kochen (1983) would have applauded. Yet information science, especially its subdiscipline of bibliometrics, consistently uses those criteria Brooks identified as "crude at best." These traditional information science standards, perhaps because they are quantifiable, have consistently been used to mean quality: awards won, positions held, prestige of institution, citation counts, being found on authority lists, being a joint author, and writing in the English language (see Narin 1976; Goffman and Warren 1980; Bruer 1985).

These sorts of criteria avoid taking into account effects on society or on individuals, effects that in many instances are immeasurable. In the physical sciences and medicine, the effects of research are visible, whether these effects are good or bad, and one can look back over history and say something about the quality of those effects in terms of humanity's quality of life.

Perhaps, in the long run, time and time alone will identify the quality ideas in the social sciences and the humanities. Counting citations and publications and awards cannot measure real quality. Charles Lindblom (1987), in his contribution to the special issue of *Knowledge: Creation, Diffusion, Utilization* on national policies for optimizing validity in applied social research, said that a "very high degree of validity" could not be achieved in the social sciences and that the great ideas of people like "Adam Smith, John Stuart Mill, Karl Marx, Sigmund Freud, Emile Durkheim, Max Weber, or J. M. Keynes" (p. 517) could not be considered in terms of validity without belittling them. Although Karl Popper (1965) rejected, as scientific theories capable of being falsified, Marx's theory of history and Freud's psychoanalysis, he did not reject the possibility that these theories could be true. He knew "very well that science often errs, and that pseudo-science may happen to stumble upon the truth" (p. 33). Lindblom (1987) did not want validity to be ignored, but it was not to be used to limit speculation and investigation. In any social science, the unqualified pursuit of validity, certainly in a quantitative sense, could lead to results that lack the necessary "feel" of reality to make them credible. As information, such results can be meaningless, at best, and deceptive misinformation, at worst.

CAUSES OF INFERIOR QUALITY

I suppose the primary cause of bad information is human imperfection—laziness, disinterest, sloppiness, greed, ambition, distraction, making (wrong) assumptions, taking things for granted, and just plain making mistakes. Carol Weiss (1978) makes a good point:

Not every social scientist functions at the peak standards that current developments permit. Many are mediocre or out-of-date in their research skills. Rather than aspire to apply existing methods creatively to novel problems, they adhere to textbook injunctions. A simple example, but by no means the most important one, is the ritualistic use of 0.05 levels of statistical significance, regardless of the statistical technique, the type of problem, the relative need for certainty, or the real-world risks that accrue to error. (p. 41)

In discussing effective research and development management, Laurence Lynn (1978) commented on the government pressure on social scientists to produce "relevant" research. The 1976 National Research Council's review of research funded by the National Science Foundation had concluded that the quality of work was "highly variable and on average relatively undistinguished, with only modest potential for useful application" (Lynn 1978, p. 5). The pressure to produce, Lynn noted, "has flooded the market with shoddy products. The resulting poor quality research, nonreplicable demonstrations, ambiguous experiments, useless data, and biased evaluations have neither policy value nor scientific merit" (p. 5).

On the other hand, politicians and civil servants do not always demand, or make decisions based on, quality in the research they hire or use. Ernst Stromsdorfer (1985), analyzing the use of information by policymakers, reported:

After reading commentary on the policy-development process and inspecting policy and budgetary documents and evaluations of actual social programs, it has become obvious that policy makers, while not totally subjective and nonrational, will use whatever data are at hand to support their case, regardless of the methodological purity by which it has been developed. Canons of scientific evidence are not ignored but are applied selectively. Taste or preference for certain methods, such as the case-study approach, are as much determinants of what data are used as is any perceived methodological purity or rigor. (p. 258)

If political pressure causes the users of research to be a little casual about the quality of research, it is surely just as political for researchers to respond in kind. Lynn (1978) quoted the comment of a psychologist who was strongly committed to socially useful research: "Paradoxically, when funding agencies under the edicts of conservative federal administrations have pressured for relevance, the effect has often been just the opposite from that which was intended—an increase occurred only in pseudo-relevancy and much re-writing of project proposals to use the 'relevance' terminology took place" (p. 6).

The pressure to do research occurs in industry as well as in universities and privately owned laboratories. Lewis Branscomb (1982), of IBM, described the issue in general terms:

As a company looks at how competitive its technological position is and as it gauges its perceptions of its competitors' technological capability, then it feels heavier pressure as the competition improves. Those pressures are communicated to the research community when the development divisions find themselves hard-pressed to remain self-sufficient in the technology required to create their product. (p. 70)

But throughout the literature on the quality of science, the main culprit is the policy of publish or perish, adopted by universities after the Second World War and striking with force at young faculty members coming into the professoriat in the 1970s. It is enlightening to read Robert Nisbet's (1971) *The Degradation of the Academic Dogma*, about the American university from 1945 to 1970, and find no mention of publish or perish. The change in universities, as Nisbet then saw it, was caused by the establishment of research centers operated by individual faculty or groups of faculty with money received directly from the granting agencies—subverting the traditional structure of the university where faculty were beholden to the central administration for funds and thus felt a certain union of interests. Of course, in the competition for grant money, it was better to have a long list of publications to indicate quality as measured by, for instance, acceptance in peer-reviewed journals or international conferences.

However, the publish-or-perish policy must have been in place at the time. Williamson (1977) quoted a 1968 article by L. M. Branscomb, who noted a "vast unusable literature," which might "indicate that society is paying a very high price for the publish-or-perish policy" (p. 2). A. J. Meadows (1974) saw publish or perish, at the time he wrote his book, as a peculiarly American phenomenon (although he did say that no major science-producing country was immune. "This impulse towards quantity of publications tends to be particularly evident in the U.S., owing to the system of tenure adopted in the universities there. The 'up-or-out' rule insists that the university staff in the lower ranks should only be allowed a fixed number of years to show their ability: if not promoted at the end of this period, they are required to leave" (p. 60). Probably because of the need for new professors to meet the postwar baby boom entering universities in the 1960s, the policy became very visible, particularly in the following decade. Promotion and tenure committees had little or no knowledge of the work of these new faculty, and so, as Meadows suggested, it was tempting, whenever the committee members were not "personally acquainted" with an individual, to count number of publications (pp. 60–61).

A number of other writers can be cited on this issue William Goffman and Kenneth Warren (1980) wrote, "It is because of the publish-or-perish syndrome that quality filtering of the scientific literature is essential" (p. 170). Franz Kaltwasser (1987), then the director of the Bavarian State Library in Munich, identified as one cause of the enormous volume of "redundant and obsolete" information (p. 115) "the growing academic aspect of our lives, the pressure for more literary production and the need to distinguish oneself in academic circles" (p. 112). A New York Times editorial entitled "Credit and Credibility in Science" (1987) commented on the case of Dr. Glueck, who had published conclusions based on data that "barely existed." The writer noted, "The more articles a researcher publishes, the better his chances for Federal grants, university jobs and academic honors." The writer then added: "Perhaps that's why two of Dr. Glueck's co-authors, though aware of problems with the results, left their names on the study. . . . with many scientists interested in the sheer quantity of publications, who is going to spoil their colleagues' game and fuss about quality?" (p. E26). The New Republic similarly editorialized: "The academic industry, as the recent Boyer Report on undergraduate education pointed out, is increasingly geared to a professionalized faculty and away from students. Faculty members, through a tenure system that prizes a journal article over evidence of good teaching, are under increasing pressure to keep pumping out the books" ("The Case for Book Burning" 1987, p. 7). Although William Broad (1988), writing about the increase in the number of scholarly journals, saw the growth as, in part, the healthy expansion of science, he added, "But experts say at least part of it is symptomatic of fundamental ills, including a publish-or-perish ethic among researchers that is stronger now than ever and encourages shoddy, repetitive, useless or even fraudulent work" (p. C1). Finally, Russell Jacoby (1987) argued that there are no longer intellectuals who speak to the general public because they are now all academics. He wrote that even when rank and security are attained by faculty publishing in order not to perish, habits of thinking small remain, for by then, "the talent, even the desire, for bold thinking has long since atrophied" (p. 159).

For twenty years, writers have identified this one cause of poor quality research, yet the publish-or-perish policy remains in place. Is the reason for inaction a case of ignoring the information, or is it some aspect of human imperfection? It's a dilemma.

THE QUALITY OF INFORMATION IN GENERAL

It is not my intention to do more than identify the fact that much, if not most, of the information coming at us through the broadcast media is biased, manufactured to sell something, and simply untrue. One need only read Ian Mitroff and Warren Bennis's (1989) book about the television industry, subtitled "The Deliberate Manufacturing of Falsehood and What It Is Doing to Our Lives." They developed a case that enables them to say that TV lulls us "silently and seductively into collective dumbness through its very banality" (p. 182). Their analysis is supported by Richard Bernstein (1989) in a discussion of movies that distort facts and add fictional episodes to historical events to "teach" the strongly held, personal point of view of producer or director. The visual reality conveyed by the settings in motion pictures tricks the viewer into believing the fiction to be as "true" as the scenery. This is what Dennis Mumby (1988) called, in the context of advertising, "systematically distorted communication" (p. 34).

The literature on propaganda, beginning at least with Jacques Ellul's (1965) classic, opens another channel of misinformation we have to live with. Lies, deceptions, and distortions of the facts have been part of the story of humanity from the beginning; they are magnified and multiplied by the technology of mass communication.

THE CURE—THE DILEMMA

Clearly there is only one way to make sure that people can tell fact from fiction and that they will *want* to know that what they hear and see is factual—or as close to factual as is humanly possible—and that way is education. Government regulations can control the advertising industry up to a point, but there is no control of "artistic" manipulation of events in order to win audiences (television news) or to speak an "eternal truth" (the movies). But people can be taught about the popular media so that they understand that what they read and see and hear is not necessarily real or accurate. They can also be taught about the world so that they can recognize distortions. One problem with this "solution" is how to teach all that is necessary in the time available for schooling. Another problem is that *what* is taught must itself be brushed with the highest quality of argument and evidence. *There* is the problem for researchers and scholars and every kind of communicator of information. *There* is the need for rigor and absolute carefulness in the creation, preparation, and production of knowledge and information. The instillation of quality consciousness in the research community, though necessary for the excellence of knowledge, is even more important for the attitudes toward their work of those who also teach. There must be a respect for knowledge and knowledge workers, a respect that is seriously eroded when it is clear to everyone in the academic and broadcast communities, for instance, that shoddy work is being done for self-serving reasons.

I have had occasion to review the problem of quality control in the scientific community (Neill 1989), and it is clear to me that the peer-review process, as practiced by the best scholarly journals (the double-blind variety), is still the best hope. Broad (1988) was concerned that the sheer growth in numbers of publications was causing an "apparent overloading of the quality control systems in science, including the watchful eyes of co-authors and referee panels that scrutinize submissions to journals." He referred to a "spate of recent cases of scientific fraud in which gross errors of fact and logic have slipped through the safety nets" (p. C11).

What is unfortunate about these cases is that those fraudulent articles that have been caught and have been formally retracted in the relevant journals continue to exist in the literature and continue to be read and cited. Mark Pfeifer and Gwendolyn Snodgrass (1990) identified eighty-two retracted articles and found 733 citations to these papers well *after* the retractions had been published. It is true that there was a reduction in the number of citations that could have been expected (by 35 percent), but still, "articles citing invalid, retracted work are abundant and ubiquitous in the scientific literature" (p. 1422) and in well-known as well as obscure journals. One particular case, that of John Darsee, received wide publicity in the popular press, "yet, despite this, Darsee's 14 completely retracted papers were subsequently cited 123 times after their retraction" (p. 1422).

On the other hand, Eugene Garfield and Alfred Welljams-Dorf (1990), in the same issue of *JAMA* (*Journal of the American Medical Association*), found that in the case of Stephen Breuning, which was also well-known, researchers "shunned" his work after retraction, although not completely. Unfortunately, the authors concluded that their study suggests "the potential value of citation indexes for limiting the spread of falsified research" (p. 1426). Garfield, as the founder and president of the Institute for Scientific Information, which publishes the citation indexes, could be somewhat self-serving in this conclusion, especially in the light of the findings of Pfeifer and Snodgrass.

Quite naturally, Pfeifer and Snodgrass raise the question of cause and cure. "These revelations have stirred debate about our 'publish-or-perish' mentality, the structure and responsibility of research institutions, the peer review process, the role of government intervention, and many issues in biomedical publishing" (p. 1420). Undoubtedly, those concerns were behind the special conference issue of *JAMA* on peer review and the quality of the medical literature, and this despite over twenty years of work on quality assurance and the quality of health care literature by Dr. John Williamson and his colleagues (see Williamson 1977; Williamson, Goldschmidt, and Colton 1986; Williamson, German, and Weiss 1989; Neill 1989, p. 8 n.4).

In the same issue of *JAMA*, Noel Nobel (1990) reported a survey of U.S. and Canadian medical schools regarding their quality guidelines—other than those concerned with human and animal rights. Of 133 schools, 17 had such guidelines, 91 were not even considering them, and 9 provided the author with copies. Nobel discovered that nonacademic institutions, in government and industry, had policies recognizing "that while research is carried out by individuals who bear specific responsibility for their own actions, the organization bears responsibility for clearly stating unambiguous standards for behavior and will not tolerate any variation from its ethical expectations" (p. 1436). This is corroborated by Branscomb's (1982) description of peer review at IBM. "The fact that the value judgments are made not by some independent government agency or by peers in distributed locations but by those directing the work, means that the judgments are less independent of the conduct but perhaps better informed." More time is spent on evaluation in "midstream than on retrospective evaluation" (p. 73), and "lots" of in-house people are involved, as well as outside reviewers.

Nobel's (1990) indictment of universities is forthright: "It is clear that the academic community has, for the most part, failed to accord sufficient priority to these issues. The academic research community has not examined the measures that nonacademic organizations use to ensure quality in an ethically, intellectually and operationally sound manner" (p. 1436). Universities have been immune from criticism because of the public's faith in their social role, faith built up over centuries, and because of the publicity given to the principle of academic freedom—essentially the freedom to pursue truth idiosyncratically. Of course, an institution operating under the publish-or-perish policy might have difficulty applying quality guidelines that involve more than merely counting awards, publications, and citations.

CONCLUSION

Quality is hard to assess in a way that allows administrators to rank faculty for promotion and tenure year after year, for true quality is subjective and unquantifiable—at least until the perspective of history can shine the light of effects-over-time on discoveries and ideas that contemporaries don't even know exist. In the last analysis, the problem of quality of information is a moral problem that only individual scholars, newspeople, moviemakers, businesspeople, politicians, and citizens can solve—and then only as individuals. Information workers, concerned with the quality of the information they acquire for organization and retrieval, must recognize this dilemma—and recognize that it is a dilemma. Information scientists, perhaps, should try to do something about it.

REFERENCES

Allison, Paul D. "Estimation and Testing for a Markov Model for Reinforcement." *Sociological Methods and Research* 8(4): 434–53 (May 1980a).

———. "Inequality and scientific productivity." *Social Studies of Science* 10(2): 163–79 (May 1980b).

———. Personal correspondence, Feb. 10, 1988.

Bernstein, Richard. "Can Movies Teach History?" *New York Times*, Nov. 26, 1989, sec. 2, p. 1.

Bookstein, Abraham, and Eve B. Podet. "Predicting Graduate Library School Performance Using a Probabilistic Retrieval Model." *Library Quarterly* 56(4): 370–88 (Oct. 1986).

Branscomb, Lewis. "Industry Evaluation of Research Quality: Excerpts from a Seminar." In La Follette 1982, 68–81.

Braun, T., W. S. Lyon, and E. Bujdoso. "Literature Growth and Decay: An Activation Analysis Résumé." *Analytical Chemistry* 49(8): 682A–688A (July 1977).

Broad, William J. "Science Can't Keep up with Flood of New Journals." *New York Times*, Feb. 16, 1988, C1, C11.

Broad, William, and Nicholas Wade. *Betrayers of the Truth*. New York: Simon and Schuster, 1982.

Brooks, Harvey. "Science Indicators and Science Priorities." In La Follette 1982, 1–32.

Bruer, John T. "The Search for Quality Information: Schistosomiasis Literature." In Kenneth S. Warren, ed., *Selectivity in Information Systems: Survival of the Fittest*, 144–53. New York: Praeger, 1985.

Bujdoso, E., W. S. Lyon, and I. Noszlopi. "Prompt Nuclear Analysis: Growth and Trends." *Journal of Radioanalytical Chemistry* 74(1–2): 197–238 (1982).

"The Case for Book Burning." *New Republic*, Sept. 14 and 21, 1987, 7–8, 10.

Cooper, Michael D. "A Cost Model for Evaluating Information Retrieval Systems." *Journal of the American Society for Information Science* 23(5): 306–12 (Sept.-Oct. 1972).

"Credit and Credibility in Science." *New York Times*, July 26, 1987, E26.

Cronin, Blaise. *The Citation Process: The Role and Significance of Citations in Scientific Communication*. London: Taylor Graham, 1984.

Drott, M. Carl, Jacqueline C. Mancall, and Belver C. Griffith. "Bradford's Law and Libraries: Present Applications—Potential Promise." *Aslib Proceedings* 31(6): 296–304 (June 1979).

Ellul, Jacques. *Propaganda: The Formation of Men's Attitudes.* New York: Knopf, 1965.

Evans, James T., Howard I. Nadjari, and Sherry A. Burchell. "Quotational and Reference Accuracy in Surgical Journals." *JAMA* 263(1): 1353–54 (March 9, 1990).

Garfield, Eugene, and Alfred Welljams-Dorf. "The Impact of Fraudulent Research on the Scientific Literature: The Stephen E. Breuning Case." *JAMA* 263(10): 1424–26 (March 9, 1990).

Garvey, William D. *Communication: The Essence of Science.* Oxford, N.Y.: Pergamon Press, 1979.

Garvey, William D., and Belver C. Griffith. "Communication and Information Processing within Scientific Disciplines: Empirical Findings in Psychology." *Information Storage and Retrieval* 8(3): 123–36 (June 1972).

Garvey, William D., Nan Lin, and Carnot E. Nelson. *The Role of the National Meeting in Scientific and Technical Communication* (NTIS Report PB 202 007). Baltimore: Center for Research in Scientific Communication, Johns Hopkins University, 1970.

Goffman, William, and Kenneth S. Warren. *Scientific Information and the Principle of Selectivity.* New York: Praeger, 1980.

Jacoby, Russell. *The Last Intellectuals.* New York: Basic Books, 1987.

Kaltwasser, Franz Georg. "Dangers for the Modern Information Society in the Computer Age." *IFLA Journal* 13(2): 111–19 (1987).

Kochen, Manfred. "Information and Society." *Annual Review of Information Science and Technology* 18: 277–304 (1983).

Kohn, Alexander. *False Prophets.* Oxford, N.Y.: Basil Blackwell, 1986.

La Follette, Marcel Chotkowsky, ed. *Quality in Science.* Cambridge: MIT Press, 1982.

Leontief, Wassily. "Theoretical Assumptions and Nonobserved Facts." In his *Essays in Economics: Theories, Facts, and Policies.* 2: 24–34. White Plains, N.Y.: M.E. Sharpe, 1977.

Lindblom, Charles E. "Alternatives to Validity." *Knowledge: Creation, Diffusion, Utilization* 8(3): 509–20 (March 1987).

Long, J. Scott. "Productivity and Academic Position in the Scientific Career." *American Sociological Review* 43(6): 889–908 (Dec. 1978).

———. "Productivity and Position in the Early Academic Career: A Study of Two Cohorts of Ph.D. Biochemists." Ph.D. dissertation, Cornell University, 1977.

Lynn, Laurence E., Jr., ed. *Knowledge and Policy: The Uncertain Connection.* Washington, D.C.: National Academy of Sciences, 1978.

Meadows, A. J. *Communication in Science.* London: Butterworth, 1974.

Mitroff, Ian I., and Warren Bennis. *The Unreality Industry: The Deliberate Manufacturing of Falsehood and What It Is Doing to Our Lives.* New York: Birch Lane Press, 1989.

Mumby, Dennis K. *Communication and Power in Organizations: Discourse, Ideology, and Domination.* Norwood, N.J.: Ablex Pub. Corp., 1988.

Narin, Francis. *Evaluative Bibliometrics: The Use of Publication and Citation Analysis in the Evaluation of Scientific Activity* (NTIS, PB 252 339). Washington, D.C.: National Science Foundation, 1976.

Neill, S. D. "The Information Analyst as a Quality Filter in the Scientific Communication Process." *Journal of Information Science* 15(1): 3–12 (April 1989).
———. Review of *Canadian Libraries in Their Changing Environment*, ed. Loraine Spencer Garry and Carl Garry (Downsview, Ontario: York University, 1977). *Library Quarterly* 48(3): 359–61 (July 1978).
———. Review of "Classification: Theory and Practice," ed. Ann F. Painter (*Drexel Library Quarterly* 10[4], October 1974). *Library Quarterly* 45(4): 434–35 (Oct. 1975).
Nisbet, Robert. *The Degradation of the Academic Dogma: The University in America, 1945–1970.* New York: Basic Books, 1971.
Nobel, Noel L. "Comparison of Research Quality Guidelines in Academic and Non-academic Environments." *JAMA* 263(10): 1435–37 (March 9, 1990).
Pfeifer, Mark P., and Gwendolyn L. Snodgrass. "The Continued Use of Retracted, Invalid Scientific Literature." *JAMA* 263(10): 1420–23 (March 9, 1990).
Popper, Karl. *Conjectures and Refutations: The Growth of Scientific Knowledge.* New York: Harper Torchbooks, 1965.
Project Progress: A Study of Canadian Public Libraries. Ottawa: Canadian Library Association, 1981.
Reskin, Barbara F. "Scientific Productivity and the Reward Structure of Science." *American Sociological Review* 42(3): 491–504 (June 1977).
———. *Sex Differences in the Professional Life Chances of Chemists.* New York: Arno Press, 1980.
Salinger, J. D. *Franny and Zooey.* Boston: Little Brown, 1961.
Salton, Gerard. "A Note about Information Science Research." *Journal of the American Society for Information Science* 36(4): 268–71 (July 1985).
Sichel, H. S. "A Bibliometric Distribution That Really Works." *Journal of the American Society for Information Science* 36(5): 314–21 (Sept. 1985).
Stromsdorfer, Ernst W. "Social Science Analysis and the Formulation of Public Policy: Illustrations of What the President 'Knows' and How He Comes to 'Know' It." In Jerry A. Hausman and David A. Wise, eds., *Social Experimentation*, 257–81. Chicago: University of Chicago Press, 1985.
Tague, Jean, and S. D. Neill. Review of *Project Progress: A Study of Canadian Public Libraries* (Ottawa: Canadian Library Association, 1981). *Ontario Library Review* 66(1): 84–87 (March 1982).
Weiss, Carol H. "Improving the Linkage between Social Research and Public Policy." In Lynn 1978, 23–81.
Williamson, John W. *Improving Medical Practice and Health Care: A Bibliographic Guide to Information Management in Quality Assurance and Continuing Education.* Cambridge, Mass.: Ballinger, 1977.
Williamson, John W., Pearl S. German, and Robin Weiss. "Health Science Information Management and Continuing Education of Physicians." *Annals of Internal Medicine* 110(2): 151–60 (Jan. 15, 1989).
Williamson, John W., Peter G. Goldschmidt, and Theodore Colton. "The Quality of Medical Literature: Implications for Clinicians, Authors, and Editors." In J. C. Bailar and F. Mosteller, eds., *Medical Uses of Statistics*, 370–91. Waltham, Mass.: New England Journal of Medicine Books, 1986.

Wolins, Leroy. "Responsibilities for Raw Data." *American Psychologist* 17: 657–58 (1962). ("Comment" column.)

Ziman, John. "From Parameters to Portents and Back." In Yehuda Elkana et al., eds., *Toward a Metric of Science: The Advent of Science Indicators*, 261–84. New York: Wiley, 1978.

6

The Dilemma of Information Overload: Managing in the Information Society

INTRODUCTION

When I started to work on this chapter I had some sources in mind—things I had come across over the years such as S. C. Bradford (1948), T. Braun, W. S. Lyon, and E. Bujdoso (1977), Nicholas Rescher (1978), Fremont Rider (1944), and Alvin Toffler (1970). I also had a clear memory of someone who had worked on the compression of texts to reduce information overload. I could remember only that his name began with a B and might be Bernal. Thinking it would be easy to find this reference, I ploughed through everything else first. Finally I went downstairs to the library to check Bernal in the H. W. Wilson Company's index to *Library Literature*. No Bernal. No term *information overload*. I looked in *Library and Information Science Abstracts*. No Bernal. No *information overload*. Nor was there anything in *Information Science Abstracts*. I was sure, then, I had the name wrong. It came to me, as I puzzled over the name that this "Bernal" was also connected with abstracting—a logical connection to compression of texts. I went to the section of the library on Abstracting and Indexing and found a bibliography (Wellisch 1980, 1984) on that topic in which were listed articles written by Charles Bernier (1970, 1975) on "terse literatures." As I thought about this search, it struck me that none of those indexes used the term *information overload* as a subject descriptor. Nor was it used in the key-word index to volumes 1–23 of the *Annual Review of Information Science and Technology*. Manfred Kochen's (1983) article on information and society has a section called "Information-Overload and Mismatch," but it mentioned only two authors who had written directly about information overload, one being

James G. Miller (1978). Then Kochen had drifted away into artificial intelligence and the cultural aspects of communication. Only one-sixth of a two-page section was about the headlined topic. Clearly, neither librarians nor information scientists perceived information overload as a problem, yet they were continually addressing it. Then I realized that, of course, for librarians and information scientists, information overload was an opportunity, a challenge, a chance to do their thing—all the positive things identified in the index terms that their indexing services *did* use.

As a matter of curiosity, I tried to find the index term for Bernier's terse literature papers. *Library Literature* was no help. *Information Science Abstracts* classified Bernier (1975) under "Computer Systems—Hardware and Software," and Bernier (1978) under "Writing and Recording of Information and Data." *Library and Information Science Abstracts* filed Bernier (1975) under "Reading," and Bernier (1978) under "Selective Dissemination of Information (SDI)," although they could also be found in the index under "Terse literatures" and "Ultraterse literatures." I wondered why Bernier's idea had not been generally adopted—until I read, in Bernier (1975): "Experience has shown that published results of research and development, including the conclusions, can nearly always be trusted" (p. 191). His ultraterse literatures included ultraterse conclusions—basically one-sentence factual statements of the conclusions in research papers. Bernier clearly had not read Lewis Branscomb (1968) on the poor quality of scientific research papers, nor the article by S. A. Goudsmit (1966) ("Is the Literature Worth Retrieving?") upon which Branscomb built his own critique.

I tried to think of any overload experiences of my own and recalled my decision to get out of little theatre because memorizing lines took up too much head space and too much time to allow me to do the kind of reading I enjoyed—or to do nothing but watch the grass grow. I had also decided, much later, to say no to memberships on more than three or four committees, and to make sure that some of those were the kind that rarely met. But being on committees is more a time overload than an information overload.

The fact was, when I thought about it, I couldn't think of anyone I knew who was suffering from information overload, yet Miller (1978) detailed many examples—from the small print on insurance contracts to crying babies and junk mail (p. 149). Toffler's (1970) *Future Shock* was grounded on information overload. William Donnelly (1986) and Ian Mitroff and Warren Bennis (1989) foresaw social disorientation coming from information overload that was an overload of disconnected and almost meaningless information. Avner Arbel and Albert Kaff (1989), analyzing the stock market crash of October 1987, identified one of the causes as an inadequate computer capacity that "led to a breakdown in the DOT (Designated Order Turnaround) system, delays in executing orders, tardy market statistics and outright mistakes" (p. 183). Fred Fedler (1989) explained journalists' vulnerability to hoaxes by saying: "Journalists are vulnerable to misinformation and always will be. Journalists cannot determine the truth of every story they publish, nor check every detail. They receive too many stories, and a single story may contain hundreds of details" (p. 236). Orrin Klapp (1982) complained that meaning took much longer to "make" than the absorbing of "mere information." As he explained, "Meaning, being subjective, and referring to synthetic or holistic properties that cannot be reduced to the sum of parts, might be called a higher sort of information that does not come easily, let alone inevitably, from a growing heap of mere information" (p. 58). Donnelly (1986) expanded the issue in his own way:

What the rhetoric, fantasy, unrootedness, and unrelatedness of much of our communications images have in common is not what is put into them, but what is left out. They are as light as confetti. Speed is what energizes these images: the speed of their arrival, the speed of adaptation to fleeting tastes and passions, the speed with which the images jump from one to the other, and the speed with which we jump between them. Thus the problem with this type of information overload is not simply quantity, but the unconnected, excited nature of the images that package and distribute this information, whether it be news of the world or stories of human interest. (p. 186)

Toffler (1980) didn't place such an information overload experience in the future: "Consensus shatters," he wrote. "On a personal level, we are all besieged and blitzed by fragments of imagery, contradictory or unrelated, that shake up our old ideas and come shooting at us in the form of broken or disembodied 'blips.' We live, in fact, in a 'blip culture' " (p. 181). I suppose Donnelly (1986) would say, "It's bad now, but it'll be worse later." Still, people do seem to manage, although Miller (1978) did note that some psychotic cases are possibly caused by information overload. "There is also suggestive clinical and experimental evidence that overloads of information may have some relation to schizophrenic behavior" (p. 167). However, a general collapsing of the population is not evident. People adjust, and I will discuss how they adjust later on. Let me conclude this introduction with a reference to Émile Durkheim's 1893 work *The Division of Labor in Society*, quoted by James Beniger (1986). Durkheim was examining the results of the global expansion of industrialization through improved transportation and communication: "The producer can no longer embrace the market in a glance, nor even in a thought. He can no longer see limits, since it is, so to speak, limitless. Accordingly, production becomes unbridled and unregulated" (Beniger 1986, p. 11). Durkheim, foreshadowing authors such as Toffler and Donnelly by nearly a century, also argued that anomie, the breakdown of norms governing individual and group behavior, resulted not from the division of labor into distinct organizations but "from the breakdown in communication among these increasingly isolated sectors, so that individuals employed in them lose sight of the larger purpose of their separate efforts" (Beniger 1986, p. 12). How we somehow survived wholesale anomie is explained in part by Beniger in *The Control Revolution*. It is a story that augurs well for our survival in a blip or confetti culture. The part that Beniger only indirectly tells is the part played by the peculiar human need to survive and the adjustments people make to create Herbert Simon's (1986) nearly empty world, "in which there are millions of variables that in principle could affect each other but that most of the time don't" (p. 104). I will return to this concept below.

OVERLOADED SCHOLARS

The writers of books and articles have known for some time that there is more information on most subjects than can be read by one person in any reasonable amount of time. Bernier (1978) made the following calculations: "It would take more than 27 centuries to read the annual biomedical research literature at two papers a day, 365 days a year; more than seven centuries to read a year's chemical literature; more than 14 years to read the annual cardiovascular literature; and more than 70 years to read the literature of one year of research in oncology (p. 446)."

However, if you wanted to read the literature comparing the effectiveness of colonoscopy, sigmoidoscopy, and barium sulfate (enema) in locating neoplasms (cancer), you would find 226 items in the Institute for Scientific Information's on-line data base *Scisearch*, of which 24 would be directly relevant from a perusal of title and abstract. And after reading half a dozen, you would realize you were no longer hearing anything new. If you had nothing else to do, and if the library you were using was well-known to you (that is, you knew the shelf location of each journal), you could read (or skim) ten articles a day, since most are short reports of effectiveness tests of the procedures. The subject has been narrowed down, you will have noticed, by the use of five limiting descriptors—the three procedures, the term *comparative*, and the language limit *English*.

Academics, and scientists generally, are responsible by profession for "creating new knowledge." They are also forced to write, through university publish-or-perish policies (see chapter 5). These are the people who are particularly aware of an overload of information. Braun, Lyon, and Bujdoso (1977), while doing a bibliometric analysis of the literature in the field of radioactivation analysis, made the more general comment that all their readers were aware of how the scientific literature seemed to be "ever expanding." They noted, "Those under the age of 35 *think* that once the literature was more manageable; those over the age of 45 *know* it was so!" (p. 682A). Peter Shaw (1989) made a similar comment about the field of literary criticism:

"It is impossible to keep up with work in the field," the professional journals repeatedly declare. Either because academic criticism cannot be read, then, or because no one wishes to read it, professionals in the field, by their own admission, do not keep up with its progress. How then, have they muddled through? Very simply by ignoring their peers, while remaining secure in the knowledge that by doing so they miss nothing of importance. (p. 49)

Russell Jacoby (1987), in his harsh criticism of academia, noted, "Economists increasingly employ complex mathematical models not simply because they might illuminate reality but because they facilitate publishing; the models allow economists to write articles without amassing any new information." Most of these models, Jacoby said, "are relegated to the stockpile after publication because they have no application or validity" (p. 159).

Though this might be true in some disciplines, it is not true in others. In his argument that something other than a virus (particularly HIV or human immunodeficiency virus) is the cause of AIDS, Adams (1989) pinpointed a portion of the problem as information overload:

Part of the reason why a newly discovered virus like HIV could be misidentified as the cause of a complex syndrome like AIDS is that all the fields of research involved in the AIDS story are themselves complex and no individual scientist has an adequate command of all of them, each having to rely on the insights and choices made by specialists in other fields in order to corroborate from other disciplines the insights of one particular specialty. Thus the epidemiologist, who studies epidemics, is obliged to believe in the choices made by the virologist, who studies viruses, and vice versa; neither will have sufficient command of the other's discipline to be capable of judgement, particularly when the other discipline is straining past the point of knowledge and into speculation as has so often been the case in the AIDS story. (p. 4)

As Bernier (1978) noted, "Major problems become so fragmented through overspecialization that nobody can solve them simply because nobody can read let alone assimilate, remember and integrate the published fragments" (p. 447).

In a survey of medical practitioners and officers and members of medical specialty boards, officers of the specialty colleges and academies, and editorial board members of official specialty journals, John Williamson et al. (1989) found that a fair percentage were unaware of certain specific newly established medical advances. The most serious deficiency was the use of digitalis (or its derivatives) "in uncomplicated congestive heart failure in the elderly." Fifty-four percent of the physicians did not seem to be aware of the current change in use of this drug in the elderly. The next two most serious deficiencies involved the use of glycosylated hemoglobin measurement (A1C) for assessing diabetic control: "39% were apparently not aware of this accepted diagnostic tool (general practitioners being significantly worse than the other specialties, with 65% being deficient); 39% of the obstetric and gynecology specialists did not use trial of labor in certain women who had previously undergone Caesarean sections" (p. 154). Both practitioners and opinion leaders concurred that "the sheer volume of scientific literature produced has created significant problems in information retrieval." Nearly two-thirds of the practitioner sample said the current volume of scientific literature was "unmanageable" (p. 155).

Information retrieval was the problem for Bradford (1948) when he did his study of abstracting and indexing services. Less than half the useful articles could be located (p. 121), since the volume of literature simply overloaded the abstracting services. Rider (1944) was also concerned about the ability of academic libraries to shelve the numbers of new publications and showed that college and university libraries, on the average, were doubling in size every sixteen years. Robert Molyneux (1986), reviewing the literature on library growth since Rider, discovered that growth between 1970 and 1980 was not exponential (p. 26), although it had been until that decade. John Ziman (1980) noted that the journal literature had doubled every fifteen years but that the expansion had "continued at a somewhat lower rate during the 1970's" (p. 369). Of course, the growth rates varied widely from one topic or field to another.

OBSOLESCENCE

Just as the growth rates differ from subject to subject, so do the rates at which the literature becomes obsolete. In spite of its obsolescence (meaning it is no longer cited by authors), this literature must be stored in libraries or archives, adding to the volume through which the search for relevant literature must be made. In 1956, when citation analyses had to be done by hand, Charles Brown remarked on the librarian's problem of knowing how many years of a journal to keep in the active collection. "In the case of entomology and zoology at least 50 years of the journals are necessary, if the library is to possess volumes which will cover 90 per cent of the citations to serials in these fields" (p. 27). On the other hand, "some conversations with nuclear scientists have reflected the rapid obsolescence of publications in this subfield of physics. In looking over an article published two years ago one scientist remarked, 'This article is too old to be of any value now' " (p. 83). M. V. Sullivan et al. (1980), in an analysis of the obsolescence of the biomedical literature, also found it was the age of the information, and not necessarily the increase in the size of the literature, that caused articles to be cited less. Then again, J. Marton (1985), examining citations in thirty-five science journals, concluded, "The decrease in the citedness of articles does not mean obsolescence; the fact is that it is not that the older articles lose their citations (and scientific value) but that the younger articles receive extra citations" (p. 153). The reason might be because it is easier to find more recent items, indicating a reluctance to conduct a literature search if it is not absolutely necessary (as it is for a doctoral dissertation, for instance).

GRAY LITERATURE

Part of the overload is the number of articles that are redundant or worse. Kenneth May (1968) evaluated the subfield of mathematical determinants and found 43 percent to be trivia and 21 percent duplication. Jean Tague, Jamshid Beheshti, and Lorna Rees-Potter (1981) examined the literature on obsolescence and found 41 percent to be popularizations, duplication, and trivia. Another aspect of particular concern to those responsible for maintaining comprehensive collections is what is called fugitive, ephemeral, or gray literature. This literature includes such documents as minutes, regulations, notices of local authorities, scientific bulletins, lists, reports, curricula and courses, in-house publications, unpublished manuscripts, and unpublished conference, congress, and symposium proceedings. *Information Hotline* (1987) reported that the System for Information on Grey Literature in Europe (SIGLE) held "over 80,000 documents from aeronautics and agriculture to space technology" (p. 4) and that 30,000 more were expected to be added in 1987. Ross Bourne (1988), reviewing the activities of the British Library, announced a "new bibliographical publication—*British Reports, Translations, and Theses*, based upon its input to the European Communities' SIGLE" (p. 62). M. S. Palnikov (1989), of the Institute of Information in Social Sciences of the USSR Academy of Sciences, reported: "Grey literature now constitutes an essential part of INION's collection of Soviet social science literature. . . . during the 1980s alone this collection has increased to 45–50,000 items" (p. 18). All of this literature cataloged and classified in library collections, is rarely taken into the count of literature growth because it does not "exist" in standard bibliographies and indexes.

BUT IS IT ALL BAD?

There is some argument that the quantity of information I have described as information overload is necessary to get at quality. Nicholas Rescher (1978) wrote:

This "quality-drag" must, however, be construed as meaning *not* that the expanding literature of science is so much useless verbiage that reflects pointless busy-work, but rather that it represents—on balance, and collectively, at any rate—the useful and necessary inputs needed for genuine advances, the indispensable grist, so to speak, for the mill of scientific progress. There is a balance in the economy of science between its various quality-levels. One cannot adequately characterize any exploratory enterprise simply in terms of its successes. While the "big" discoveries are the determinants of *progress* proper, the unsuccessful and less successful efforts are an integral part of the whole venture. We are driven to a holistic view of science which denies the prospect of divorcing the important from the routine. (p. 109)

Recent critics of higher education would disagree completely (Jacoby 1987; Sykes 1988; Smith 1990). However, Ziman (1980) argued as did Rescher: "The speciation of scientific journals is not a pathological sign, it is a natural accompaniment of the dynamic change and growth of scientific knowledge" (p. 371). In another place (Ziman 1978), he wrote, "It is the accumulation, mutual interaction, and eventual transformation of this mass of information by various intellectual and social processes that turns it into knowledge, which is what we are really seeking" (p. 268). A. I. Yablonsky (1980), of the Institute for Systems Studies in Moscow, discussed the distribution regularity of scientific publications whereby a small percentage of authors produces a large percentage of the literature. One comment is relevant to the present issue:

In other words, the background of scientists with low productivity is, to a certain extent, inseparable from the background of the nucleus of highly productive scientists, and this inevitable overhead has to be taken into account in practical planning and organization of science. Even when the small number of highly productive scientists is singled out, the stability of their high productivity cannot be guaranteed if all the remaining scientists with low productivity are eliminated. (p. 22)

Yablonsky then quoted from Norbert Wiener's (1956) autobiography that it was "quite possible that 95% of original scientific papers were produced by fewer than 5% of professional scientists, but the greater part of them would not have been written at all if the remaining 95% of scientists did not contribute to the high level of science" (Yablonsky 1980, p. 23). Wiener (1956) did not use the words "papers" or "written" but rather scientific "work done" or not done. His comment was made in the context of an approval of universities that housed a body of professional scientists engaged in "disinterested scholarship," not many of whom would do "really original" work but who were a necessary part of the scientific enterprise. We have to remember that Wiener's was the old traditional university, the loss of which Robert Nisbet (1971) bemoaned.

Wiener (1956) was less approving of large-scale scientific laboratories, either private or government-sponsored. He saw the major defect of these "mass attacks" on problems to be the loss of many "really good results" in the "unreadable ruck of fifth-rate reports." "If a new Einstein theory were to come into being as a government report in one of our super-laboratories," Wiener wrote, "there would be a really great chance that nobody would have the patience to go through the mass published under the same auspices and discover it" (pp. 364–65). He was more concerned to have a redundancy of *time* to ripen his ideas, rather than be a clock-punching scientist who has to give an "accounting of the last minute of his research" (p. 361).

Another argument for redundancy, of a different kind but supporting the principle of the need for information redundancy (shall we say "approaching" information overload), comes from decision making in politics. Alexander George (1980) gives the following example:

A seldom-noted aspect of Khrushchev's behavior during the Cuban missile crisis was that he quickly established multiple channels for securing information on Kennedy's intentions. Too much was at stake for the Soviet government for it to wait passively for Washington to provide deliberate or inadvertent signals regarding the president's intentions. Faced with the need to make important decisions momentarily, the Soviet premier grasped the value of redundancy in information coverage of critical aspects of the situation. In striking contrast, U.S. leaders have allowed themselves in several crises to remain dependent on a single channel of information about critical aspects of the situation. . . . Among the many malfunctions of the policymaking process evident in planning the Bay of Pigs fiasco in 1961 was the fact that Kennedy and his advisers, including the JCS, depended on the CIA's estimates of Castro's military and political strength. Both were miscalculated and underestimated by CIA. It was incorrectly estimated that there was a substantial anti-Castro underground, which would lead to an uprising when the invasion by Cuban exiles took place. It was erroneously believed that Castro's air force was weak and vulnerable and that he did not have the air power to defeat the invading force. CIA argued that the invasion should not be delayed since Cuba would soon receive modern air power from the Soviets. As a matter of fact, Castro had already received these modern aircraft. (p. 129)

Ole Holsti (1972) saw that stress in crisis situations resulted in a tendency to reduce the size of decision-making groups and the numbers of people consulted, creating a situation worse than, or at least no better than, those caused by information overload. Here are two of his examples:

Similarly, John Foster Dulles's decision to cancel a loan for the Aswan Dam, precipitating the 1956 Suez crisis, was made virtually on his own. He refused to consult with, much less accept the advice of, the American ambassador to Egypt, Henry Byroade, whose assessment of the situation—a correct one as it turned out—did not correspond to his own. During the months that followed Dulles's action, Anthony Eden believed that Nasser couldn't keep the Suez Canal open because European pilots would quit and there were no trained Egyptians to replace them. In contrast to the Norwegian government, which had learned from captains who had been through the canal that little training or skill was required to become a pilot, Eden made no effort to confirm or disconfirm his erroneous belief. (p. 21)

In any dilemma, there are always arguments on all sides. James Sisson, Eric Schoomaker, and Jon Ross (1986) set out the hypothesis that "more data applied to a clinical problem may make the decision on management an inferior one" (p. 355). That is, when there are numerous interacting factors affecting clinical judgment, "a physician using intuitive thinking may be unable to comprehend their aggregate meaning" (pp. 354–55). The authors argued for a "modest" form of decision analysis tree that could be consulted "in the outpatient office or at the bedside" (p. 363).

Finally, in this argument for (and against) quantities of information, the following example, with a tongue-in-cheek commentary on the nature of social science experiments, is given by Ernst Stromsdorfer (1985):

I sometimes wonder what would have happened if Franklin Roosevelt had had the good fortune to be president when economics was further advanced than it was in the 1930s. Instead of appointing the committee for Economic Security in 1935, he might have fielded a social experiment to find out how people would respond to retirement benefits, welfare for the aged, and cash payments to the unemployed. By 1937 we might have had the research design completed instead of the legislation Congress actually enacted. By 1940 we might have seen the completion of payments to the first wave of experimental subjects instead of the initiation of benefits under a new program. The Second World War, alas, would have interrupted the analysis of results and perhaps payments to the cohorts who were still receiving treatments to test duration effects. But we could have resumed treatments in, say, 1946 and completed analysis by the mid-1950s. We could have spent some time debating whether the decline in saving that we observed was attributable to the experiment or magnified by the expectation of the end of the Great Depression or by the postwar consumption boom, whether the increase in duration of unemployment was a steady-state reaction or was magnified by the change of postway [sic] labor-market conditions and hence transistory [sic]. Oh, what a missed opportunity! (pp. 276–77)

MANAGING INFORMATION OVERLOAD

Studies of decision making by political figures yield a quantity of insights into the effects of information overload and how individuals adjust—not always with positive results, but with an instinct for survival. We know from David Braybrooke and Charles Lindblom (1970) that policymakers normally make decisions effecting "small or incremental change and not guided by a high level of understanding" (p. 71). This reflects the limited capacities of human beings to "understand and solve complex problems and an unsettled, shifting compromise of conflicting values" (p. 71). It is, in other words, a strategy to avoid or, rather, manage information overload. Philip Tetlock (1989) summarized the problems:

Policymakers must deal with incomplete and unreliable information on the capabilities and intentions of other states (sometimes even of their own states). The range of response options confronting them are indeterminate. The probable consequences of each option are shrouded in uncertainty. Policymakers must compare options on many conflicting, seemingly incommensurable, value dimensions (for example, the impact of options on economic interests, international prestige, domestic popularity, human rights, and even lives). Finally, to compound the difficulty of the task, policymakers must sometimes work under intense stress and time pressure. (pp. 341–42)

Tetlock then identified several known problem strategies: (1) reliance on simple historical analogues or precedents to interpret new situations; (2) reluctance to modify preconceptions in response to challenging evidence; and (3) dependence on easy-to-execute heuristics in assessing the likely behavior of other states (p. 342). He then warned that the cognitive economy and efficiency resulting from having made these adjustments to information overload "frequently have a steep price: susceptibility to error" (p. 342). Tetlock concluded, "Balancing the possible benefits of cognitive efficiency against the possible increases in error is a perplexing normative problem with no widely acknowledged solution" (p. 342). It is, in fact, a dilemma.

A number of authors refer to James G. Miller's research on information-input overload and various adjustment processes, indicating the acceptance of these as accurate descriptions of some of the ways people manage information overload. Holsti (1972), although he recognized the impossibility of replicating reality in laboratory experiments (p. 24), nevertheless used Miller's list. "A survey of experimental findings has identified a number of strategies for coping with the problem: omission, error, queuing, filtering, cutting categories of discrimination, employing multiple channels, and escape" (p. 115). Bernier (1978) also referred to Miller, although he used the word "approximation" for "cutting categories of discrimination," and he added "chunking" (p. 446). Miller's (1978) definitions of these concepts are slightly different from the earlier references used by Bernier and Holsti. For instance, Miller uses "abstracting" instead of "approximation." It should be noted that Miller describes some of these processes in terms of *transmitting* (or failing to transmit) information. As an example, in the Khrushchev story above, the use of multiple channels of incoming information was the point, whereas Miller's "multiple channels" are described as "simultaneously transmitting messages over two or more parallel channels," not as *receiving* from two or more channels. For the record, Miller's (1978) adjustment processes follow:

Omission—failing to transmit certain randomly distributed signals in a message. *Error*—incorrectly transmitting certain signals in a message. *Queuing*—delaying transmission of certain signals in a message, the sequence being temporarily stored until transmission. *Filtering*—giving priority in processing to certain classes of messages. *Abstracting*—processing a message with less than complete detail. *Multiple channels*—simultaneously transmitting messages over two or more parallel channels. *Escape*—acting to cut off information input. *Chunking*—transmitting meaningful information in organized "chunks" of symbols rather than symbol by symbol. This last adjustment process, unlike the others, cannot be used with signals which do not convey meaning to the receiving system based on previous learning by it. (p. 123)

Bernier (1978) added to Miller's list his own methods of adjusting to overload. These methods have, he said, "approached, but not solved" the problem of having too much relevant material to read, assimilate, remember, and integrate: "(1) specialization, (2) condensed surrogation, (3) skipping, (4) reference-retrieval systems, and (5) disbelief in the existence or the severity of the problem" (p. 446).

THE NEARLY EMPTY WORLD

The picture I have presented so far is of decision-making situations as crowded with information as is a Brueghel painting with people or a Jackson Pollock with swirls and splotches. Herbert Simon (1986) presents a different point of view, namely that we live in what might be called a "nearly empty world." This is the world in which all of us live, even top administrators. Although their "narrow" world is full to the brim with messages, and although political leaders, dealing with worldwide events, seem to be affected by all the worries in the universe, they do not, in fact, deal with all those worries or all the information and emotions attached to them. You and I do that.

In presenting the empty world concept, Simon first described the *ideal* decision-making situation. The theory assumes the decision maker has a "well-defined utility function," a "well-defined *set of alternatives*," and that a "joint *probability distribution*" can be assigned to all future sets of events. Finally, the theory assumes the decision (choice of strategy) made will "*maximize the expected value*" in terms of the utility function (p. 100). Such a theory is not unlike the classical, rational decision-making model that Holsti (1989) identified before arguing against it. This concept of decision making is based on the premise that "crisis concentrates the mind" and increases the decision maker's motivation and ability to cope with threat, complexity, and uncertainty (p. 9). The model has been applied, theoretically at least, to individuals, groups, and organizations. Holsti (1989) questioned anyone's ability to approach challenging crises with "high motivation, extraordinary energy, more accurate perceptions of the situation and relevant actors, an enhanced ability for processing information, and increased capabilities and resources for creative problem solving" (p. 10). Simon (1986) was unequivocal in saying that this "Olympian" model "has never been applied and never can be applied—with or without the largest computers—in the real world" (p. 101). In opposition, Simon offered what he called the "behavioral model" of "bounded rationality"—the nearly empty world.

Within the behavioral model of bounded rationality, one doesn't have to make choices that are infinitely deep in time, that encompass the whole range of human values, and in which each problem is interconnected with all the other problems in the world. In actual fact, the environment in which we live, in which all creatures live, is an environment that is nearly factorable into separate problems. Sometimes you're hungry, sometimes you're sleepy, sometimes you're cold. Fortunately, you're not often all three at the same time. Or if you are, all but one of these needs can be postponed until the most pressing is taken care of. You have lots of other needs, too, but these also do not all impinge on you at once. (p. 104)

This describes how we get along in the world, and especially in a world, such as ours, that is bludgeoned by information.

As an addition to the behavioral model, Simon proposed "intuitive rationality," which is built upon years of experience. That is, great quantities of information on a particular subject—chess, coins, snow, mathematics, painting, baseball statistics, makes of automobiles—garnered over years of careful study (Simon referred to research indicating at least ten years [p. 109]), are stored and used to "search through complex spaces" in "snail-like fashion" (p. 109) because of information overload. Perhaps Roosevelt, in the example cited above, intuitively made his decision based on years of experience in thinking about and dealing with political and social affairs. Certainly Sisson, Schoomaker, and Ross (1986) attributed the diagnosis of the experienced physician to intuition (p. 354). Patricia Benner (1984), using different terminology, identified the same (intuitive) process of handling quantities of information and at the same time gave an explanation of how it "works":

Proficient and expert nurses develop clusters of paradigm cases around different patient care issues, so that they approach a patient care situation using past concrete situations much as a researcher uses a paradigm. Past situations stand out because they changed the nurse's perception. Past concrete experience therefore guides the expert's perceptions and actions and allows for a rapid perceptual grasp of the situation. This kind of advanced clinical knowledge is more comprehensive than any theoretical sketch can be, since the proficient clinician compares past whole situations with current whole situations. (pp. 8–9)

Mihaly Csikszentmihalyi's (1990) concept of "flow" fits into this category. Reminiscent of Simon's nearly empty world, Csikszentmihalyi wrote, "While everything we feel, smell, hear or remember is potentially a candidate for entering consciousness, the experiences that actually do become part of it are much fewer than those left out" (p. 26). He defined consciousness as "intentionally ordered information" and intentions as "the force that keeps information in consciousness ordered" (p. 27). Referring to George A. Miller (1956) and others on the limitation of (normal) human information-processing capacity, Csikszentmihalyi pointed out, "Information enters consciousness either because we intend to focus attention on it or as a result of attentional habits based on biological or social instructions" (p. 30). That is, we are asked or forced or we choose to focus our attention, but attention "cannot notice or hold in focus more information than can be processed simultaneously" (p. 31). In a sense, then, we have no choice but to take information overload avoidance procedures.

Before moving on to the next section, we might as well take a closer look at exactly what George Miller (1956) said. His paper seems to be generally used to indicate that human information-processing capacity has a very small upper limit—seven (plus or minus two) bits. Miller looked at studies of one-dimensional discrimination tasks (e.g., pitch, tone) to support this figure. However, he also said, "The addition of independently variable attributes to the stimulus increases the channel capacity, but at a decreasing rate" (p. 88). That is, in an experiment in which two variables are available (pitch *and* tone) for making discriminations, the information-processing capacity increases. Think of the number of faces you can differentiate and the number of variables involved. The "7 + or − 2" limitation can be overcome. Miller said, "We have a variety of techniques for getting around it and increasing the accuracy of our judgments" (p. 90). The limitation of laboratory experiments to "replicate" reality should be remembered here. "We can extend the span of absolute judgment," Miller wrote, "from seven to at least 150. Judging from our every day behavior, the limit is probably in the thousands, if indeed there is a limit" (p. 91). He mentioned that experts are five to ten times better at making even unidimensional judgments, although he backed off from discussion, claiming ignorance of how the expert's mind worked. Redundancy of information certainly seems to be a factor—or the controlling of overload by constant, daily, dedicated mastery of each information item in a narrow field.

THE PRINCIPLE OF LEAST EFFORT

The idea of "bounded rationality" refers to the limited capacities of humans to deal with all the information that comes at them. These limitations encourage, if they do not force, human beings to follow the principle of least effort (Zipf 1949). The principle states, "An individual's entire behavior is subject to the minimizing of effort" (p. 6). That is, "in simple terms," as George Kingsley Zipf put it, "a person in solving his immediate problems will view those against the background of his probable future problems, *as estimated by himself.* Moreover he will strive to solve his problems in such a way as to minimize the *total work* that he must expend in solving *both* his immediate problems *and* his probable future problems" (p. 1). Although Zipf's attempts to test this principle mathematically (statistically) across a number of phenomena (such as word usage, size of cities, kinds of occupations, movement of persons by highway bus travel between twenty-nine arbitrary cities) can be questioned (see Herdan 1962), we know, just by common sense, that the general idea behind the principle holds true. People tend to take the most convenient, least troublesome route when possible. Thus we make a small fraction of the words in our vocabulary do most of the work—words that have developed a kind of "companionship" over a long period of time in a culture. These are the words G. Herdan (1962) said "have no difficulty in finding words with which to combine in sentences." It seems the nature of words and languages also has something to do with word choice. He explained further, "As we pass to the less common words, i.e. words of less general use, the hesitation in combining with other words increases . . . and this continues until we come to the rare words . . . the least sociable . . . [which] find it most difficult to find a suitable partner among the population of words in the universe of discourse" (p. 212). The difficulty of using rare words is due not just to their "anti-social" nature but to the difficulty we have in finding them. It's like the need to consult a thesaurus. The act is not consistent with the Principle of Least Effort. Nevertheless, as Arthur Iberall and Harry Soodak (1987) noted, "Language usage tends to be economical—as much is encoded into a particular set of units as possible" (p. 511). As a consequence of the "significant degree of design tolerance because of redundancy," they said, language is "highly robust in the face of noise" (p. 510).

When we read that "as much is encoded into a particular set of units as possible," we are reminded of Miller's (1978) concept of "chunking" and the conjecture of Michael Nelson and Jean Tague (1985) as they puzzled over the reason for the widespread occurrence of the Zipfian distribution. They proposed that there was "some underlying assumption about human behavior such as the principle of least effort, success-breeds-success, or the optimization of information transmitted per symbol" (p. 283). As M. K. Buckland and A. Hindle (1969) said, "Convenience or something in the nature of a Principle of Least Effort is a dominant factor in at least some aspects of information transmission" (p. 55).

Information *transmission* is, of course, the other side of information reception, but the least-effort principle works both ways. In the first published article that showed that a few authors in a field produced most of the published literature, Alfred Lotka (1926) found that "the number of persons making 2 contributions is about one-fourth of those making one; the number making three contributions is about one-ninth, etc . . . , and the proportion, of all contributors, that make a single contribution, is about 60 per cent" (p. 323). In terms of least effort, most authors take the easy way out, at least in the area of publications (now as then), thus managing their own information overload and reducing ours.

OTHER WAYS OF MANAGING
INFORMATION OVERLOAD

As J. G. March (1978) puzzled over the problem of the "engineering of choice," he wrote this about "bounded rationality":

Ideas of *limited rationality* emphasize the extent to which individuals and groups simplify a decision problem because of the difficulties of anticipating or considering all alternatives and all information. They introduce, as reasonable responses, such things as step-function tastes, simple search rules, working backward, organizational slack, incrementalism and muddling through, uncertainty avoidance, and the host of elaborations of such ideas that are familiar to students of organizational choice and human problem-solving. (pp. 591–92)

There are other ways, and James Beniger's (1986) *The Control Revolution* is all about one kind of way. One example will do as a representative—the book needs to be read in its entirety.

> Equally important to the rationalization of industrial society, at the most macro level, were the division of North America into five standardized time zones in 1883 and the establishment the following year of the Greenwich meridian and International Date Line, which organized world time into twenty-four zones. What was formerly a problem of information overload and hence control for railroads and other organizations that sustained the social system at its most macro level was solved by simply ignoring much of the information, namely that solar time is different at each node of a transportation or communication system. (p. 16)

Donnelly (1986), who was much concerned about the effects of the present and projected communications technology, envisioned ways of coping that were quite different: "The trick is to scan with a clear idea of what you are personally looking for, to scan the headings, graphs and charts, pictures and captions, and, assuming that the text is well written, the first and last paragraphs. We are already living with these kinds of video reading habits, now encouraged even more by the computer, which is itself a speed-reading instrument" (p. 187). He is referring to a modified version of George Bugliarello's (1988) hyperintelligent computer system. Donnelly's (1986) solution was to improve and increase education, particularly in the humanities. Bugliarello's (1988) solution was to develop global networks of personal computers linked into a kind of "hyperbrain" so that each individual would have "the capacity to receive information in real time from a very large number of intelligent stations (human and PC or workstation) all over the world" (p. 69). He said nothing about information overload and completely ignored, or had not considered, the problem of meaning. As Klapp (1982) noted, "Meaning, being subjective, and referring to synthetic or holistic properties that cannot be reduced to the sum of parts, might be called a higher sort of information that does not come easily, let alone inevitably, from a growing heap of mere information" (p. 58). We have, of course, considered various aspects of the development of meaning in the first two chapters.

Meaning, or what Csikszentmihalyi (1990) would, perhaps, call "intentionally ordered information," is drawn from the mass of information we encounter. This information is given meaning as it is shaped into our knowledge. We cannot make sense out of *all* the information in the world, or even all that impinges on our senses. One way we do make sense is by talking. Klapp (1982) wrote, "Talk has always been a major process of meaning formation whatever its form—discussion, debate, brainstorming, counseling, psychotherapy, encountering, group therapy, chat, gossip, rumor" (p. 60). Wiener (1956) agreed. "The scientist," he thought, "must live in a world where science is a career, where he has companions with whom he can talk and in contact with whom he may bring out his own vein" (p. 360). In this milieu he saw the scientist, "and the very young scientist in particular," as having the "leisure to ripen his own ideas" (p. 361).

An extreme example of talk as a means of making sense is rumor, particularly in tense situations. It is extreme not in its lack of use but in its unreliability as a method of getting control over information. Ralph Rosnow and Gary Alan Fine (1976) cited a study showing that the people who kept rumors going (rumormongers) were those who were caught up in the activities of the situation about which rumors were circulating—"due to their greater involvement and need to know" (pp. 35–36). Kitao Abe's (1978) field study of the 1964 Niigata earthquake found that although most people used transistor radios to obtain information, radios were not "the final determinant of individuals' actions in the confusion and disturbance following the disaster. . . . People were generally influenced by passers-by, who were not particularly reliable" (pp. 148–49). That is, what people knew was based on rumor, but it was the face-to-face character of the information that was meaningful (if wrong). However, only 40.3 percent admitted to hearing rumors.

Rumors themselves can become distorted, and this is clearly caused by information overload. Rosnow and Fine (1976) explain, "Because of the natural porosity of human memory and the tendency to simplify and bring order to things, the most common rumor distortions are the result of leveling (elimination of some details), sharpening (selective attention given to particular information), and assimilation (twisting of new material to build a better overall structure)" (p. 36). Except for the last, we have met these processes before. The authors are very clear that rumors, at least those that are not deliberate, are grounded in the effort to manage confusing information (which could include, naturally, a lack of information).

Human beings are motivated to make sense of their environment; there is an "effort after meaning." Our minds strive to illuminate chaos and uncertainty. When the truth is not directly forthcoming we piece together information as best we can, giving rise to rumors, rationalizations, and a search for a definition of the situation. The reason rumors circulate is that they explain things and relieve the tensions of uncertainty. (p. 51)

In this vein of people needing to bring meaning out of the welter of information, Patricia Meyer Spacks (1985) reviewed the social science literature on gossip and listed the variety of uses of gossip, all leading to the development of meaning.

It provides groups with means of self-control and emotional stability. It circulates both information and evaluation, supplies a mode of socialization and social control, facilitates self-knowledge by offering bases for comparison, creates catharsis for guilt, constitutes a form of wish-fulfillment, helps to control competition, facilitates the selection of leaders, and generates power. It provides opportunity for self-disclosure and for examination of moral decisions. (p. 34)

Here is an information retrieval "device" untouched by information science.

Spacks (1985) was more concerned, however, with the kind of gossip closest to talk, the kind that "involves two people, leisure, intimate revelation and commentary, ease and confidence. . . . They weave their web of story . . . speaking the language of shared experience, revealing themselves as they talk of others, constructing a joint narrative—a narrative that conjures up yet other actors, offstage, playing out their own private dreams" (p. 3), and in the process, getting control of all the information from their world they decide to keep.

Mention of "story" brings me to the last means that I wish to consider for combating information overload—the use of stories. I will never forget the experience of reading Mary Moorman's (1957, 1965) intimately detailed description of the life of William Wordsworth. She seemed to follow him footstep by footstep, constructing the poet's world complete and comprehensible. I was reminded of that experience when I read J.R.R. Tolkien's (1954, 1955) *The Lord of the Rings*. All the information that was necessary to feel and understand that world was present—there was no chaotic overload of meaningless bits of news, announcements, warnings, and advice. (Not, that is, until Tolkien's son began publishing his father's literary remains.) Thus I knew what Donnelly (1986) was getting at when he saw the "increasing consumption of fantasy and science fiction" as an escape "into a very hierarchical and simple society not the least bit reflective of or analogous to our own" (p. 186). However, I could not agree that the works I had read were about "simple" societies or that they were not reflective of the present world. Indeed, they gave meaning to the present in a way that quantities of information could not. Neil Postman (1989) described the place of stories—not just fantasies but stories of all kinds, including a person's own story—in a culture "inundated" with information. He wrote:

Without stories as organizing frameworks we are swamped by the volume of our own experience, adrift in a sea of facts. Merely listing them cannot help us, because without some tale to guide us there is no limit to the list. A story gives us direction by providing a kind of theory about how the world works—and how it needs to work if we are to survive. Without such a theory, such a tale, people have no idea what to do with information. They cannot even tell what is information and what is not. (p. 123)

There is a set of scholarly literature on the use of and the need for story in contemporary society. This is not the place to review that literature, but the following will provide an introduction: Bruno Bettelheim (1976), Robert

Coles (1989), Mihaly Csikszentmihalyi and Olga Beattie (1979), Olga Beattie Emery and Csikszentmihalyi (1981), and Joseph Gold (1990).

CONCLUSION

In the introduction to this chapter, there was a reference to the information overload with which we are all familiar—junk mail. However, it is not information overload for those who just throw it in the recycling box. Nor is it information overload for those who search through the ads and coupons for bargains and who get pleasure as well as profit from applying the knowledge so gained to their shopping responsibilities.

Before the growth of bureaucracies and the welfare state, the information we needed to cope with life's ordinary problems was found in conversation with friends and neighbors. The megalopolis practically forbids that. Part of information overload is sheer size—in miles to go and numbers of people— from less than a million people in 1500 to over five billion in 1990. To find our way around in the myriads of agencies, organizations, and departments, we have had to invent community information centers to act as clearinghouses of local information in the areas of legal, health, educational, civic, social, and recreational information.

There is evidence that the effects of information overload can be negative. Miller (1978) cited research that told us that the "modern city dweller rarely considers himself his brother's keeper. Good Samaritans are rare. Strangers in need are commonly passed by, and no help is offered or given them. Since so many individuals are in need in big cities, people fear that their personal resources would be exceeded if they were to give aid to all the needy people they encounter" (p. 150). Miller also described a number of cases of "pathological effects of information input overload" (pp. 164–69). Csikszentmihalyi (1990) seemed to suggest that some teenage suicides and other ills of society were due to information overload (p. 15). Indeed, his book as a whole is about controlling and using information for what he calls "optimal experience." He described, briefly, the pathology of information as follows: "One of the main forces that affects consciousness is psychic disorder—that is, information that conflicts with existing intentions, or distracts us from carrying them out" (p. 36).

Nevertheless, most people, as we have seen, make adjustments—for better or worse. It is only futurologists who thump the information overload drum—so that they can tout the new technology as a cure. But there is no cure. Information breeds information as one thought leads to another and as answers lead to questions. The dilemma for information scientists is how to reduce the instances where the results of information overload lead to decisions of the "worse" kind. Developing better information control and retrieval systems for recorded information is only one way of doing that job. Do information scientists have the responsibility to go beyond that job and into the wider world of information use, misuse, and avoidance? Perhaps this is the real dilemma.

REFERENCES

Abe, Kitao. "Levels of Trust and Reactions to Various Sources of Information in Catastrophic Situations." In E. L. Quarantelli, ed., *Disasters: Theory and Research*, 147–58. Beverly Hills, Calif.: Sage Publications, 1978.

Adams, Jad. *AIDS: The HIV Myth*. New York: St. Martin's Press, 1989.

Arbel, Avner, and Albert E. Kaff. *Crash: Ten Days in October . . . Will It Strike Again?* New York: Longman Financial Services Publishers, 1989.

Beniger, James R. *The Control Revolution: Technological and Economic Origins of the Information Society*. Cambridge: Harvard University Press, 1986.

Benner, Patricia. *From Novice to Expert: Excellence and Power in Clinical Nursing Practice*. Menlo Park, Calif.: Addison-Wesley, 1984.

Bernier, Charles. "Reading Overload and Cogency." *Information Processing and Management* 14(6): 445–52 (1978).

———. "Terse Literatures I: Terse Conclusions." *Journal of the American Society for Information Science* 21(5): 316–19 (Oct. 1970).

———. "Terse Literature II: Ultra-Terse Literatures." *Journal of Chemical Information and Computer Science* 15(3): 189–92 (Aug. 1975).

Bettelheim, Bruno. *The Uses of Enchantment: The Meaning and Importance of Fairy Tales*. New York: Knopf, 1976.

Bourne, Ross. "The British Library." In *British Librarianship and Information Work, 1981–1985*, 2: 55–72. London: Library Association, 1988.

Bradford, S. C. *Documentation*. London: Crosby Lockwood & Son, 1948.

Branscomb, Lewis M. "The Misinformation Explosion: Is the Literature Worth Reviewing?" *Scientific Research* 3(11): 49–56 (May 27, 1968).

Braun, T., W. S. Lyon, and E. Bujdoso. "Literature Growth and Decay: An Activation Analysis Résumé." *Analytical Chemistry* 49(8): 682A–688A (July 1977).

Braybooke, David, and Charles E. Lindblom. *A Strategy of Decision: Policy Evaluation as a Social Process*. New York: Free Press, 1970.

Brown, Charles Harvey. *Scientific Serials*. Chicago: Association of College and Research Libraries, 1956.

Buckland, M. K., and A. Hindle. "Library Zipf." *Journal of Documentation* 25(1): 54–57 (March 1969).

Bugliarello, George. "Toward Hyperintelligence." *Knowledge: Creation, Diffusion, Utilization* 10(1): 67–89 (Sept. 1988).

Coles, Robert. *The Call of Stories: Teaching and the Moral Imagination*. Boston: Houghton Mifflin, 1989.

Csikszentmihalyi, Mihaly. *Flow: The Psychology of Experience*. New York: Harper & Row, 1990.

Csikzentmihalyi, Mihaly, and Olga Beattie. "Life Themes: A Theoretical and Empirical Exploration of Their Origins and Effects." *Journal of Humanistic Psychology* 19(1): 45–63 (Winter 1979).

Donnelly, William J. *The Confetti Generation: How the New Communications Technology Is Fragmenting America*. New York: Henry Holt & Co., 1986.

Emery, Olga Beattie, and Mihaly Csikzentmihalyi. "The Socialization Effects of Cultural Role Models in Ontogenetic Development and Upward Mobility." *Child Psychiatry and Human Development* 12(1): 3–18 (Fall 1981).

Fedler, Fred. *Media Hoaxes.* Ames: Iowa State University Press, 1989.

George, Alexander L. *Presidential Decision-Making in Foreign Policy: The Effective Use of Information and Advice.* Boulder, Colo.: Westview, 1980.

Gold, Joseph. *Read for Your Life: Literature as a Life Support System.* Post Mills, Vt.: Fitzhenry & Whiteside, 1990.

Goudsmit, S. A. "Is the Literature Worth Retrieving?" *Physics Today* 19(9): 52–55 (Sept. 1966).

"Grey Literature Database." *Information Hotline* 19(1): 4 (Jan. 1987).

Herdan, G. *The Calculus of Linguistic Observations.* The Hague: Mouton, 1962.

Holsti, Ole R. "Crisis Decision Making." In Philip E. Tetlock et al., eds., *Behavior, Society, and Nuclear War,* 1: 8–84. New York: Oxford University Press, 1989.

———. *Crisis, Escalation, War.* Montreal: McGill-Queen's University Press, 1972.

Iberall, Arthur S., and Harry Soodak. "A Physics for Complex Systems." In F. Eugene Yates, ed., *Self-Organizing Systems: The Emergence of Order,* 499–520. New York: Plenum Press, 1987.

Jacoby, Russell. *The Last Intellectuals: American Culture in the Age of Academe.* New York: Basic Books, 1987.

Klapp, Orrin E. "Meaning Lag in the Information Society." *Journal of Communication* 32(2): 56–66 (Spring 1982).

Kochen, Manfred. "Information and Society." *Annual Review of Information Science and Technology* 18: 277–304 (1983).

Lotka, Alfred J. "The Frequency Distribution of Scientific Productivity." *Journal of the Washington Academy of Sciences* 16(12): 317–23 (June 19, 1926).

March, J. G. "Bounded Rationality, Ambiguity, and the Engineering of Choice." *Bell Journal of Economics* 9(2): 587–608 (Autumn 1978).

Marton, J. "Obsolescence or Immediacy? Evidence Supporting Price's Hypothesis." *Scientometrics* 7(3–6): 145–53 (March 1985).

May, Kenneth O. "Growth and Quality of the Mathematical Literature." *ISIS* 59 (Pt. 4, No. 199): 363–71 (Winter 1968).

Miller, George A. "The Magical Number Seven, Plus or Minus Two: Some Limits on Our Capacity for Processing Information." *Psychological Review* 63(2): 81–97 (March 1956).

Miller, James Grier. *Living Systems.* New York: McGraw-Hill, 1978.

Mitroff, Ian I., and Warren Bennis. *The Unreality Industry: The Deliberate Manufacturing of Falsehood and What It Is Doing to Our Lives.* New York: Birch Lane Press, 1989.

Molyneux, Robert E. "Patterns, Processes of Growth, and the Projection of Library Size: A Critical Review of the Literature on Academic Library Growth. *Library and Information Science Research* 8(1): 5–28 (Jan.-March 1986).

Moorman, Mary. *William Wordsworth: A Biography.* 2 vols. Oxford: Clarendon Press, 1957, 1965.

Nelson, Michael J., and Jean M. Tague. "Split Size-Rank Models for the Distribution of Index Terms." *Journal of the American Society for Information Science* 36(5): 283–96 (Sept. 1985).

Nisbet, Robert. *The Degradation of the Academic Dogma: The University in America, 1945–1970.* New York: Basic Books, 1971.

Palnikov, M. S. "Small-Circulation ('Grey') Literature in the Institute of Information in Social Sciences of the USSR Academy of Sciences." *Interlending and Document Supply* 17(1): 16–19 (Jan. 1989).

Postman, Neil. "Learning by story" (A review of E. D. Hirsch, Jr., *Cultural Literacy*, and Allan Bloom, *The Closing of the American Mind*), *Atlantic* 264: 119–24 (Dec. 1989).

Rescher, Nicholas. *Scientific Progress: A Philosophical Essay on the Economics of Research in Natural Science.* Pittsburgh: University of Pittsburgh Press, 1978.

Rider, Fremont. *The Scholar and the Future of the Research Library.* New York: Headham Press, 1944.

Rosnow, Ralph L., and Gary Alan Fine. *Rumor and Gossip: The Social Psychology of Hearsay.* New York: Elsevier, 1976.

Shaw, Peter. *The War against the Intellect: Episodes in the Decline of Discourse.* Iowa City: University of Iowa Press, 1989.

Simon, Herbert A. "Alternative Visions of Rationality." In Hal R. Arkes and Kenneth R. Hammond, eds., *Judgment and Decision Making: An Interdisciplinary Reader*, 97–113. Cambridge: Cambridge University Press, 1986.

Sisson, James C., Eric B. Schoomaker, and Jon C. Ross. "Clinical Decision Analysis: The Hazard of Using Additional Data." In Hal R. Arkes and Kenneth R. Hammond, eds., *Judgment and Decision Making: An Interdisciplinary Reader*, 354–63. Cambridge: Cambridge University Press, 1986.

Smith, Page. *Killing the Spirit: Higher Education in America.* New York: Viking, 1990.

Spacks, Patricia Meyer. *Gossip.* New York: Knopf, 1985.

Stromsdorfer, Ernst W. "Social Science Analysis and the Formulation of Public Policy: Illustrations of What the President 'Knows' and How He Comes to 'Know' It." In Jerry A. Hausman and David A. Wise, eds., *Social Experimentation*, 257–81. Chicago: University of Chicago Press, 1985.

Sullivan, M. V., et al. "Obsolescence in Biomedical Journals—Not an Artifact of Literature Growth." *Library Research* 2(1): 29–45 (Spring 1980).

Sykes, Charles J. *Profscam: Professors and the Demise of Higher Education.* Washington, D.C.: Regnery Gateway, 1988.

Tague, Jean, Jamshid Beheshti, and Lorna Rees-Potter. "The Law of Exponential Growth: Evidence, Implications, Forecasts." *Library Trends* 125–45 (Summer 1981).

Tetlock, Philip E. "Methodological Themes and Variations." In Philip E. Tetlock et al. eds., *Behavior, Society, and Nuclear War*, 1:334–86. New York: Oxford University Press, 1989.

Toffler, Alvin. *Future Shock.* New York: Bantam Books, 1970.

———. *The Third Wave.* New York: William Morrow, 1980.

Tolkien, J.R.R. *The Lord of the Rings.* 3 vols. London: George Allen & Unwin, 1954, 1955.

Wellisch, Hans H. *Indexing and Abstracting: An International Bibliography.* 2 vols. Santa Barbara, Calif.: ABC-Clio, 1980, 1984.

Wiener, Norbert. *I Am a Mathematician.* New York: Doubleday, 1956.

Williamson, John W., Pearl S. German, Robin Weiss, Elizabeth A. Skinner, and

Frederick Bowes. "Health Science Information Management and Continuing Education of Physicians." *Annals of Internal Medicine* 110(2): 151–60 (Jan. 15, 1989).

Yablonsky, A. I. "On Fundamental Regularities of the Distribution of Scientific Productivity." *Scientometrics* 2(1): 3–34 (Jan. 1980).

Ziman, John. "From Parameters to Portents and Back." In Yehuda Elkana et al., eds., *Toward a Metric of Science: The Advent of Science Indicators*, 261–84. New York: Wiley, 1978.

———. "Proliferation of Scientific Literature: A Natural Process." *Science* 208(4442): 369–72 (April 25, 1980).

Zipf, George Kingsley. *Human Behavior and the Principle of Least Effort*. New York: Hafner Publishing Co., 1949.

7

The Dilemma of Unknown Information: The Enigma of Complexity

SOCIAL EPISTEMOLOGY

The idea that society has knowledge, that society can know, was placed before us by Jesse Shera (1972). He saw libraries as directly involved in that process and "social epistemology" as a basic study for librarianship. For some reason, however, he did not develop the idea fully, whether from lack of time, changing interests, or the problems inherent in the development of the concept.

The first problem the concept of social epistemology presents is the idea that society can know as a person knows. It is quite clear that society cannot know in this way, except metaphorically. But if we think in terms of living systems, after James Miller (1978) and Lane Tracy (1989), it is possible to perceive society, as a social organization, gathering and using knowledge. Of course, the gatherers and users are persons who work for the organization. The information they use in decision making is relevant to the goals of the organization. Society, as an organization, "has knowledge" in that way.

There is another way in which we can speak of society as having knowledge, and that is culturally. In any society there is a conventional wisdom that is shared by its members—rules of behavior without which there would be distrust and anarchy. These are the sorts of rules the economist F. A. Hayek (1949) sees as having developed over time to keep the market system operating on a more or less even keel—in equilibrium. They are also the sorts of rules Robert Fulghum (1988) so neatly identified as "all I needed to know I learned in kindergarten."

Another kind of knowledge that could be said to be "known" by a society is the body of knowledge that is taught to everyone as being necessary for survival in the world. Jomo Kenyatta (1938) described what was needed by a Gikuyu villager in Africa. In another society, the curriculum and textbooks from the years of compulsory education would give us a pretty fair idea of what each citizen was expected to know.

Although much specialized knowledge is necessary for individual roles in a society, the basic knowledge needed by everyone to keep the social organization running can be thought of as what society "knows."

Another question for social epistemology is how knowledge is communicated in society. This question is more easily answered, since the media of communication are quite obviously relevant. Institutions such as schools and libraries are also easily listed.

Donald Schon (1971) has shown how different institutions come into being to address problems in society, particularly in a society where change is rapid and old institutions no longer match the new problems. He also indicates the role of neighborhoods and word-of-mouth communication with respect to community agencies. Manfred Kochen (1989) collected a number of studies that investigated social networks—how news can travel long distances with only a few people involved (someone who knows someone who knows someone else).

In all information communication, there is the problem of reliability and distortion. I have addressed these matters elsewhere in this volume, but I would like to refer the reader to Ian Mitroff and Warren Bennis (1989), which will be relevant to what I have to say about complexity later on. The book describes two sets of forces operating on the future of any technologically developed nation or, more to the point, any technologically *dependent* nation. One set is called the "Complexity from Without"; the other set is the "Rot from Within."

The Complexity from Without describes the "highly interdependent, highly coupled global economy" that has arisen since World War II. The effect is "that *everything* is not only interconnected but potentially capable of affecting everything else." The authors give as examples the Bhopal and Chernobyl tragedies.

The Rot from Within concerns the general effects of the American television and show business culture, which affects "every facet of our society from education to politics" and results in a "growing inability to handle complex issues." The basic argument on the effects of TV states: "When no 15- to 30-second blip need bear any logical or coherent relation to any other blip, and when blips follow one another faster than anyone can make sense of them, the inevitable result not only is a society that is uninformed about anything, but one that has lost the even more fundamental ability to know that it is uninformed. In short, *it is ignorant of the fact that it is ignorant. It doesn't know that it doesn't know*" (Mitroff and Bennis 1989, pp. 178–79). The lack of *that* knowledge is far more serious than not being able to corral *all* the information needed for making decisions, which is the theme of this chapter. It is the effect of the Complexity from Without that is central to and supportive of the other evidence on that topic I present below.

THE DILEMMA

The epistemological questions (what can we know, how do we know, and how can we know that what we know is valid) can be answered, for our purposes, quite directly. We *can* know everything we experience. (Whether we do or not is another question.) The degree of depth or detail can vary depending on exposure and motivation. How we know can be answered in two ways—through the human cognitive mechanisms and through the knowledge and information communicated to the society's members. We know that our knowledge is valid by constant testing against experience, empirically and logically, and by this I mean all that Karl Popper (1965) meant by "conjecture and refutation."

Shera postulated that librarians need to know the role of information in society—how it is used—in order to refine access systems to the "graphic record." Although the information scientist is also concerned with access systems, of even greater concern are the flaws in the overall information world. Taking the three epistemological questions, we can say: (1) we cannot know everything, since we cannot experience everything, (2) our *ways* of knowing are flawed because they are idiosyncratically subjective (see chapters 1 and 2), and (3) the quality (validity) of our knowledge is often questionable because of the nature of the human enterprise (see chapters 3–6).

In this chapter I wish to consider the dilemma that much we need to know *cannot* be known. That dilemma belongs to information science because this discipline claims to study information phenomena in general. When Kochen (1983) urged information scientists to take action on some of the critical issues in American society, he was speaking under that claim. The thrust of Kochen's article was that information scientists ought to get control over information related to social problems. One of those problems is planning, and the key issue in planning is, as Kochen noted, "the need for correct decisions from incomplete or incorrect data" (p. 294). It is the point of this chapter that such data will always be incomplete, hence the dilemma.

SOCIAL PLANNING

In 1963, David Braybrooke and Charles Lindblom published a study of policy-making and concluded that the normal method for deciding on policies was that of "disjointed incrementalism." It was incremental in that it was not revolutionary on the grand scale. Small, or relatively small, problems were involved, and the solutions were prepared and proposed by individuals or by committees. Incremental change seems to be what people can handle most comfortably. Any large change is psychologically threatening, and in any case, the necessary information to predict the consequences of action simply isn't available.

Incremental policy analysts, we are told, "often rule out of bounds the uninteresting (to them), the remote, the imponderable, the intangible, and the poorly understood, no matter now important" (Braybrooke and Lindblom 1963, p. 90). We are faced yet again with the dilemma of the subjective and human imperfection and with the effect of these dilemmas on the quality of the information used in planning.

Another information issue arises from the "disjointed" nature of policy-making. Because the various aspects of public policy, or of any problem, are analyzed by different people in different places, with no apparent coordination or articulation (p. 105), planning is disjointed. It's not as if a general problem, such as the building of a subdivision or a jail, is addressed holistically, with each problem area subdivided and given to the relevant sector to study, much as a scientific laboratory would break a problem into workable units and articulate the work of teams as they tried to solve each unit in order to come to a solution of the whole. It seems that in public policy issues, the invisible college is lacking.

But social problems cannot be reduced to a size that ensures complete control. Popper (1965) was aware that long-term prophecies could be derived from scientific predictions "only if they apply to systems which can be described as well-isolated, stationary, and recurrent. These systems are very rare in nature; and modern society is surely not one of them" (p. 339). Indeed, no society, ancient or modern, is one of them.

The incompleteness of the information we have in hand when we address social problems is uniquely highlighted in Douglas Schuler and Jonathan Jacky's (1989) introduction to a special section on "responsibility" in the *Communications of the ACM*. The titles of the three articles indicate areas not dissimilar to those suggested by Kochen (1983): "The Potential of Artificial Intelligence to Help Solve the Crisis in our Legal System," "Computing, Research, and War: If Knowledge Is Power, Where Is Responsibility," and "Computer Accessibility for Federal Workers with Disabilities: It's the Law."

Schuler and Jacky (1989) tell us that computers are now being proposed for use in the solution of problems that were formerly "the exclusive preserve of human judgment." The authors caution computer professionals who venture into the arena of social and political questions to "appreciate their richness and complexity, and acknowledge the compromise and incompleteness that is characteristic of most workable solutions" (p. 927).

This caution will be familiar to professional planners. The literature on planning fully recognizes the uncertainties in the planning process, all of which are due to the complexity of dealing with institutional structures in the hands of human "organisms." John Sillince (1986) delineates some of these uncertainties: individual political values, planning decisions that are based on implicitly held ideas rather than explicitly stated ones, the need to bargain with various departments with partisan interests, assumptions about the future operating environment undermined by unexpected events, and the difficulty of defining aesthetic quality in designs (pp. 165–72).

Peter Hall (1980), in a close analysis of a number of large ventures that went awry, such as the Anglo-French Concorde and the opera house in Sydney, Australia, identified three types of uncertainty similar to those of Sillince. The first is uncertainty about the relevant planning environment when there is little or no information about the future mass behavior of people in the community or society, for example their propensity to have children, to move about, or to demand different goods and services. The second is uncertainty about decisions being made in areas other than the planning department. Whether these other decision makers are individuals or groups, they all have some area of discretion outside the area of the planners. As independent agents, they respond to planning decisions in ways that cannot be known in advance and cannot be ignored. The third area of uncertainty is that of values. This includes "all the problems where information has been assembled, but where the final decision turns upon questions of value" (p. 5).

In chapter 3 we saw how the values of individuals influenced their use of information. Now we see that it is important, in our dealings with others, to know their values. Yet information about the values of others can never be secure, since values change, not only over long time periods but also sometimes overnight, and values held under one situation might not hold under different circumstances. For instance, the construction industry long held the value of hard work encapsulated in the saying "early to bed and early to rise makes a man healthy, wealthy, and wise." Thus the ten-hour day was justified or rationalized. Today, building projects in residential areas start at nine in the morning, out of consideration for the neighbors.

FRIEDRICH HAYEK

Having presented a rough idea of what unknown information is by looking at planning, I am now going to examine the relevant work of the Noble-prize-winning economist F. A. Hayek. Hayek has argued persuasively, over a long career, against the feasibility of large-scale central planning, particularly as exemplified by the socialist states influenced by the theories of Karl Marx. There are two underlying factors: (1) in a complex situation, everything quite simply cannot be known, and (2) much of the conduct of people is guided by values and rules that have developed over centuries and so are not articulated even by the people themselves. In the sphere of the complex phenomena of life, of the mind, and of the society, theories and techniques of investigation used in the interpretation of observed facts (in physics, for example) cannot help in discovering all the particulars that enter into the determination of complex patterns. "Concerning our modern economic system" Hayek (1978) wrote, "understanding of the principles by which its order frames itself shows us that it rests on the use of knowledge (and of skills in determining relevant information) which no one possesses in its entirety, and that it is brought about because individuals are in their actions guided by certain general rules" (p. 13). J. G. March (1978) describes this as "systemic" choice, not calculated choice. That is, the system makes the choice. He then imagines what Hayek states as a fact: "Suppose we imagine that knowledge, in the form of precepts of behavior, evolves over time within a system and accumulates across time, people and organizations without complete current consciousness of its history. Then sensible action is taken by actors without comprehension of its full justification" (March 1978, p. 592). There is inherent common sense in this supposition, which makes Hayek's position easy to understand.

The economic problem is "how to secure the best use of resources known to any of the members of society, for ends whose relative importance only those individuals know. Or, to put it briefly, it is a problem of the utilization of knowledge which is not given to anyone in its totality" (Hayek 1949, p. 78).

Much of the information used by individuals in making decisions cannot be known in advance because it is generated at the point of having to decide. "One person's actions are the other person's data" (Hayek 1949, p. 38). People learn from experience. The whole market acts as if it were one, "not because any of its members survey the whole field, but because their limited individual fields of vision sufficiently overlap so that through many intermediaries the relevant information is communicated to all" (p. 86).

It is clear that we have come back to Shera's social epistemology. The symbols, the rules, and the institutions we rely on to inform ourselves about what to do and about what is happening have been integrated into our society over time. Periods of trial and error long forgotten, or never recognized at all, built certain guidelines into our understanding—honesty in dealing with others, for instance. The price system is a good example of a "sign" communicating information that individuals can only assume. Hayek (1949) explains how much knowledge a person needs to fit his decisions into the pattern of changes in the larger economic system:

There is hardly anything that happens anywhere in the world that *might* not have an effect on the decision he ought to make. But he need not know of these events as such, nor of all their effects. It does not matter for him *why* at that particular moment more screws of one size than of another are wanted, *why* paper bags are more readily available than canvas bags, or *why* skilled labor, or particular machine tools, have for the moment become more difficult to obtain. All that is significant for him is how much more or less difficult to procure they have become compared with other things with which he is also concerned, or *how much more or less* urgently wanted are the alternative things he produces or uses. (p. 84)

The individual's knowledge of events is based on the changing prices of things.

For Hayek (1960), knowledge exists only as the knowledge of individuals. "Society" does not know. "It is not much better than a metaphor," he wrote, "to speak of the knowledge of society as a whole. The sum of the knowledge of all the individuals exists nowhere as an integrated whole. The great problem is how we can all profit from this knowledge, which exists only dispersed as the separate, partial, and sometimes conflicting beliefs of all men" (pp. 24–25). The means of communication are human institutions of various kinds, from universities to business organizations. The historical development of some of these has been described by James Beniger (1986) in his book *The Control Revolution: Technological and Economic Origins of the Information Society.*

One further ingredient Hayek insists is necessary is the provision of freedom for "unknown" individuals to learn facts others are unaware of and to make use of them. These unknown individuals are those outside the state planning body. "It is because freedom means the renunciation of direct control of individual efforts that a free society can make use of so much more knowledge than the mind of the wisest ruler could comprehend" (Hayek 1960, p. 31). The political events in the Communist bloc since the winter of 1989 speak volumes for Hayek's thesis and are highlighted in a quote by Mikhail Gorbachev, cited by George Gilder (1990): "The Soviet Union is in a spiritual decline. We have had to pay for this by seriously lagging behind and we will be paying for it for a long time to come. We are one of the last to realize that in the age of information science, the most valuable asset is knowledge—the breadth of mental outlook and creative imagination" (p. A12).

Hayek's theory is verified by these words and events, although the necessity for freedom in the Communist countries, from the economic point of view, was advocated years ago by Jan Marczewski's (1974) analysis of Soviet planning. In a different vein, Martin Cave's (1980) study of the use of computers in Soviet planning also showed the inability of even an all-powerful central government to achieve economic efficiency—to gain control over the information in a complex market.

CHAOS

When Hayek noted that there is hardly anything that happens anywhere in the world that will not have an effect on a decision maker, we are reminded of Mitroff and Bennis's (1989) "Complexity from Without." We can also relate this phenomenon to those situations that the discipline of Chaos describes as being "sensitive to initial conditions." The classic example is the tornado in Texas caused by the flutter of a butterfly's wings in Brazil (see Gleick 1987, p. 322 n. 20). A more realistic example is the action of a swing. To push an empty swing demands careful and balanced placement of the hands if a smooth motion is to be maintained. A very slight alteration will cause the swing to oscillate until it is out of control.

Chaos, as an area of scientific investigation, is the study of complex *physical* occurrences that involve turbulence, or nonlinear dynamics. The event that starts the chaotic action is only *analogous* to a bit of information. The information scientist is concerned with meaning, with information that is an "object" only in the sense of being an object in Popper's World 3. Yet, in the context of unknown information, which affects decisions nevertheless, the analogy is exact. The complexity of various human systems creates the dilemma of how to know everything so as not to be surprised. Ilya Prigogene and Isabelle Stengers (1984) discuss "modelizations of complexity," where the models are of "an unstable world where small causes can have large effects." But, they continue, it is not an arbitrary world. "On the contrary, the reasons for the amplification of a small event are a legitimate matter for rational inquiry" (p. 206). It is important to realize that Prigogene and Stengers are referring not to physical but to social systems. The authors cite the example of a slum-clearance program that resulted in a situation worse than before because the new buildings attracted more people, for whom there were not enough jobs; the people remained poor, and the dwellings became more overcrowded. The authors then conclude that making models of human situations is risky because "in complex systems, both the definition of entities and of the interactions among them can be modified by evolution. Not only each state of a system but also the very definition of the system as modelized is generally unstable" (p. 204).

After the stock market crash of October 1987, Avner Arbel and Albert Kaff (1989) wrote a book to explain what happened. At one point they compared the global network of securities, futures, and commodities, which drove prices up and down like waves, to a nonlinear dynamic system. Certainly there was evidence of chaotic behavior, one eminent economist was quoted as saying, and another, looking for new methods to study stock market behavior, saw "behavior that begins to be amenable to the ideas of chaotic dynamics" (p. 143). However, the authors concluded with a reference to the efforts of Shelley Zacks, an applied mathematician at the State University of New York at Binghamton, to apply some mathematical models to the market. The models did not work, and Zacks was quoted as saying, "A lot of research still has to be done, using huge data bases before any conclusions about chaos theory and the market can be made seriously" (p. 143).

The analogy between nonlinear, "chaotic" dynamics and any complex information communication event is appealing—just as it is appealing to see the two hemispheres of the brain as two distinct brains (see chapter 4). There are *not* two brains, and information is not a fluid. It is entirely possible, however, that a network of interlinked computers could experience a chaos event if the electrons were somehow merged and nudged (by some initial condition) into a doubling wave pattern leading to "turbulence" in the flow of electricity. But that is a physics and engineering problem, not an information problem. There were information problems in the October 1987 crash, but these were caused by "opening delays, trading halts and computer failure" (Arbel and Kaff 1989, p. 183) and not by any turbulence in strictly physical phenomena. The situation was turbulent, but it was not the kind of turbulence measured consistently by the Feigenbaum number.

Even if we accepted the analogy, finding the event that created the bit of information that created the end effect would be like finding the one Brazilian butterfly whose fluttering wings caused the Texas tornado.

COMPLEXITY

The modeling of complexity has also been addressed by mathematicians with the development of probability theory and fuzzy sets. The most recent effort to solve problems of uncertainty and incomplete information has been motivated by the increased use of computers, particularly in artificial intelligence. Here the aspect of lexical elasticity, or the vagueness of word meanings, has led to what is being called possibility theory. Didier Dubois and Prade (1988) preface their introductory text on the theory by pointing to the expectation of solving more and more complex problems with computers. The need to gather very sophisticated data has meant that much of the information "cannot be obtained as precise and definite numbers, that purely symbolic treatment can be inadequate, and that for various reasons . . . the information is imprecise, incoherent, and in any case incomplete" (p. ix).

The following example from Dubois and Prade (1988) will illustrate the type of complex problem demanding a theory of possibility:

A good example of a sequence of fuzzy instructions that must have nonfuzzy execution is provided by commands intended to guide the movement of a person (or a robot) toward a target. The following itinerary is fairly typical of plans of action used, and communicated, by human beings:

"Continue till you reach a junction about 100 yards away."
"Turn right."
"Continue for about 50 yards till you reach an Asiatic restaurant."
"Turn left."
"Continue for 20–30 yards till you reach a post box." (pp. 192–93)

The problem in this sequence of imprecisely specified instructions is to allow, in a "fuzzy" computer program built on possibility theory, for backtracking and reinterpretation (in accordance with the program specifications).

Table 7.1
Complexity and Relationships

M (Math)	P (Physics)	S (Science)
Good	Fairly good to good	Good
Fairly good to good	Good	Good
• • •	• • •	• • •
Fairly good to good	About 10	Fairly good
Fairly good	Fairly good	Fairly good
• • •	• • •	• • •

Another example from Dubois and Prade (1988) considers a question asked of a data base of information on students' attainments in different subjects, their age, and their degrees of liking for each other. The most complex question asked of this data base was "Who are good in science in the first term?" The authors tell us this is more complex than the other questions (e.g., "Who are good in math or in physics?" and "Who are friends of Jane?") because it "introduces a compound universe of discourse—'science.'" Table 7.1 lists the possible relationships. The word *science*, for this particular data base, is made more precise by translating the query into "Find all the students who are good in math and fairly good to good in physics or fairly good to good in math and good in physics in the first term" (p. 243). There is still a quantity of uncertainty because the word *fairly* is as "lexically elastic" as the word *about* in the first example.

As a method for meeting the dilemma of measuring complexity, possibility theory more appropriately belongs in the chapter on research methods. I mention it here to show the range of disciplines concerned with situations containing incomplete (unknown) information and to show the range of situations themselves—from the world market to single sentences.

CONTROL IS IMPOSSIBLE

John Gray (1989), in his essay on the liberalism of Karl Popper, discusses Popper's argument against a holistic method in social science because it ignores "the inevitable selectivity of all observation and description." Gray comments, "Indeed, as Popper has reminded us, 'there are infinitely many possibilities of local, partial, or total disaster,' so there may well be 'important historical situations' in which there is no 'viable solution to the problems faced by people in a given society'" (p. 17). The point I am making is not whether Popper is right here, but that he is reinforcing the problematic of the information scientist in dealing with the complex information system that is the world's people in contact. It is not possible to control all or even nearly all social relations because, says Popper, "with every new control of social relations we create a host of new social relations to be controlled. In short, the impossibility is a logical impossibility" (Gray 1989, p. 16–17). Since all social relationships are relationships of communication, they are information relationships and are the legitimate field of study of information scientists, even if *control* of the information is logically impossible.

In fact, it is also theoretically impossible. As we have seen, the essence of human social life is change—evolution. The essence of that change lies in the meeting and solving of problems. Problems come from the outside, as a block in life's path, or from the inside, as an innovative idea (the problem being how to put that idea into practice). In either case, there is a problem to be solved. If there were a problem-solving theory that could predict success, inevitable and unvarying success, all the variables would need to be identifiable in order to be taken into consideration in the process of solution. To attempt to identify these variables is to step into a complex world in which the thoughts and emotions and beliefs of individuals are at play in situations where not even all the observable facts can be known. After years of scrutiny in psychology and cognitive science, the method or strategy of how to go about solving problems has been described for many disciplines and fields of work, but there is no theory of problem solving. Margaret Boden (1988) directly addressing the question, concluded: "There cannot in principle be a psychological theory of problem-solving capable of generating—still less, predicting—all the details of every instance of human problem-solving behavior. . . . Any theorist who tried to specify all the indefinitely many thoughts that might possibly arise, or even all those which might in fact have arisen, during adventurous thinking would be doomed to failure" (p. 172). Problem solving can be influenced not only by facts and conjectures but also by desires and beliefs and, as we saw in chapter 2, by the physical actions of the body.

So the possibility of resolving the dilemma of unknown information seems to be out of the question. But it is possible to study information transfer and information transformation and thus come to a clearer understanding of the communication of information (social epistemology), if not a "scientific" explanation of all aspects of its generation and use. Considering the need for freedom in gathering and applying information, it might, in fact, be counterproductive or, rather, countercreative to try to gain absolute control over *all* information.

STUDYING THE "UNKNOWN"

Information science does not lack investigations that could be seen as efforts to trace the paths of information in society. Bibliometrics is the most obvious as it analyzes literature growth and configurations through citation analysis and author productivity. The journal *Scientometrics* focuses on this area. Although much of bibliometrics deals with the literature itself, as observable documents, some work is also done to discover patterns in the spread of ideas. Charlotte Cottrill, Everett Rogers, and Tamsy Mills (1989), for example, use a method of cocitation cluster analysis, developed by Henry Small (1973) of the Institute for Scientific Information, to examine ideational links between the discipline of technology transfer and the discipline of diffusion of innovations. Their study looks at knowledge generation, exchange, and utilization.

One of the more enduring concepts in the field of bibliometrics has been William Goffman's epidemic theory of the communication of ideas. There are some difficulties with the analogy between the spread of an idea and the spread of a disease, particularly in light of the above discussion of the impact of beliefs and values on whether or not an idea is accepted. The world of ideas is complex, as the first part of this chapter has shown, and there are more forces at work than the mere writing for and reading of the literature. Society's needs, the mission of government granting agencies, and political events all act on the process of development and transmission of ideas. Perhaps it was a consciousness of this that caused Goffman to switch from the disease analogy. As noted in Goffman and Kenneth Warren (1980), "This model of scientific communication can be removed from the purview of disease and inserted in the province of ecology" (p. 59).

Having said that, we can make a clear link between Goffman and the work of the science historian Stephen Toulmin (1972) and his evolutionary approach to the growth of disciplines through conceptual change. As John Losee (1987) noted in commenting on Toulmin's work, "To take seriously the evolutionary analogue is to emphasize the importance of 'ecological considerations' in conceptual development" (p. 126).

Other students of information transfer have looked at the more or less informal means of getting knowledge. William Garvey's (1979) research into how scientists do their work and when and how they use informal communication channels, such as conferences and the invisible college, is a classic example. It is in this area that we get closer to the domain of "unknown" information. The informal sphere provides an area of overlap between people, an area that is ephemeral and difficult to trace, unlike the stable character of the literature with which bibliometrics works.

Other studies of informal communication have been done in the business community. Tom Wilson (1988), in Britain, observed people at work in social services departments, recording all aspects of communication over a twenty-two-week period. His work corroborated the results of Henry Mintzberg's (1973) ground-breaking investigation of managers. Wilson synthesized Mintzberg: "Managers exhibit a preference for *oral* communication, and meetings constitute an important part of such communication" (Wilson 1988, p. 47).

I mention Mintzberg to emphasize the fact that people other than information scientists study information and that there is a need to get outside the narrow confines of bibliometrics and the application of technology to information access problems. A case in point is the journal *Knowledge: Creation, Diffusion, and Utilization,* for it is as relevant, and often more relevant, in the context of "unknown" information, than is *Scientometrics.*

There are other sources of knowledge about unknown information, such as histories and biographies, which can stand as case studies if they are done well. Sociological studies of knowledge workers, such as Karin Knorr-Cetina's (1981) anthropological analysis of a year in a scientific laboratory, are also relevant. But perhaps the most relevant and most interesting work is that of Don Swanson, who has explored the logical connections of "implicit" citations, as distinct and different from other citation studies that simply count items explicitly cited by authors. Swanson's (1990) research has shown that there are "mutually oblivious literatures related by implicit, unnoticed connections" (p. 33). That is, in two literatures, mutually isolated from each other—or "noninteractive," having no authors or articles in common and therefore not citing each other—there can be in one or the other findings relevant to problems unsolved in one or the other. Swanson (1990) clarifies the relationship in this logical model:

Suppose that one literature reports that, under certain circumstances, A causes B (e.g. drug A alters blood levels of hormone B). Such a causal statement is denoted by "AB." Assume that a second literature reports a similar causal connection, BC (e.g. hormone B influences the course of disease (C). Presumably, then, anyone aware of the two premises AB and BC would notice that A might influence C (denoted "AC"). (p. 30)

What Swanson is doing is unquestionably searching for that which is unknown—information in the form of a logical connection that has not been made before or, if it has, has gone unnoticed. One of his searches discovered a connection between magnesium and migraine headaches, and afterward a single article was found that reported a clinical test of this relationship. It was an article that had not been found in the extensive literature search Swanson had conducted and was not cited in any of the normal indexing and abstracting services.

The point to be made here is that even in the published literature, the dilemma of the unknown abides. Mendel's article on heredity is the famous example of this phenomenon. Swanson is well aware of the difficulty. In an earlier paper (Swanson 1986), he concluded that since new information is being published while searches are under way, any information search "is essentially incomplete, or, if it were complete, we could never know it" (p. 114). His own experience shows that it is not just new knowledge (i.e., published knowledge) that is the problem. Indexing services are not perfect; indexers are not consistent in their choice of terms, nor are users' choices of words predictable. As Swanson (1986) describes the situation: "A new solution to a problem may be based on a wholly new and different point of view. That is, not only do we seek what we do not understand, we often do not even know at what level an understanding might be achieved" (p. 115). Other work, similar to Swanson's, has been reviewed by Roy Davies (1989), and he provides a good background to this most interesting approach.

CONCLUSION

Swanson's work grew out of his application of Karl Popper's philosophy of science to work in libraries (Swanson 1979). Popper's World 3 is, among other things, the world of the logical content of books and articles. It is this world with which Swanson and other information scientists are concerned. It was this world that interested Shera when he conceived the idea of social epistemology. If we broaden social epistemology beyond library work with the graphic record to include all communication of information between individuals in a society (and the effects of those communication events), then we must include the study of what I have here called "unknown" information. There seems little doubt that there will always be some potentially useful information that is unknown yet that has its effects, like the flap of the wings of the butterfly in Brazil and its effect on the weather in Texas.

There is another reason why there will always be unknown information—a reason other than the complexity of the world. It is found in the last symbol of Popper's problem-solving schema, P_1-TT-EE-P_2 (problem one-tentative theory-error elimination-problem two). The solution is not the final answer. It is another problem. Human beings are question-asking creatures—it is the model of their "eternal" nature. Laurens Van Der Post (1982) expressed this appropriately in the following autobiographical story.

One afternoon, on the bridge of the whaling ship *Larsen II*, the captain, a man named Kaspersen, made a comment on the horizon, which was particularly clear and precise and round. In effect, he said he hated the horizon because it cut off his vision, saying, as it were, "That's as far as I will let you see—and no further." To Kaspersen, the effect was like being in a "travelling prison." Van Der Post commented:

At the time I thought the outburst merely a result of the tensions which stretched him to well-nigh unbearable extremes as the time between one expected killing and another had lengthened. But I soon realized that he was unknowingly speaking in the code of his own inner unrest. He had reached the point when the human being realizes that no amount of knowing diminishes the amount of the unknown. Knowledge moves and searches for meaning, just as our little ship was moving through the sea and looking for whales with the inexorable horizon insisting on keeping us always at the same distance. It was as if the unknown infinite made a mockery of the known infinitesimal. (pp. 73–74)

REFERENCES

Arbel, Avner, and Albert E. Kaff. *Crash: Ten Days in October—Will It Strike Again?* New York: Longman Financial Services Publishers, 1989.

Beniger, James R. *The Control Revolution: Technological and Economic Origins of the Information Society.* Cambridge: Harvard University Press, 1986.

Boden, Margaret A. *Computer Models of Mind: Computational Approaches in Theoretical Psychology.* Cambridge: Cambridge University Press, 1988.

Braybrooke, David, and Charles E. Lindblom. *A Strategy of Decision: Policy Evaluation as a Social Process.* New York: Free Press, 1963.

Cave, Martin. *Computers and Economic Planning: The Soviet Experience.* Cambridge: Cambridge University Press, 1980.

Cottrill, Charlotte A., Everett M. Rogers, and Tamsy Mills. "Co-citation Analysis of the Scientific Literature of Innovation Research Traditions." *Knowledge: Creation, Diffusion, and Utilization* 11:2: 181–208 (Dec. 1989).

Davies, Roy. "The Creation of New Knowledge by Information Retrieval and Classification." *Journal of Documentation* 45(4):273–301 (Dec. 1989).

Dubois, Didier, and Henri Prade. *Possibility Theory: An Approach to Computerized Processing of Uncertainty.* Trans. E. F. Harding. New York: Plenum Press, 1988.

Fulghum, Robert. *All I Really Need to Know I Learned in Kindergarten.* New York: Random, 1988. (Here are some of the rules and regulations Fulghum learned: "Share everything. Play fair. Don't hit people. Put things back where you found them. Clean up your own mess. Don't take things that aren't yours. Say you're sorry when you hit somebody. Wash your hands before you eat. When you go out into the world, watch out for traffic, hold hands, and stick together. Live a balanced life" (6–7).

Garvey, William D. *Communication: The Essence of Science.* Oxford, N.Y.: Pergamon Press, 1979.

Gilder, George. "The Drexel Era." *Wall Street Journal,* Feb. 16, 1990, A12.

Gleick, James. *Chaos: Making a New Science.* New York: Viking, 1987.

Goffman, William, and Kenneth S. Warren. *Scientific Information and the Principle of Selectivity.* New York: Praeger, 1980.

Gray, John. *Liberalism: Essays in Political Philosophy.* London: Routledge, 1989.

Hall, Peter. *Great Planning Disasters.* London: Weidenfield and Nicolson, 1980.

Hayek, F. A. *The Constitution of Liberty.* Chicago: University of Chicago Press, 1960.

———. *Individualism and Economic Order.* London: Routledge & Kegan Paul, 1949.

———. *New Studies in Philosophy, Politics, Economics, and the History of Ideas.* London: Routledge & Kegan Paul, 1978.

Kenyatta, Jomo. *Facing Mount Kenya.* London: Secker & Warburg, 1938.

Knorr-Cetina, Karin. *The Manufacture of Knowledge: An Essay on the Constructivist and Contextual Nature of Science.* New York: Pergamon, 1981.

Kochen, Manfred. "Information and Society." *Annual Review of Information Science and Technology* 18: 277–304 (1983).

———, ed. *The Small World.* Norwood, N.J.: Ablex Publishing Corp., 1989.

Losee, John. *Philosophy of Science and Historical Enquiry.* Oxford: Clarendon Press, 1987.

March, J. G. "Bounded Rationality, Ambiguity, and the Engineering of Choice." *Bell Journal of Economics* 9(2): 587–608 (Autumn 1978).

Marczewski, Jan. *Crisis in Socialist Planning: Eastern Europe and the USSR.* Trans. Noel Lindsay. New York: Praeger, 1974.

Miller, James Grier. *Living Systems.* New York: McGraw-Hill, 1978.

Mintzberg, Henry. *The Nature of Managerial Work.* New York: Harper & Row, 1973.

Mitroff, Ian I., and Warren Bennis. *The Unreality Industry: The Deliberate Manufacturing of Falsehood and What It Is Doing to Our Lives.* New York: Birch Lane Press, 1989.

Popper, Karl. *Conjectures and Refutations: The Growth of Scientific Knowledge.* New York: Harper & Row, 1965.

Prigogene, Ilya, and Isabelle Stengers. *Order Out of Chaos: Man's New Dialogue with Nature.* Boulder, Colo.: Shambhala Publishers, 1984.

Schon, Donald A. *Beyond the Stable State: Public and Private Learning in a Changing Society.* London: Temple Smith, 1971.

Schuler, Douglas, and Jonathan Jacky. "Responsibility." *Communications of the ACM* 32(8): 925–27 (August 1989).

Shera, Jesse H. *The Foundations of Education for Librarianship.* New York: Becker & Hayes, 1972.

Sillince, John. *A Theory of Planning.* Aldershot: Gower Publishing Co., 1986.

Small, Henry. "Co-citation in the Scientific Literature: A New Measure of the Relationship between Two Documents." *Journal of the American Society for Information Science* 24(4): 265–69 (July–August 1973).

Swanson, Don R. "Libraries and the Growth of Knowledge." *Library Quarterly* 49(1): 3–25 (Jan. 1979).

———. "Medical Literature as a Potential Source of New Knowledge." *Bulletin of the Medical Library Association* 78(1): 29–37 (Jan. 1990).

———. "Undiscovered Public Knowledge." *Library Quarterly* 56(2): 103–18 (April 1986).

Toulmin, Stephen. *Human Understanding.* 2 vols. Princeton: Princeton University Press, 1972.

Tracy, Lane. *The Living Organization: Systems of Behavior.* New York: Praeger, 1989.

Van Der Post, Laurens. *Yet Being Someone Other.* London: Hogarth Press, 1982.

Wilson, Tom. "Information, Managers, and Information Technology." *Argus* 17(2): 47–50 (June 1988).

8

The Dilemma of Method for Information Research: Is Information Science a Science, Social Science, or Humanity?

THE GENERAL PREDICAMENT

At one time I studied for my master's degree in education. The instructor for the Introduction to Research Methods course was a senior member of the faculty. His opening remark was that 95 percent of the research in education was trash. I remember nothing else from that course. That remark stayed with me as I read the literature on educational theory, most of which seemed to have come out of "experimental" schools or laboratory classrooms where the professor and a team of graduate student assistants "taught" a class of ten or twelve bright girls and boys. When I taught high school, I realized what the word *trash* meant. The research itself was rigorous enough, and the theories might well have been valid, for an experimental school. But the theories had no credibility for someone facing twenty-five to thirty reluctant teenagers. The irrelevance of it all was highlighted for me when I taught a tenth-grade class of boys in the technical program, boys whose IQs ranged from 80 to 140. It wasn't that the *research* was trash, but the method simply wasn't relevant outside the controlled atmosphere of the laboratory.

I was reminded of this when I read the first sentence in the abstract to D. Ellis's (1984) discussion of the difficulties he had encountered in a study of on-line searching. He wrote, "There is a critical lacuna in information retrieval research between the theoretical framework employed in laboratory tests to explain the performance of information retrieval systems, and the sorts of factors which bear on their operational effectiveness" (p. 261). His conclusion was that the circumstances of the real environment of any information retrieval system had to be studied. The complexity of the situation, including the backgrounds and personalities of the searchers, their affective as well as their cognitive characteristics, made laboratory testing of abstract models and small, controlled collections simply inappropriate.

Information is a social construct, and communication of information is a social event. Attempts to develop "proofs" for arguments related to social phenomena are bound to fail. As Charles Lindblom and David Cohen (1979) put it, "Problem complexity denies the possibility of proof and reduces the pursuit of fact to the pursuit of those selective facts which, if appropriately developed, constitute evidence in support of relevant argument" (p. 81). The argument developed in the chapter on unknown information is relevant here—in any human problem-solving endeavor, there is inevitably an incompleteness of data that blocks any credible law or rule. That is why results of research based on physical science methods have little or no impact on practice in education or in information work.

It is also, I imagine, why Pranas Zunde (1987) quickly qualified his use of the word *laws* in his title ("Information Science Laws and Regularities: A Survey") to mean "soft" laws. He makes a clear distinction between laws of human behavior and laws of physics. The laws that "control" human social actions and interactions may be "subject to rapid change." He confesses, "In the domain of study of information science, there are, as yet, very few observed regularities which have been sufficiently verified and confirmed" (p. 244). He does not identify those few, but since some of the "hypothesized" laws "may not survive a more rigorous experimental testing," he decides to refer to "all reported observations of empirical relationships as regularities rather than laws" (p. 245).

Friedrich Hayek's (1967) discussion of laws is directly relevant to Zunde's statement that laws about social interactions may be subject to rapid change:

It would seem, therefore, that the conception of law in the usual sense has little application to the theory of complex phenomena. . . . I believe this to be in a great measure true of social phenomena: though we possess theories of social structures, I rather doubt whether we know of any "laws" which social phenomena obey. It would then appear that the search for the discovery of laws is not an appropriate hall-mark of scientific procedure but merely a characteristic of the theories of simple phenomena as we have defined these earlier; and that in the field of complex phenomena the term "law" as well as the concepts of cause and effect are not applicable without such modification as to deprive them of their ordinary meaning. (pp. 41–42)

Some of the regularities Zunde lists are rank-frequency distribution of phonemes, probability distribution of word types by the number of their lexical meanings, correlational dependencies of title length and the number of keywords it contains, probability distribution of library users by number of tasks they perform during a single library visit, rank-frequency distribution of scientists by publication productivity, and correlational dependencies of usage and age of a periodical. Clearly these are findings based on statistical measures. Whether such "regularities" find their way into the practice of the librarian or information analyst, or whether they are used by information scientists in research to help the practitioner (Zunde gives some examples, pp. 256–57), there is not, on the (qualified) evidence presented, much reason to think these regularities are or will be seen to be important in the field. In any case, they are likely to be, as J. Tague (1987) suggests, "little more than textbook exercises rather than procedures that could actually be used by a decision-maker" (p. 271).

Tague (1987) directly addressed the question of the use of research in that area of information science "heralded as the theoretical base" (p. 271) of the discipline. She comments, "Those of us who have studied the forms and relationships of these models have done so, primarily, because of their intrinsic interest and because of the pleasure we take in this kind of analysis" (p. 271). The two examples of the *possible* uses of bibliometrics are given with the qualification that more research is needed to get a closer fit to the problem areas.

The dilemma in the area of research methods in information science is that information creation and use is complex, imprecise, and subjective. Quantitative measurement just cannot address the major problems, which are human-human, human-machine, and human-language. To be measured with any accuracy, phenomena must be observable, whereas the most vital aspects of information work are cognitive and affective. The use of fuzzy set or possibility theory in an effort to put some numbers on uncertainty is too limited to handle the intricacies and scope of the social issue that is information retrieval and knowledge production.

Statistics, model building, and simulation exercises deal with the problem of large numbers by eliminating complexity, particularly the complexity of structural relations. These tools give us a snapshot of phenomena that are hard, or impossible, to see whole. Such pictures are invaluable as building blocks for thinking about complex affairs but cannot be taken for explanations of them. F. A. Hayek (1967) noted:

The statistical method is therefore of use only where we deliberately ignore, or are ignorant of, the relations between the individual elements with different attributes, i.e., where we ignore or are ignorant of, any structure into which they are organized. Statistics in such situations enables us to regain simplicity and to make the task manageable by substituting a single attribute for the unascertainable individual attributes in the collective. It is, however, for this reason irrelevant to the solution of problems in which it is the relations between individual elements with different attributes which matters." (p. 30)

What Hayek is talking about is very nicely illustrated in a qualifying remark in a paper on the problem of processing fuzzy queries (Kamel, Hadfield, and Ismail 1990). The authors use an example to illustrate fuzziness:

Consider the following fuzzy natural language query:

"Give me some of the names of the people who make a high salary and like their job" In this query, "some" is a quantification descriptor, "high" is a qualitative numeric descriptor, and "like" is a qualitative nonnumeric descriptor.

In this paper, we will be concerned only with Qualitative Numeric Descriptors. Quantifiers can be answered by explicitly defining each term and using a random record selection process. Nonnumeric descriptors require not only the information contained in the database, but also a very extensive knowledge base about the world, and will not be considered further here. (p. 280)

It is that "extensive knowledge base about the world" with which we need to be concerned in any study of human social interactions.

Ellis (1984) became well aware of the inadequacies of model searches and the artificial simulation of the real retrieval situation, to the extent that he concluded, "The experience of the operational situation bears no resemblance to its simulated analogue" (p. 267).

Numbers are trustworthy at fairly simple levels and for a limited number of variables. As complexity increases, a realistic representation is possible only with extremely complex mathematics. At that point, as James Johnstone (1974) commented in a review of educational planning models: "The model is not easily managed or manipulated, and thus concise description is impossible. The model becomes more difficult to manipulate than the situation itself" (p. 192).

Hayek (1978), in his Nobel Memorial Lecture, argued against the "scientistic" attitude of economists, seeing it as a "mechanical and uncritical application of habits of thought to fields different from those in which they have been formed" (p. 23). He argued, "In the study of such complex phenomena as the market, which depend on the actions of many individuals, all the circumstances which will determine the outcome of a process . . . will hardly ever be fully known or measureable" (p. 24). He then pointed out that, in research depending on making quantitative measurements in the social sciences, what is investigated will be what is amenable to measurement and not what is important. The danger then lies in perceiving what has been measured *as* important.

Ellis (1984) noted this circumstance in his study. In the interviews with the researchers he was describing, he discovered that the educational and occupational experience of the individuals "had affected their definition or perception of the task they were engaged on" (p. 268). These factors were disregarded "as being incidental to their information problems rather than hints at the existence of a larger and more complex frame within which their information seeking activities might be understood" (p. 268). The reason for ignoring these cognitive and affective aspects was, essentially, because the model of information retrieval developed in the laboratory was restricted by the desire to be able to count relevant retrieved documents resulting from matching the question statement and the document representation.

FROM BRILLOUIN TO HERMENEUTICS

The dilemma of conducting credible and useful research in information science has not gone unrecognized. It is enlightening to trace the radical change of thinking over a quarter of a century. Leon Brillouin (1962), one of the early and important writers in the field of information theory, described the parameters within which he was working, in both the first and second editions of his book *Science and Information Theory*. He wrote:

The methods of this theory can be successfully applied to all technical problems concerning information: coding, telecommunication, mechanical computers, etc. In all of these problems we are actually processing information or transmitting it from one place to another, and the present theory is extremely useful in setting up rules and stating exact limits for what can and cannot be done. But we are in no position to investigate the process of thought, and we cannot, for the moment, introduce into our theory any element involving the human value of information. This elimination of the human element is a very serious limitation, but this is the price we have so far had to pay for being able to set up this body of scientific knowledge. The restrictions that we have introduced enable us to give a quantitative definition of information and to treat information as a physically measurable quantity. This definition cannot distinguish between information of great importance and a piece of news of no great value for the person who receives it. . . . All these elements of human value are ignored by the present theory. (pp. x–xi)

Gerard Salton (1968), the creator of the SMART system and author of a major text on automatic indexing, did not use the phrase "human element," but that element is directly responsible for the difficulties in the theoretical problems regarding meaning. Salton delineated these problems:

This text, then, is an attempt to examine the principal technical and intellectual problems arising in information processing and to determine the extent to which they are amenable to solution by automatic or semi-automatic methods. The structure and properties of scientific information are of principal concern, as reflected in a semantic content analysis of the documents (but not a qualitative evaluation concerning their accuracy, veracity, or conciseness).

In many ways, a study of the analytical aspects of scientific information in a mechanical environment must appear as a hopeless endeavor, because so many of the important theoretical problems are unsolved. What exactly is the content or meaning of a document? To what extent can individual words, or word groups, in a text be said to carry and maintain a well-defined, controlled meaning? How can one isolate the content-bearing units if they exist? And so on.

Since the answers to these fundamental questions are unclear, it becomes impossible to justify the text-manipulating procedures introduced in this volume for purposes of content analysis other than as *ad hoc* devices. (pp. 2–3)

Years later, Salton recognized the multitude of factors at play in natural language processing: "The free manipulation of unrestricted natural language data is not a likely prospect for the foreseeable future. In particular, no agreement exists about the best way of formalizing document content, about the world knowledge (above and beyond the specialized knowledge in a given subject area) that may be needed to understand texts and interpret natural language statements, and about reasoning strategies, inferences, and deductions that may be needed in order actually to respond to user inquiries" (Salton and McGill 1983, p. 420). In spite of this, the evaluation results in the text "are based on recall and precision, because these measures remain the standard" (p. 192).

So while Salton continued to work with theoretically unjustified procedures, K. Otten and A. Debons (1970) tried to found a discipline on the same basis. In this piece of evidence, Brillouin's position is repeated, leaving the application to man for some distant point in time:

Man sets the limit to what can be done with information. As ultimate user and, in many cases, as generator of information, his information processing capabilities determine the usefulness of information systems to him individually and collectively. This statement concerning man as the point of reference applies even to the functions of hypothesized supermachines exhibiting artificial intelligence exceeding that of exceptional human performance.

It must be recognized, however, that the complexity of man's relation to information and of his information processing, prevent man, at this time, from being the test bed for information sciences. The theories forming the body for the metascience of information may have to evolve slowly. They have to be based on elementary information conditions in manmade form and environment. The application of these fundamental laws and relations in more and more complex systems ultimately have to be applicable to man and always have to serve man. (p. 92)

We have here an unbelievable situation. Brillouin recognizes the "very serious limitation" of ignoring the human. Salton does so as well but continues to work at a "hopeless endeavor," and Otten and Debons reluctantly struggle with the development of an argument for a metascience that must, seemingly of necessity, do without its "point of reference" and its limiting factor. Is it any wonder that the results of such a peculiar science should be found to be inapplicable to a society made up of human kind? Dilemma indeed!

At the same time, some consideration for the human element can be found. Tefko Saracevic (1971) reported on a four-year project inquiring into the testing of information retrieval systems. The first of his general conclusions simply identified the importance of the human element, which information scientists had always known about but had chosen to ignore. "The human factor, i.e., variations introduced by human decision-making, seems to be the major factor affecting the performance of every and all components of an information retrieval system" (p. 138). In another article in the same issue of the *Journal of the American Society for Information Science*, Caryl McAllister and John Bell (1971), from IBM, actually attempted to identify "human factors" in their design of a computer system for total library management. They were, of course, concerned with a very narrow range of human activities, but it was a step in the right direction. Their final sentence is an apt comment on the Brillouin-Salton dilemma:

Yet system designers and programmers really know very little about what happens when a person sits down in front of a terminal. Generalized modes of man-machine communications are often limited in scope. Skirting the complex problems of experimental control or statistical analysis of this kind of interaction, theoreticians sometimes produce equally complex equations based on purely hypothetical systems. (p. 104)

In spite of this recognition, the quantitative approach continued to dominate the field, but objections were heard more and more frequently because of the failure of the research to produce results. One example of the debate is seen in two articles on retrieval effectiveness in *Communications of the ACM* (Association of Computing Machinery). The first, by D. C. Blair and M. E. Maron (1985), reported a study in a legal context where automated, full-text searches were successful in recalling only 20 percent of the relevant items. It was reasoned that a full-text retrieval system has difficulty retrieving documents by subject "because its design is based on the assumption that it is a simple matter for users to foresee the exact words and phrases that will be used in the documents they will find useful, and *only* in those documents" (p. 295). The reality was quite the opposite. The following year, Salton (1986) argued that manual indexing was no better than automatic indexing, even for large data banks, a suggestion made by Blair and Maron. Of course, the point is that *neither* system works well, and Michael Eisenberg and Linda Schamber (1988) identify the reason: "The communication paradigm (the source-to-destination model of information retrieval) is too linear, too system-oriented, to provide a realistic understanding of the human judgment process" (p. 167).

Mark Rorvig (1989), particularly concerned with the human judgment process, reviewed the work on psychometric measurement and related it to information science. But even more relevant was Brenda Dervin and Michael Nilan's (1986) review article, which exhibited a somewhat missionary approach in describing a research orientation starting with the user, rather than the system, as a "call" to address the fundamentals of the human condition. "Almost without exception," they wrote, "information needs have not been defined as what users think they need but rather in terms that designate what it is in the information system that is needed. The definitions have not focused on what is missing for users (i.e. what gaps they face) but rather on what the system possesses" (p. 17). Their review identifies scholars who are "now calling for supplementing quantitative approaches with inductive, qualitative approaches" (p. 16).

Three other, widely different, examples will illustrate the distance information science has come from the days of Brillouin. Donald Owen Case (1988), taking into consideration the proliferation of personal computers and the need to understand how individual knowledge workers organize their information, applied ethnographic or anthropological methods in a study of academic historians. The idea was to find out how historians "digest" written information and thus to "find clues that may help us to design better retrieval systems" (p. 89).

The second example is Daniel Benediktsson's (1989) analysis of hermeneutics and its relevance to information science. In his opening remarks he states: "Quantitative statistical methods can be used only in those areas in which the human perception of a situation is not a factor. The presence and validity of human perception is a clear indication for the application of phenomenological-hermeneutical methods" (p. 205). One is reminded of the statements in the Ellis (1984) article: "It was the notion of relevance to the subject of the request which was itself 'open-textured'. . . , being open to systematic redefinition according to the perception of the individual researchers. . . . What seemed to be required to effect such an explanation and to develop such an understanding was a more holistic and interpretive approach to the problems experienced" (pp. 265, 266). As Benediktsson concludes, working with texts clearly involves interpretation, including "texts and their representation on various levels of complexity (from indexing terms to simple bibliographic references to detailed bibliographic records to documentation units like abstracts)" (p. 226). Added to these, of course, are the individual and social relationships in query negotiation in institutions designed for certain purposes—information centers and services of all kinds.

The third example emphasizes the argument for research methods relevant to individuals interacting with each other in "socially constructed information systems." Julian Warner (1990) reminds us that "the established domains of information science are social not natural" and that "methodologies for investigation modelled on the physical sciences and technology, either by explicit derivation or as an accepted inheritance, are therefore radically misplaced, and have not been productive" (p. 18). If we refer back to Blair and Maron's (1985) criticism of an automatic text retrieval system that used the formal aspects of text to predict meaning (e.g., location and frequency of words), the kind of change Warner (1990) calls for becomes very clear. Warner insists that the act of interpretation is complex, "resorting to inference, rather than the simpler act of linking equivalent terms implied by the dictionary entry" (p. 23). In suggesting the use of semiotics in information science, Warner tells us that one aspect of semiotics is "a resistance to final definitions. . . . A linguistic term obtains its meaning from its place in an indefinite network of slightly or greatly differing terms and its meaning is accordingly subject to change with alterations in the senses of other terms" (p. 21).

These few examples of suggestions for new methods of doing research in information science clearly indicate the existence of a dilemma of staggering importance for a field with pretensions to be a scientific discipline.

THE DILEMMA IN LIBRARY SCIENCE

Running parallel to this search for an appropriate methodology in information science has been a similar battle with logical positivism in the sister discipline of library science. The dilemma for librarians, however, has been how to avoid being "scientific" in any way, insisting that librarianship is not a science but an art. Michael Harris (1986a) mounted an attack on positivism with the intention of rethinking the "epistemological foundations of research in library and information science" by drawing on work in critical theory and hermeneutics. He outlined the tendency of positivism "to remain on the surface of appearances," thus describing phenomena but not explaining them (p. 525). He also identified the objective of such science as "instrumentalism"—the use of laws and theories to predict and control (p. 518). We shall meet this word again in the final section. The result, said Harris (1986b), in another article, has been "too much trivial work on the wrong questions" (p. 212), with most research problems being technical and administrative in nature. Referring to the contemporary rejection of positivism by social science in general, he proposed the reason was that "the social sciences simply cannot sustain the essential division between the subject and the object of research so central to the positivist epistemology" (p. 220).

These same concerns were expressed by Curtis Wright (1979), who identified librarianship as the "polar opposite" of applied science. "It studies ideas (information). The metaphysical subsistents that lie beyond the reach of science in the *terra infirma* of philosophy, and reduces physical existents to its means of dealing with them. Librarianship is the art of providing orientation to knowledge—a service that constitutes its entire project. . . . Librarianship, in other words, is the very antithesis of science as a knowledge system" (p. 74). Some years later, Wright (1986) followed this with a scathing attack on both librarianship and information science. He claimed that librarianship had made an error, following the example of information science, in the use of the "scientific method." The result was "the scientizing of a humanistic idea-business that cannot be scientized: and the only possible remedy for this condition is to return librarianship to its humanistic foundation" (p. 743).

Wright is not saying that research should be abandoned but that we should find a way to study the "phenomena" in the world of librarianship so that a human being is not seen as "a complex adaptive (cybernetic) system," as do Valery Frants and Craig Brush (1988, p. 86).

All of this evidence points to the conflict between the desire for control—from cataloguers and information searchers to the information and library professions and their long pursuit of universal bibliographic control—and the recognition that complete control is impossible. Many information scientists began as natural scientists interested in controlling science information. They brought with them the scientist's attitude that problems could be solved by breaking them down into workable (researchable and measurable) parts. Hence Brillouin set aside the human element for the time being. But information systems come down at last to information retrieval, and it is there that the human element resides. It is impossible to avoid the triad, the social triad, of inquirer/intermediary/collection of information. There are at play human beings and their artifacts, books and machines, in conversation, in doubt, from different backgrounds, with peculiar ways of interpreting that other human artifact, language. At this juncture in the information transfer process, interpretation, understanding, intuition, imagination, intelligence, personality, and character all come into the dance, and the question arises—is this science or art? At the point of action, it certainly feels like art.

DILEMMA: ART OR SCIENCE?

Librarianship had an opportunity to debate the question of art versus science in the 1930s, when the Chicago Graduate Library School began. The "nonlibrarians" hired as professors in that educational experiment took reading as their project and applied the current sociological research methods to reading as a social phenomenon, both in the mass of the population and in categories of people. The story is told in detail in Stephen Karetzky's (1982) history. Practicing librarians objected to any statistical analysis of the books they loved and the individuals they served. How could anything worthwhile, arrived at by surveys, be said about the highly personal experience of reading? Karetzky quoted at length Helen Haines, who was the author of the standard selection text *Living with Books* (1950) and who stated the opinion that librarianship was an art.

The sociological studies of reading were not widely read, and with the changes in the faculty and the purpose of the Graduate Library School, and the fact that in other library schools faculty came from the field, librarians coming into the profession were not introduced to scientific works or scientific methods. Library education was basically technical—how to run a library—and literary, in the sense of knowing the titles and contents of a wide range of books. It remained that way until the last quarter of the century. During those years, research methods—quantitative research methods at that—became part of the curriculum of library schools. These schools frequently became schools of library and information science, and the professors were required to have doctorates and to do research (Grotzinger 1976; Heilprin 1980; Heim 1986; Lynch 1984). I think it is fair to say that this change was due in part to the existence of information science and the (necessary) use by information scientists of library collections as testbeds. Library schools could easily add courses on information science, at a time when the universities in which the schools were housed began to enforce the publish-or-perish policy. Since publications, under that policy, are rated by the quality of the research, and since measurement is the key to science, quantitative methods became more and more attractive. In the world of librarianship, articles on "how I run my library good," which were useful, were criticized by academics as opinion pieces lacking grounding in reliable and generalizable evidence.

At the same time, at least one critique has said that library science education is *not* research oriented and is not scientific (Houser and Schrader 1978). In a review of Lloyd Houser and Alvin Schrader's book, Boris Raymond (1978) argued that library science is not a science and has no intention of being one. "It is not now, and never will be a science in the sense that astronomy, physiology, or psychology are sciences. . . . The reader is quite at liberty to argue that library educators . . . wisely preferred to teach . . . the current state of the art, rather than a non-existent and improbable science" (p. 461). Two other reviewers, Michael Buckland (1979) and Glynn Harmon (1979), suggested that Houser and Schrader look at information science for what is scientific in schools of library and information science, citing as examples Bradford's law and bibliometrics.

Houser (1988) did just that and analyzed the articles in the first fifteen volumes of *Journal of the American Society for Information Science*. He must have smiled as he wrote the following words in the abstract:

The empirical evidence shows that information science is merely library science, that the majority of *JASIS* authors which could be identified were from library science (and the majority of them taught in library science), and that *JASIS* authors are not scientists. There is no scientific community of information scientists. In fact there is no justification for naming a new branch of science *information science*. Logically, therefore, there cannot be any inter- or multidisciplinarity in the enterprise and there can be no justification for people to term themselves "information scientists." (p. 3)

Whatever one might say about Houser's research, it was statistical and it was published in a journal known for its orientation to the scientific method. In Wayne Wiegand's (1989) *Library and Information Science Research* review of George Bennett's (1988) dissertation (which used a hermeneutic approach to analyze a selection of literature), we find the conflict still alive and well.

In some respects, however, it is ironic that a book like this should be reviewed so favorably in the pages of a journal which generally focuses on publications emanating from a different kind of research. Yet the potential for effecting change in professional behavior may be greater if the conclusions emerging from the unscientific methodology manifested here are ultimately found to be persuasive." (p. 80)

RESEARCH AS AN ART OR A SCIENCE

The position of librarians was that librarianship is an art and that hard science methods are inappropriate for the "object" studied. The art-or-science dilemma exists in the social sciences generally, but there the dilemma is the research methods themselves, not the phenomena studied. Years ago, the eminent sociologist Robert Nisbet (1968) published the article "Sociology As an Art Form." He did not argue against the scientific method, but against that method as the only way. Indeed, in contrast to Houser's opinion about information science, Nisbet wrote: "Nothing I say is intended to imply that sociology is not a science. I am quite willing, for present purposes, to put sociology on the same line with physics and biology, applying to each of these the essence of what I say about sociology" (p. 143). What he had to say about the various sciences was that "each is indeed a science, but each is also a form of art, and if we forget this we run the risk of losing the science, finding ourselves with a sandheap of empiricism or methodological narcissism, each as far from science as art is from billboard advertisements" (p. 144). Both artist and scientist desire to understand, interpret, and communicate their thoughts of the world they find around them. Nisbet was concerned with the focus on methodology, which seemed to mean that method was all that was needed to solve problems, not imagination and sensitivity. This sort of thinking, Nisbet said, "has done much to drive sociology into areas of study chosen not because of their intrinsic intellectual importance, but because in them quantitative methodologies can work frictionlessly" (p. 152). It is appropriate to think of bibliometrics and citation analysis in this context.

Nisbet was reacting to the dominance of statistical methods in sociology in the 1950s, which was the result of the influence of positivism in all the social disciplines. As the century drew to a close, he might have welcomed the approach of scholars such as Dennis Mumby (1988), who wrote, "Traditional research has adopted a policy of objectivity à la natural science, while current interpretive approaches favor active engagement with the subject of study, and styles of presenting research results which blur the distinction between art and science" (pp. 5–6). On the other hand, R. Rosenthal (1984), noting that more and more reviews of the literature of the social sciences "are moving from the traditional literary format to the quantitative format" (p. 10), went on to state:

There is nothing in the set of meta-analytic procedures that makes us less able to engage in creative thought. All the thoughtful and intuitive procedures of the traditional review of the literature can also be employed in a meta-analytic review. However, meta-analytic reviews go beyond the traditional reviews in the degree to which they are more systematic, more explicit, more exhaustive, and more quantitative. (p. 17)

Of course, quantification of the results of the individual studies in such reviews requires that the quantitative results be present in those studies themselves.

And so we come to Martyn Hammersley's (1989) exploration, *The Dilemma of Qualitative Method*. Hammersley wrote:

Qualitative researchers claim that operationalization of sociological concepts in terms of quantitative indicators squeezes the meaning out of those concepts. Similarly, they argue that conceptualizing the social world in terms of variables and the relationships among them abstracts away the character of social life and produces distorted, inconclusive, irrelevant, banal, or even plainly false results. (p. 1)

Qualitative methods try to match the complexity of the social world, emphasizing, therefore, process rather than structure, understanding rather than explanation, to "develop insights that illuminate our lives" (p. 215). To do so means to "study local and small-scale social situations" (p. 2). Ellis (1984) came to the conclusion that "the sort of studies necessary to come to a better understanding of the factors influencing the operational effectiveness of retrieval systems may only be possible on a small scale" (p. 271). He referred to other information science researchers who were concerned with the "determining factors" of user behavior and who saw the need for in-depth studies of all types of people. Brenda Dervin's (1983) time-line approach was developed to do just that—for groups such as the 82 cancer patients, the 80 blood donors, the 6 developmentally disabled adults, and the 114 children in a television-viewing study. Then there is the work of Nick Belkin and his associates (Brooks, Daniels, and Belkin 1985), analyzing "six dialogues, recorded in two different online retrieval services, with four different intermediaries" (p. 193).

Hammersley, discussing the work of Herbert Blumer at the University of Chicago's School of Sociology, calls our attention to the fact that Blumer, classified as a qualitative researcher, referred to the "dilemma" facing social research. "On the one hand, social phenomena cannot be understood without taking account of subjective as well as objective factors; yet, at present we have no way of capturing subjective factors that meet the requirements of science" (p. 4). Dervin and Belkin both consider themselves empirical scientists, and both have struggled to find a method to identify quantitatively the two factors mentioned by Blumer.

Hammersley concluded, "We need to work on both fronts simultaneously, examining and if necessary modifying whatever is genuinely questionable" (p. 220). There is no solution to the dilemma. Information science, like all the other social sciences, studies human actions, and the students of those actions themselves bring prejudices of background and culture to their interpretation of what is observed and what is important.

I would like to conclude this chapter by suggesting two cultural factors that might be contributors to the tension between quantitative and qualitative methods and the dilemma of doing any research in the field of library and information science. Just as the arguments in the social sciences generally apply to library and information science, so the arguments I propose here apply to all the social sciences.

THE UNDERLYING SOURCE OF THE METHODOLOGICAL DILEMMA

One source of tension is the essentially oral nature of human society and of the actions undertaken by each member of that society. I realize this raises the various views about print and oral cultures and the view that the electronic media of communication are oral in form. I have never been convinced that all the meetings I attend and all the other events in daily life are not as full of face-to-face talk as any so-called primitive tribe's preliterate confabulations. A society is an organization. It is also an organization of organizations. The open market mentioned earlier, diffuse as it is, is an organization, even if it is not consciously organized. That, indeed, was Hayek's major point. And as Lee Thayer wrote in the preface to Mumby (1988), "To speak of organization is to speak of communication" (p. x). Although there is a quantity of printed communication in organizations, whether on paper or computer screen, most connections are made face-to-face. Conversation pulls onto the stage of research all the facets of personal and interpersonal relationships identified in the first two chapters in particular. Two information science examples, which I have discussed elsewhere (Neill 1979), will illustrate the conflicts involved.

S. R. Ranganathan, who invented much of the language we use to talk about the theory of classification, recognized the oral nature of the universe of knowledge. He saw it as "multi-dimensional," and he knew he faced the "insoluble problem" of mapping multidimensional space into one linear dimension (Ranganathan 1965, p. 33). The multiple and simultaneous relationships of the world of knowledge were well understood by Ranganathan, whose roots were in the oral tradition of India, but he was also a person who had "an extremely scientific attitude" and who suffered "sleepless nights and nightmares" as he struggled with the "maddening" problem (p. 34).

Jason Farradane was another who grappled with the problem of the classification and indexing of knowledge. Indeed, he felt that it was a fallacy to think that any sort of permanent or universal classification could be devised

(Farradane 1961). Classification schemes, out of practical necessity, identify standardized subject areas, freezing the concepts in classes and hierarchies. Farradane's attempt at constructing a classification system ended with a tentative arrangement based not on subjects but types of observables: entities, abstracts, activities, and properties. He knew that process was the fundamental property of knowledge, and so his relational operators, which were based on perceptions rather than concepts (Neill 1975), were structured on a time element—increasing clarity of perception and association over time (Farradane 1967, p. 305). Milic Capek (1961), discussing the changes in physics since Einstein, remarked, "Time is least conspicuous in the realm of visual and tactile sensations, but no so with ordinary sensations, which have the dynamic character of becoming" (p. 372). Farradane's "model" is a model of becoming. Conversation is becoming.

Yet Farradane (1967), as a scientist and a science information officer, felt that for "exact scientific work," for problems of measurement and calculation, for exact expression of knowledge and meaning, it was "necessary to develop a semantic equivalent of mathematics" (p. 298). In practice, however, he refused to define his relational operators in precise and static definitions, using examples in "ordinary language," such examples not to be "taken as limiting definitions" (p. 305).

I have chosen these examples from knowledge classification particularly to show that even in studying the product of human communication—the graphic record—we find that the difficulties of complete control are insurmountable. When we examine the information retrieval process, from question (and questioner) to answer, when we attempt to study information in all its manifestations, we face even more difficulties. We face the dilemmas described in this book.

Another factor at play in the social sciences is the essentially feminine nature of the "objects of study." This is particularly so for library and information science, where the goal of the profession is to help others. Indeed, librarians have traditionally used the word *mission* to describe their efforts to enrich the lives of people through the reading of the great literary works. Dervin and Nilan's (1986) review of the literature on information needs and uses consistently used the word *call*—a call to focus on the user—as if writing about a mission. This style was most unusual for the *Annual Review of Information Science and Technology*. Whether in the research laboratory or in the public library, there is a "caring" factor at work, and the caring professions are female professions—that is, the human nature of the workers (men or women) matches the nature of the work. Let me fill this in a little.

Physicists have not had to face the research methods dilemma. But, remembering the reference to Capek (1961), we find him saying that physics needs to find a model that will show us the acoustic nature of the universe: "The search for imageless models of the universe will become imperative. In this search the observed isomorphism of psychological duration and phys-

Table 8.1
Summary of Attitudinal Orientations, Main Attributes

Instrumentalism	Contextualism
• views self as autonomous	• views self in connection with community/others
• sees human interactions as separate and competitive	• sees human interactions as part of a continuous web of relationships
• distinguishes between objective and subjective knowledge: favors objective	• integrates objective and subjective knowledge; believes both have "bias"
• main focus is protecting individual's rights	• main focus is addressing needs
• separates the public and private spheres	• sees the interaction between the public and private spheres

Source: Lyn, Kathlene, "A New Approach to Understanding the Impact of Gender on the Legislative Process," in Joyce McCarl Nielsen, ed., *Feminist Research Methods* (Boulder, Colo.: Westview Press, 1990), p. 254.

ical becoming will constitute one of the most significant clues" (p. 380). And then we find Evelyn Fox Keller (1990) alluding to the pressure for change in science: "Of particular interest among recent developments *within* science is the growing interest among physicists in a process description of reality. . . . In these descriptions object reality acquires a dynamic character" (p. 55). But Keller's article is about the belief that science, and objectivity, are masculine. She is not saying that scientific work is "intrinsically" masculine or that "men are by nature objective" (p. 51). She is presenting the reasons why we might believe these characterizations to be true. What is interesting for my argument that information work is feminine is what she says might happen if more women engaged in science, for it corroborates my relating certain aspects of human nature, the feminine aspects, to information work. Keller says that if our beliefs about gender differences are true, then more women in science would cause a different science to emerge. "Our very conception of 'objective' could be freed from inappropriate constraints" (p. 55). My point is quite different. I argue that it is the nature of the field of study that allows certain methods to "work." A woman physicist would need to be as objective as allowed by the objects studied. If the physical objects become less concrete, more dynamic, then some variation in method is likely necessary. It so happens that the "becoming," or dynamic, character of contemporary physics appeals more to feminine characteristics, whether found in men or women. Table 8.1 delineates those characteristics.

These orientations are gender related, those under "instrumentalism" being male attributes and under "contextualism," female attributes. These characteristics are given scientific support in other works (see Chodorow 1974; Gilligan 1982; Kathlene 1989). However, it should be said that these orientations are conditioned by culture and are not necessarily inherent in the nature of either male or female. Nor is there ever, in reality, as neat a dichotomy as the list suggests. Nevertheless, the characteristics, as a model simplifying complexity, allow us to think productively about the world.

Now, rather than reading these lists as attributes of people, read them as descriptions of jobs. Apply them to the work of information professionals, and it is obvious that the contextual list describes the nature of the field as presented throughout this chapter. This is not the place to further this surmise, but it is at least interesting to pose the question of the cause of the dilemma of method in this way. My argument is that, in part, the work of the information profession, *by its nature*, is responsible for the dilemma over which type of research is most valid for information science.

CONCLUSION

All conversation is a making, and all making is art. Whether the conversation is face-to-face, one-on-one, live or recorded (print, sound, or image), it entails a creation—an expression of thought and feeling, an articulation of ideas. Whether consciously or unconsciously, in all such making there is design. After that act, we can talk about the degree of elegance of the design, in terms of function and beauty. Function denotes what works. Beauty, being in the eye of the beholder, is open for discussion. After the act of making, we can also talk about the importance of the conceptual content, but that is a matter for time to decide.

Since the human element cannot be ignored in information science, that which is crucial in information science must be understood as an art and therefore must be studied as an art. The dilemma of how to do this has been the burden of this chapter.

REFERENCES

Benediktsson, Daniel. "Hermeneutics: Dimensions toward LIS Thinking." *Library and Information Science Research* 11(3): 201–34 (July–Sept. 1989).

Bennett, George E. *Librarians in Search of Science and Identity: The Elusive Profession*. Metuchen, N.J.: Scarecrow Press, 1988.

Blair, D. C., and M. E. Maron. "An Evaluation of Retrieval Effectiveness for a Full-Text Document Retrieval System." *Communications of the ACM* 28(3): 289–99 (March 1985).

Brillouin, Leon. *Science and Information Theory*. 2d ed. New York: Academic Press, 1962.

Brooks, H. M., P. J. Daniels, and N. J. Belkin. "Problem Descriptions and User Models: Developing an Intelligent Interface for Document Retrieval Systems." In *Advances in Intelligent Retrieval, Informatics 8: Proceedings of a Conference . . . ,Oxford, 1985*, 191–214. London: Aslib, 1985.

Buckland, Michael K. Review of Houser and Schrader 1978. *Library Research*, Spring 1979, 85–88.

Capek, Milic. *The Philosophical Impact of Contemporary Physics*. New York: Van Nostrand, 1961.

Case, Donald Owen. "The Use of Anthropological Methods in Studying Information Management by American Historians." In *Proceedings of the 51st ASIS Annual Meeting, 1988*, Vol. 25, 87–93. Medford, N.J.: Learned Information, 1988.

Chodorow, Nancy. "Family Structure and Feminine Personality." In Michelle Zimbalist Rosaldo and Louise Lamphere, eds., *Woman, Culture, and Society*, 43–66. Stanford: Stanford University Press, 1974.

Dervin, Brenda. "An Overview of Sense-Making Research: Concepts, Methods, and Reports to Date." Presented at the International Communications Association Annual Meeting, Dallas, May 1983.

Dervin, Brenda, and Michael Nilan. "Information Needs and Uses." *Annual Review of Information Science and Technology* 21: 3–33 (1986).

Eisenberg, Michael, and Linda Schamber. "Relevance: The Search for Definition." In *Proceedings of the 51st ASIS Annual Meeting, 1988*, Vol. 25, 164–68. Medford, N.J.: Learned Information, 1988.

Ellis, D. "The Effectiveness of Information Retrieval Systems: The Need for Improved Explanatory Frameworks." *Social Science Information Studies* 4(4): 261–72 (Oct. 1984).

Farradane, J. "Concept Organization for Information Retrieval." *Information Storage and Retrieval* 3(4): 297–314 (Dec. 1967).

―――. "Fundamental Fallacies and New Needs in Classification. In D. J. Foskett and B. I. Palmer, eds., *The Sayers Memorial Volume*, 120–33. London: Library Association, 1961.

Frants, Valery, I., and Craig B. Brush. "The Need for Information and Some Aspects of Information Retrieval Systems Construction." *Journal of the American Society for Information Science* 39(2) 86–91 (March 1988).

Gilligan, Carol. *In a Different Voice*. Cambridge: Harvard University Press, 1982.

Grotzinger, Laurel. "Characteristics of Research Courses in Masters' Level Curricula." *Journal of Education for Librarianship* 17(2): 85–97 (Fall 1976).

Hammersley, Martyn. *The Dilemma of Qualitative Method: Herbert Blumer and the Chicago Tradition*. London: Routledge, 1989.

Harmon, Glynn. Review of Houser and Schrader 1978. *Journal of Library History* 14(1): 102–4 (Winter 1979).

Harris, Michael H. "The Dialect of Defeat: Antinomies in Research in Library and Information Science." *Library Trends* 34(3) 515–34 (Winter 1986a).

―――. "State, Class, and Cultural Reproduction: Toward a Theory of Library Service in the United States." *Advances in Librarianship* 14: 211–52 (1986b).

Hayek, F. A. *New Studies in Philosophy, Politics, Economics, and the History of Ideas*. London: Routledge & Kegan Paul, 1978.

―――. "Theory of Complex Phenomena." In his *Studies in Philosophy, Politics, and Economics*, 22–42. Chicago: University of Chicago Press, 1967.

Heilprin, Lawrence. "The Library Community at a Technological and Philosophical

Crossroads: Necessary and Sufficient Conditions for Survival." *Journal of the American Society for Information Science* 31(6): 389–95 (Nov. 1980).

Heim, Kathleen M. "The Changing Faculty Mandate." *Library Trends* 34(4): 581–606 (Spring 1986).

Houser, Lloyd. "A Conceptual Analysis of Information Science." *Library and Information Science Research* 10(1): 3–34 (Jan.–Mar. 1988).

Houser, Lloyd, and Alvin M. Schrader. *The Search for a Scientific Profession: Library Science Education in the United States and Canada.* Metuchen, N.J.: Scarecrow Press, 1978.

Johnstone, James N. "Mathematical Models Developed for Use in Educational Planning: A Review." *Review of Educational Research* 44: 177–201 (1974).

Kamel, M., B. Hadfield, and M. Ismail. "Fuzzy Query Processing Using Clustering Techniques." *Information Processing and Management* 26(2): 279–93 (1990).

Karetzky, Stephen. *Reading Research and Librarianship: A History and Analysis.* Westport, Conn.: Greenwood Press, 1982.

Kathlene, Lyn. "A New Approach to Understanding the Impact of Gender on the Legislative Process." In Joyce McCarl Nielsen, ed., *Feminist Research Methods*, 238–60. Boulder, Colo.: Westview Press, 1990.

———. "Uncovering the Political Impacts of Gender: An Exploratory Study." *Western Political Quarterly* 42(2): 397–421 (June 1989).

Keller, Evelyn Fox. "Gender and Science." In Joyce McCarl Nielsen, ed., *Feminist Research Methods*, 41–57. Boulder, Colo.: Westview Press, 1990.

Lindblom, Charles E., and David K. Cohen. *Usable Knowledge: Social Science and Social Problem Solving.* New Haven: Yale University Press, 1979.

Lynch, Mary Jo. "Research and Librarianship: An Uneasy Connection." *Library Trends* 32(4): 367–83 (Spring 1984).

McAllister, Caryl, and John M. Bell. "Human Factors in the Design of an Interactive Library System." *Journal of the American Society for Information Science* 22(2): 96–104 (March–April 1971).

Mumby, Dennis K. *Communication and Power in Organizations: Discourse, Ideology, and Domination.* Norwood, N.J.: Ablex Publishing Corp., 1988.

Neill, S. D. "Farradane's Relations as Perceptual Discriminations." *Journal of Documentation* 31(3) 144–57 (Sept. 1975).

———. "McLuhan and Classification." In A. Neelameghan, ed., *Ordering Systems for Global Information Networks: Proceedings of the Third International Conference on Classification Research, Bombay, 1975,* 177–87. Bangalore: FID/CR and Sarada Ranganathan Endowment for Library Science, 1979.

Nisbet, Robert A. "Sociology as an Art Form." In his *Tradition and Revolt: Historical and Sociological Essays,* 143–62. New York: Random House, 1968.

Otten, K., and A. Debons. "Towards a Metascience of Information: Informatology." *Journal of the American Society for Information Science* 22(1) 89–94 (Jan.–Feb. 1970).

Ranganathan, S. R. *The Colon Classification.* New Brunswick, N.J.: Rutgers University Graduate School of Library Science, 1965.

Raymond, Boris. Review of Houser and Schrader 1978. *Canadian Library Journal* 35(6): 461 (Dec. 1978).

Rorvig, Mark E. "Psychometric Measurement and Information Retrieval." *Annual Review of Information Science and Technology* 23: 157–89 (1988).

Rosenthal, R. *Meta-Analytic Procedures for Social Research*. Beverly Hills, Calif.: Sage, 1984.

Salton, Gerard. "Another Look at Automatic Text-Retrieval Systems." *Communications of the ACM* 29(7): 648–56 (July 1986).

———. *Automatic Information Organization and Retrieval*. New York: McGraw-Hill, 1968.

Salton, Gerard, and Michael J. McGill. *Introduction to Modern Information Retrieval*. New York: McGraw-Hill, 1983.

Saracevic, Tefko. "Selected Results from an Inquiry into Testing of Information Retrieval Systems." *Journal of the American Society for Information Science* 22(2): 126–39 (March–April 1971).

Tague, J. "What's the Use of Bibliometrics?" In Leo Egghe and Ronald Rousseau, eds., *Informetrics 87/88: Select Proceedings of the First International Conference on Bibliometrics and Theoretical Aspects of Information Retrieval, August, 1987*, 271–78. Amsterdam: Elsevier Science Publishers, 1987.

Warner, Julian. "Semiotics: Information Science, Documents, and Computers." *Journal of Documentation* 46(1): 16–32 (March 1990).

Wiegand, Wayne A. Review of Bennett 1988. *Library and Information Science Research* 11(1): 80–82 (Jan.–Mar. 1989).

Wright, H. Curtis. "The Symbol and Its Referent: An Issue for Library Education." *Library Trends* 34(4): 729–76 (Spring 1986).

———. "The Wrong Way to Go." *Journal of the American Society for Information Science* 30(2): 67–76 (March 1979).

Zunde, Pranas. "Information Science Laws and Regularities: A Survey." In Jens Rasmussen and Pranas Zunde, eds., *Empirical Foundations of Information and Software Science III*, 243–70. New York: Plenum Press, 1987.

9

On the Style of Some Philosophers: The Dilemma of Debate

> I would not be much use, Socrates, nor would Euthyphro differ in any way from the majority of men, if I did not know all such things with strict accuracy.[1]

It was a day in late winter when I took down from the shelf Lucretius's *Of the Nature of Things* with the intention of reading it through from the beginning. The snow on the lawns was sagging with age and was dirty brown along the edges of the road. The skies were overcast. Spring was not yet in the air, but even now winter was over. I had been puzzling my way through another convolution of sentences purporting to be a description of consciousness. Suddenly the only thing of which I was conscious was the boxed copy of Lucretius's works sitting on the shelf where it had always sat, unread, acting as a support for Wittgenstein, Kant, Koestler, Heisenberg—a baker's dozen of mixed philosophers.

An ill-remembered line from Keats came to mind. I was barely conscious of the words: "O for a beaker of the warm South." Simultaneously, I was conscious of the wine-red binding of the Lucretius book. Then I was conscious that I was conscious of these (mind?) events. For a moment, I allowed myself to be conscious that I was conscious of being conscious. But only for a moment. Afraid of being torn from my moorings by that infinite regression, I pulled back to the surface of my Rylean self and did something practical. I checked my Keats and found these lines from his "Ode to a Nightingale":

> O, for a draught of vintage! that hath been
> Cool'd a long age in the deep-delved earth,

Tasting of Flora and the country green,
  Dance, and Provençal song, and sunburnt mirth!
O for a beaker full of the warm South,
  Full of the true, the blushful Hippocrene,
  With beaded bubbles winking at the brim,
    And purple-stained mouth;
That I might drink, and leave the world unseen,
  And with thee fade away into the forest dim.[2]

I had almost faded away into the dim forest of introspection. I opened *On the Nature of Things* in order to fade into a less frustrating philosophic time.

The first few pages of Book I soothed me, as "puissant Mars" was lulled by Venus, "o'ermastered by the eternal wound of love." Lucretius poetically explained primal matter and the eternal void and gracefully conceded the reader some intellectual ability:

And still I might by many an argument
Here scrape together credence for my words.
But for the keen eye these mere footprints serve,
Whereby thou mayest know the rest thyself.[3]

Thus relaxed, I was thunderstruck when I came upon the excoriation of a fellow philosopher in terms as current as last month's issue of *Mind*, my favorite journal of philosophy.

And on such grounds it is that those who held
The stuff of things is fire, and out of fire
Alone the cosmic sum is formed, are seen
Mightily from true reason to have lapsed.
Of whom, chief leader to do battle, comes
That Heraclitus, famous for dark speech
Among the silly, not the serious Greeks
Who search for truth. For dolts are ever prone
That to bewonder and adore which hides
Beneath distorted words, holding that true
Which sweetly tickles in their stupid ears,
Or which is rouged in finely finished phrase.[4]

Marking the page, I put the book aside. Are all philosophers the same, I asked myself? Has it always been the custom for philosophers, while manipulating arguments and words with the care taken by the farmer's daughter in gathering eggs, to slam their opponents to the mat with the battle-joy of puissant Mars himself?

Only the other day I had found U. T. Place accusing Sir Charles Sherrington, all psychologists, all physiologists, and many (past) philosophers of being unable to discover a simple logical mistake. "Sherrington's argument," opined Place, "for all its emotional appeal depends on a fairly simple logical mistake, which is unfortunately all too frequently made by psychologists and physiologists and not infrequently in the past by the philosophers themselves."[5]

I also remembered having read a long professorial harangue by R. J. Nelson on the complete incompetence of two of his colleagues, Richard Rorty and William Kalke. Referring to something they had said about computers in their articles on functionalism, Nelson mercilessly took them to task:

These declarations are plainly false. Only a madman would attempt to predict or control the behavior of a computer from a knowledge of its hardware. Further, it is not true that the level of abstraction at which a computer qua computer is described is merely one among many essentially arbitrary levels. And, contrary to what Kalke says, an engineer or a computer-systems designer distinguishes *easily* between internal (logical) states and external states. These simple facts need not and will not be argued here; it suffices to recall that computers are designed to fit a priori logic and program schemes. If Kalke and, following him, Rorty, here mean to imply that a necessary condition for an adequate functionalism in philosophy of mind is an adequate "functionalism" in computer science and that the latter does not obtain, they are wide of the mark. A good dose of the computer literature beginning with Turing and Von Neumann and ending with any student's computer-engineering handbook seems to be called for.[6]

I had, of course, noticed this anvil chorus style of argument before but somehow had thought the practice limited to certain eminent and irascible graybeards. R. G. Collingwood, for instance, called Herbert Spencer's attempts at a (pre-Darwinian) philosophical exposition of the concept of evolution "amateurish and inconclusive."[7] A charitable person could have allowed Spencer some justification for his amateurishness.

Collingwood did not qualify his statement in any way, as he did in the following corkscrew remark about Baruch Spinoza: "But if Spinoza's theory of the relation between body and mind is at bottom unintelligible, it is obviously the work of an exceedingly intelligent mind.[8] Sir Isaac Newton, however, fared much worse: "Of the theoretical difficulties lurking among the foundations of his natural philosophy Newton seems quite unaware, although many of them had been familiar for a very long time." In a final gesture of dismissal of this great man who was not great enough, Collingwood concluded, "It is perhaps legitimate to infer that the careless and second-hand thinking on fundamental questions of cosmology, to which I have called attention, proved his undoing in the end."[8]

Not fear, favor, or affection, it seems, hinders the philosopher in his search for errors in the work of his contemporaries, his teachers, or his intellectual ancestors. Collingwood made no bones about it and even managed to compliment those he had attacked, in the preface to his autobiography: "I have written candidly, at times disapprovingly, about men whom I admire and love. If any of these should resent what I have written, I wish him to know that my rule in writing books is never to name a man except *honoris causa*, and that naming any one personally known to me is my way of thanking him for what I owe to his friendship, or his teaching, or his example, or all three."[9]

I assume this does not cover Spencer, Spinoza, or Newton. Given Collingwood's position, it seems only just that Alan Donagan, in his work on Collingwood, would write, "The first obstacle to understanding Collingwood's later philosophy is his own narrative of its development, which beyond doubt is untrue."[10]

Whether or not Gilbert Ryle followed the principle of never naming "a man except *honoris causa*," he certainly did not hesitate to name. "Now I think that Mr. Collingwood's general views are wrong," wrote Ryle when he was thirty-five, "but I want only to discuss, and if possible to refute, certain theories which he expounds. . . . And I confess at once that I intend to be destructive only."[11] Years later Ryle, feeling safe, perhaps, as Waynflete Professor (as had been Collingwood), or feeling he had eliminated the danger by eliminating the ghost in the machine, ignored Bertrand Russell's assertion "that there is a perculiarly painful chamber in hell inhabited solely by philosophers who have refuted Hume."[12] Ryle confidently asserted, "Hume's attempt to distinguish between ideas and impressions by saying that the latter tend to be more lively than the former was one of two bad mistakes."[13]

David Hume would not, I think, have been nearly as harsh as Russell. Hume was well aware of the philosopher's problem. "It is easy for a profound philosopher to commit a mistake in his subtle reasonings; and one mistake is the necessary parent of another, while he pushes on his consequences, and is not deterred from embracing any conclusion, by its unusual appearance, or its contradiction to popular opinion." Seeing Ryle undeterred "in the pursuit of his consequences," Hume would have invited him over for a good meal and a glass of claret, for he knew the dangers of unrelieved philosophical research and cited Nature's admonishment: "Abstruse thought and profound researches I prohibit, and will severely punish, by the pensive melancholy which they introduce, by the endless uncertainty in which they involve you, and by the cold reception which your pretended discoveries shall meet with, when communicated. Be a philosopher; but, amidst all your philosophy, be still a man."[14]

The experience of a "cold reception" is nowhere as plaintively expressed as on the first page of Karl Popper's *Objective Knowledge*:

I think that I have solved a major philosophical problem: the problem of induction. (I must have reached the solution in 1927 or thereabouts.) This solution has been extremely fruitful, and it has enabled me to solve a good number of other philosophical problems.

However, few philosophers would support the thesis that I have solved the problem of induction. Few philosophers have taken the trouble to study—or even to criticize— my views on this problem, or have taken notice of the fact that I have done some work on it. Many books have been published quite recently on the subject which do not refer to any of my work, although most of them show signs of having been influenced by some very indirect echoes of my ideas; and those works which take notice of my ideas usually ascribe views to me which I have never held, or criticize me on the basis of straight-forward misunderstandings or misreadings, or with invalid arguments.[15]

These concluding clauses bring Popper into the attack position.

It is not only professional philosophers who use the argument of ignorance and bad thinking to place themselves in a strong redoubt. The late media philosopher Marshall McLuhan was well known for his put-downs of other thinkers. A reviewer, obviously unfamiliar with the philosophical style, once said of him, "He makes a habit of saying that somebody like Plato, Kant, Einstein, Toynbee, Spengler, Mumford 'failed to grasp' what he grasps so easily."[16] But McLuhan, like most philosophers who are truly philosophical, knew that he was, after all, a man, and I have always assumed, surely rightly, that he was thinking as much of himself as of every other famous person when he said, "For it has always been an advantage to have direct contact with eminent men, if only because proof positive of their essential mediocrity spurs younger talent."[17]

It is now standard practice in all social science research (fortunately not in philosophy?) to include a final section indicating other studies that are needed to advance the field. The purpose of this is to cover the author in two ways. First, by identifying further research, one can show one's own dissertation to be crucial to the development of the discipline. Here are several other important topics, in other words, that need investigation and that would have been completely ignored had not the present analysis been undertaken.

The second purpose is to cover the author's physical and intellectual failings. Knowing that several vital qualifications have not been taken into consideration—because it has not been known how to handle them, because they haven't been understood, or simply because the author has been too tired or too disinterested to bother—the author can hide these errors and omissions under the guise of "further research."

So it is with the present essay. Here we have opened up a new field for researchers—Otsogmenology (the study of the Stupidity of Great Men).[18] Crucial to the understanding of the development of ideas, a whole new discipline could be identified that undertakes to analyze why one author has been brutally critical of another and whether that criticism has been just. For instance, when Ryle identified two of Hume's "bad mistakes," the in- vestigation would involve an examination of Hume's "mistakes" to test for the truth or falsity of the accusation. Also entailed would be a critical inquiry into the "corrections" made by the individual who has blurted *"J'accuse."* Collingwood's theory of the forms of error would be a useful underpinning to this subject.[19]

The discipline would, of course, find its metatheory in detailed analyses of the meanings of such linguistic counters as "bad mistakes," "distorted words," "dark speech," "plainly false," "second-hand thinking," "straight-forward misunderstandings," and so on. But these matters must wait. A month has passed since I began this essay. Today the sun is warm, and I intend to take my lunch to the high bank of the river, sit by the tumbling waters, and absorb the odors of spring.

NOTES

1. R. E. Allen, *Plato's "Euthyphro" and the Earlier Theory of Forms* (London: Routledge & Kegan Paul, 1970), p. 19.

2. *The Poems of John Keats*, ed. Aileen Ward (New York: Heritage Press, 1966), p. 263.

3. Titus Lucretius Carus, *De Rerum Natura* (Of the nature of things). Trans. William Ellery Leonard (New York: Heritage Club, 1957), p. 17.

4. Ibid., p. 26.

5. U. T. Place, "Is Consciousness a Brain Process?" *British Journal of Psychology* 47(1): 44–50 (Feb. 1956), p. 49.

6. R. J. Nelson, "Mechanism, Functionalism, and the Identity Theory," *Journal of Philosophy* 73(13): 365–85 (July 15, 1976), p. 380.

7. R. G. Collingwood, *The Idea of Nature* (New York: Oxford University Press, 1945), p. 11.

8. Ibid., pp. 106, 108, 110.

9. R. G. Collingwood, *An Autobiography* (London: Oxford University Press, 1939), preface.

10. Alan Donagan, *The Later Philosophy of R. G. Collingwood* (Oxford: Clarendon Press, 1962), p. 1.

11. Gilbert Ryle, "Mr. Collingwood and the Ontological Argument," *Mind* 137–51 (April 1935), p. 137.

12. Ernest Campbell Mossner, *The Life of David Hume*, 2d ed. (Oxford: Clarendon Press, 1980), p. 5 (citing Russell's *Nightmares of Eminent Persons*).

13. Gilbert Ryle, *The Concept of Mind* (London: Hutchinson's University Library, 1949), p. 250.

14. David Hume, *Enquiries Concerning the Human Understanding and Concerning the Principles of Morals*, 2d ed. (Oxford: Clarendon Press, 1902), pp. 7, 9.

15. Karl Popper, *Objective Knowledge: An Evolutionary Approach* (Oxford: Clarendon Press, 1973), p. 1. A Bertrand Russell quote that calls for investigation leads off Popper's first chapter: "The growth of unreason throughout the nineteenth century and what has passed of the twentieth is a natural sequel to Hume's destruction of empiricism." Mossner, *David Hume*, overly enamored of his subject, in interpreting the *Nightmares* quote as being supportive of Hume, was probably deaf to Russell's satiric tone. Russell is another irascible graybeard. "I do not respect respectable

people," he once wrote, "and when I pretended to do so it was humbug" (cited in Ronald W. Clark's *The Life of Bertrand Russell* [London: Jonathan Cape, 1975], p. 5).

16. David Cort, "Any Number Can Play," *New York Times Book Review*, May 1, 1966, p. 26.

17. Marshall McLuhan, "Space, Time, and Poetry," *Explorations* 4: 56–62 (February 1955), p. 56.

18. I realize this should say "on the stupidity of great men and women." The result would be Otsogwomenology, the word *men* thus being contained in the word *women*. I certainly did not like Otsogmenandwomenology and rejected outright Otsogw'm'nology, which seemed meaningless except as an on-line search term with truncation problems. I did wonder if great women might not be just as happy to be left out of this one, but the more I worried about the problem, the more I began to appreciate the full meaning of Otsogwomenology, especially in the light of recent feminist criticism, and find myself leaning toward that choice.

19. R. G. Collingwood, *Speculum Mentis* (Oxford: Clarendon Press, 1924). There are, of course, different opinions about the nature and degrees of error. Agnes Arber, the distinguished botanist, provides us with the following concise statement in *The Mind and the Eye* (Cambridge: University Press, 1954), pp. 72–73:

The idea that scientific truth is inevitably partial and relative, brings us to the consideration of error and falsity. Error must not be confused with meaninglessness; as Hobbes wrote in 1651, "if a man should talk to me of a *round Quadrangle* . . . I should not say he were in Errour, but that his words were without meaning; that is to say, Absurd." If then we set aside statements that are without significance, and consider the category of actual falsity, we find much reason to accept Spinoza's dictum that erroneousness is not a positive quality, but that it consists simply in privation of knowledge. From this point of view, error is truth in an imperfect and incomplete form; and there is thus no duality of truth and falsity to reconcile, since we are left with a graded series of "truths," beginning with those so imperfect and partial that they are classed as errors, and passing upwards through every gradation of conditional truth.

Bibliographical Essay

Most of the evidence to support the argument of the chapters in this book has been found in the literature of other disciplines, each touching on one or two aspects of the information issues I am raising. There is, therefore, no set of works to suggest for "further reading," although the Information and Behavior series edited by Brent Ruben, referred to in the Introduction, has as its purpose the exploration of topics relevant to information science *and* communication studies. As the reader will have noticed, a number of papers from this series have been used in this book. Indeed, judging from the series title, I had thought more papers would be directly relevant to the problem areas I had in mind than I found to be the case, but there is a scatter of articles that avoid technology, government policies, and information systems and focus on the human issues at play.

Other items referred to in the Introduction, particularly the unusual slants of Manfred Kochen and John Swan, will provide an opening for interesting thinking. Two works not mentioned in the Introduction, but referred to elsewhere, will give the reader insight into the production and control of information—one a view from the bottom, Karin Knorr-Cetina's *The Manufacture of Knowledge: An Essay on the Constructivist and Contextual Nature of Science* (New York: Pergamon, 1981) and the other a view from above, James R. Beniger's *The Control Revolution: Technological and Economic Origins of the Information Society* (Cambridge: Harvard University Press, 1986).

If I refer the reader to David Braybrooke and Charles E. Lindblom's *A Strategy of Decision: Policy Evaluation as a Social Process* (New York: Free Press, 1963), it is because that book confirmed my own experience of the way in which human beings make administrative or organizational decisions, and because the words "disjointed incrementalism" have been part of my vocabulary for many years. The authors have kept my eyes open, so to speak, to the difficulties of making decisions for other people, particularly for large communities most of whose members are not known to the decision makers.

The other book that caused an unusual number of sparks in my imagination was

Friedrich Hayek's *Individualism and Economic Order* (London: Routledge & Kegan Paul, 1949). I came to this and others of Hayek's writings (see chapter 7) when I was reading Peter Drucker's *The New Realities* (New York: Harper & Row, 1989) and he mentioned that Hayek had something to say about the nature of information (see Drucker's footnote on p. 60). Although Hayek is often very theoretical, his approach to economics is more humanistic than statistical, and we are, after all, very much involved in economics as workers and consumers. Hayek gave me the key to the idea of complexity in the world of information and knowledge.

A final comment: the one journal that is "on topic"—*Knowledge: Creation, Diffusion, Utilization*—is not one of the core information science periodicals. Of the core, the *Journal of Documentation* is the best, perhaps because of its broader selection criteria. For instance, the first chapter of this book, "The Dilemma of the Subjective," had been rejected by another information science journal in part because one reviewer thought the "poetry" would not be appreciated by that journal's audience. I immediately realized (or assumed) that a British journal might be more welcoming of my "literary" style and that the journal could only be "*J. Doc.*," with its sympathies leaning, shall we say, away from the technological and toward the human, its sympathies in sympathy with those of its readers.

Name Index

Subject Index

Dalkon Shield, 48–49
Data, quality of. *See* Quality of information
Debate, 56, 159–68
Decision making, 11–12, 31, 41–43; in complex situations, 27, 129; in confusing situations, 62; ideal situation, 110; and inconclusive evidence, 44–45; influenced by the past, 44–45; influenced by standardized forms, 64–66; in politics, 106–7, 108; and stress, 107, 110; and values, 127
Disjointed incrementalism, 125–26
Dissertations, 82, 84
Distant data, 80–85
The Division of Labor in Society (Émile Durkheim, 1893), 101
Documentary reality, 64–65
Document representation. *See* Representations of documents
Drawing on the Right Side of the Brain (Betty Edwards, 1979), 72
Drug abuse, 56

Earthquakes, 57–59, 72, 115
Ecological nature of knowledge growth, 33, 134
Econometric models, 80
Economic system and use of knowledge, 128–29
Economists, "scientistic" attitude, 142
Education, 51, 61, 72, 91–92; and research in, 139; and social epistemology, 124
Effective use of information, 55, 56
Electronic media, 67, 152. *See also* Broadcast media
Enactive representations, 30
Engineers, 41–42, 57
Ephemeral literature. *See* Gray literature
Epidemic theory of communication. *See* Communication theory, epidemic theory
Epistemological questions, 125
Errors, 27, 40, 49, 72, 85; of fact, 78–79; from information overload management, 109; in philosophical argu-

ment, 161–68; in science, 88; suggested study of, 163–64; of thinking, 78, 161–68; truth in incomplete form, 165. *See also* Citations, errors; Judgment, errors of
Eskimos. *See* Inuit
Ethnographic methods. *See* Research methods, ethnographic
Evidence, concealment of, 51; impressionistic, 59, 60; inconclusive, 45; questionable, 79–80; and selected facts, 140; use of, 28, 62, 67, 71, 92; validity of, 56, 78–79, 80–87
Experience: and learning, 29, 31, 125, 128; and thinking, 25, 27–28, 30
Experientialism, 33. *See also* Thinking, role of the human body
Experts, 56, 112. *See also* Military experts
Expert systems, 28

Face-to-face communication. *See* Oral communication
Facts, interpretation, 42. *See also* Interpretation
Factual errors. *See* Errors of fact
Falsifications. *See* Lies, distortions, and fraud
Fat lady (in J. D. Salinger's *Franny and Zooey*), 85
Federal Drug Administration, 48
Feedback, 31, 32
Feeling, relation to thinking. *See* Thinking, role of the human body
Feigenbaum number, 131
Felt meaning. *See* Thinking, role of the human body
Felt thought. *See* Thinking, role of the human body
Feminine nature of information work, 153–55
Filters, Robert Taylor's five filters, 15
Flow, 111
Forms, 64–65
Forward Air Control (FAC), in Vietnam, 64–65
Fraud. *See* Lies, distortions, and fraud
Freedom, and information, 129, 133

About the Author

S. D. NEILL, one of the founding faculty members of the School of Library and Information Science at the University of Western Ontario, has published widely on many aspects of librarianship and information science. His main teaching areas are reference work, storytelling for children, and the philosophy of the profession.